"Mr. California" Autobiography of
ROCKWELL D. HUNT

"MR. CALIFORNIA"

Autobiography of

ROCKWELL D. HUNT

FEARON PUBLISHERS

2450 Fillmore Street

San Francisco 15, California

Library of Congress Catalog Card Number: 56-7132

PREFACE

I waited a long time before actually undertaking the task of writing the story of my own life. I was in my eighty-seventh year; I had entered upon my second "retirement" period, and there were other literary projects as well as thoughts of leisure and recreation inviting me.

For several years a few of my closest friends had been urging me to write my autobiography, stating that I owed it to the public, as well as to my family, to put on record my connection with the development of education in California and my reflections on what might be called the philosophy of living.

After writing other books the feeling grew within me, as the requests of certain friends became more urgent, that perhaps I might be justified in undertaking the task — which I judged would be somewhat formidable — and from the effort expended on it I probably would derive personal satisfaction provided it were actually brought to completion. But if never completed, I should not repine, for in the reviewing of memories of the past I could find certain pleasure. I shall not deny that an element of personal conceit might have entered into my decision to attempt the preparation of an autobiography. I was fully aware, however, that the task would demand many days of determined effort. In any event, I became persuaded.

The decades of my own life stretch over a far greater period of time in the history of California than the entire period preceding my birth, beginning with the earliest phases of the American conquest down to the year in which I was born. California was not yet eighteen years old as a state in the Union at the time of my birth in its capital — I may almost claim to have grown up with the state. So my active incumbency at the University of Southern California—thirty-seven years, beginning at forty, in 1908—covers a far longer period than all the preceding history of that University. Perhaps my life as a native of all California and my intimate association with the development of education in the state may offer some justification for my presenting this personal account.

One of my personal traits, from early childhood, has been the saving of old diaries, note books, letters, clippings, and keepsakes, as well as my own published writings. It has been simply a life-long habit. Now I find it greatly simplifies the preparation of my memoirs, while assuring a higher degree of accuracy.

As George Creel wrote, "Autobiographies are the stuff of which much of history is made.... When one is written by an actor as well as an eye witness, the result is not only compelling in its interest, but has importance as a historical document."

I have never yet found a definition of an autobiography that seems to satisfy all requirements. The principal reason for this, I suspect, is that no standard and acceptable norm for the literary product called autobiography has ever been established — how can an adequate definition be drafted when the object to be defined itself contains so many nebulous elements?

Perhaps the lack of a standard definition may incline the reader to be more charitable in judging this work, since in its scope and character it may not wholly conform to his own particular ideas.

After long personal acquaintance with Professor Thomas N. Carver, and with sincere appreciation of his career as a leading American economist, I cannot quite agree that the title of his autobiography, while it is typically Carverian, is altogether accurately applied to his long and fruitful life — *Recollections of an Unplanned Life*. I am disposed to be even more critical of the

statement of William Allen White in the Preface to his masterful
Autobiography, that "is necessarily fiction," — "only a tale that is
told." Granted, no autobiography can embody the entire truth
regarding the author's life, White has marshalled an incredible
number of facts in his volume, while fiction plays a very minor
rôle indeed. Still, I think both Carver and White have, in title and
preface, revealed truthfully something of their own personalities,
thus expressing the candor and humility that characterized them
both. But the title of Albert Jay Nock's autobiography, *Memoirs
of a Superfluous Man*, frankly, shocks me. It is truly a most
provocative book; but if the brilliant writer is "superfluous," what
is the *raison d'étre* of the *Memoirs*? If, as he avers, society is still
paleolithic, would not a more ingenuous title be *The Memoirs of
an Indispensable Man*? All of which gives accent to the difficulty
of choosing an appropriate title and reinforces the ancient maxim,
"Well begun is half done."

In this volume I have attempted the rather difficult task of
presenting an accurate self-portrait, with historical framework
and individual focus, of avoiding the pitfall of self-praise on the
one hand and false modesty on the other, with a modicum of what
may be called literary quality overall — in summary, an account
of my life, in just perspective, written with self-imposed restraint.
At any rate, I have felt keenly the need to be intellectually honest.

Problems of perspective and relative values, however, are not
easy of solution. As one example, I have given space to my travels,
because these have constituted a significant part of my equipment
and have enriched my life. I conceive that complete omission of
them from the narrative would be doing an injustice to the subject
— they are vital chapters in my life story. The same may be said of
my experiences in the mountains of California, which constituted
a large part of my recreational life, beginning with the first camping trip in early childhood.

Since entering upon the task of preparing this autobiography a little contemplation of earlier decades has tended to make me feel like a California pioneer myself. A simple narration of the persons and things that have touched my life will appear like the voice of history to the present generation. It is well over a century since my own parents came to the Golden State. What has happened in California since 1850 constitutes one of the marvels of human history. My own humble place in the dynamic century, projected back to the days when my pioneer parents arrived, makes meaningful the expression of my friend George P. Hedley in a personal letter, saying:

> It is good to know a man who is so thoroughly at home in 1953, as well as in the middle 1850's—natural enough, though, for it is knowledge of yesterday that makes possible a sane understanding of today.

My life has covered significant parts of two centuries. The changes I have witnessed in California, as well as in the world at large! which hold much in common — are, in the perspective of the years, truly sensational.

ROCKWELL D. HUNT

CONTENTS

xi

L IST
of ILLUSTRATIONS

Note: For the preparation of illustrations to be used in this volume, the author gratefully acknowledges the capable assistance of his friend, V. Covert Martin, of Stockton, California.

INTRODUCTION

All the readers of this autobiography will agree that it is written in an easy-to-comprehend and smooth-flowing style; although prepared by an educator, the choice of words is that of a literary person. Even a connoisseur of literature will find the diction both stimulating and pleasing.

Other autobiographies have been written by Californians, but none, so far as I know, by anyone who can compare with Rockwell D. Hunt as "a life-long Californian." In this volume its author, who has few if any equals in embodying in his life and work the spirit of California at its best, reviews and interprets nearly nine decades of experiences in a State which is not yet eleven decades old.

Other autobiographies have been written by pioneers, but this one has been thoughtfully prepared by the pioneer son of rugged pioneer parents, one of whom came from New York by the Isthmus of Panama and the other by covered wagon from Illinois, and who thus has been well-grounded in the meaning of the hardship and the hopefulness involved in pioneering. The author of this book is a pioneer in his own right in historical research, in educational administration, in training scholars. His most fruitful educational work is represented by the new procedures that he helped to initiate during his thirty-seven years of continuous service at the University of Southern California.

It is uniquely appropriate that the author of the life story of a lifelong Californian is a California historian. It has been composed by no ordinary writer of California history, but by one who alone holds the distinction of having been officially pro-claimed by a governor of the state "Mr. California."

Some autobiographies are submitted to the public by men of affairs, and some by men of books, but this one has been written by one who throughout many decades has happily combined in his daily life a wide range of activities from those of devoted husband and deeply interested parent on one hand, to those connected with analyzing and writing upon themes with worldwide ramifications. Always in touch with the latest books and current periodicals, Dean Hunt has never been more than a step away from a call to help solve a current educational problem. While his library is overflowing with carefully marked and underlined documents of many kinds, he has been continually at work testing ideas by personal experiences, by practical activities, and by appropriate research. Thus, he is able to bring to the reader of this life story a well-balanced integration of practice and theory.

This is the autobiography of an able educator whose academic training began in California but which reached a culmination in the conferring on him of the degree of doctor of philosophy in 1895 at the Johns Hopkins University, where he had studied under the direction of some of the most distinguished educators in the nation. The honorary doctor degrees that he has received constitute high appreciation of his educational achievements.

This is the life account of one who has sought to educate, with an eye to the kinds of uses to which ideas might be put, of one who has taught economics and history as aspects of a world in which human character is a primary value, of one who has presented economic and historical data within a moral and spiritual frame of reference, of one who in the classroom has discussed economic systems and historical changes not as social fragments, but as integral parts of a larger dynamic whole that is not moving blindly in a circle, but according to plan, toward "one far-off divine event to which the whole creation moves."

While this is an autobiography of a Californian, it is more. It describes a citizen of the United States whose loyalty has led him repeatedly to defend, and at times to suggest improvements in, the democratic procedures which his nation has sought to put into effect both at home and abroad. It reveals the growth of thought of one whose penetrating analyses and proposals encompass international and world affairs.

This is the autobiography of a distinguished administrator, but it is more, for it tells of the activities of a graduate school dean who for more than a quarter of a century showed a deep personal interest in the welfare of each graduate student who came within the range of his administrative desk. This is the autobiography of an author of many volumes, but it is more, for it reflects the spirit of one who writes to arouse people to do some original thinking. It is the autobiography of one interested in social reforms, but it is more, for Dr. Hunt taught that improvements in the social environment, by themselves, might be dangerous, unless accompanied by a broadening of social responsibility and a deepening of ethical character on the part of the beneficiaries.

It is the autobiography of an orderly and scholarly mind, but it is more, for it reflects not only attention to a painstaking filing and record-keeping system, but it rises above categories and classifications, and lays hold of the symbols of creative thinking. It is the autobiography of a personal friend, but more, it is sent forth by one who is a friend to man, and to all who represent whatever things are true, just, and of good report.

If the readers of this volume will exercise even a small degree of empathy, they will find their sights regarding the meaning of life being lifted, their visions of things to come being clarified, and their determination to put their shoulders to the wheel of progress being immeasurably stimulated.

EMORY S. BOGARDUS

UNIVERSITY OF SOUTHERN CALIFORNIA

CHAPTER ONE

BEGINNINGS

I had not expected ever to see New York City again — there appeared to be no particular reason why I should visit the metropolis, and I had no great hankering for the trip. But when my son Lloyd, and his lovely wife Dorothy, urgently and generously invited me to go with them to attend the wedding of their only daughter, my charming granddaughter Nansanna, in Dr. Ralph Sockman's Methodist Church on Park Avenue, August 28, 1954, I yielded to their importunity.

It was a non-stop flight from Los Angeles International Airport to New York. On the return flight, the great Constellation plane took to the air close to 12:30 o'clock, mid-day, and it was some time before dark that afternoon when it circled for a landing at Los Angeles.

On the way back to California, cruising in ease and comfort, 340 to 360 miles per hour, at an elevation of 20,000 feet, I could not help thinking of the young woman of twenty-four, later to become my mother, who in that very month of August, exactly 100 years earlier, reached Sacramento by way of the "prairie schooner" from Joliet, Illinois, after three laborious months across the plains and over the mountains! What could more perfectly illustrate the fantastic changes in transportation in America and the modern world during the span of a single century! And yet transportation is only one of the many phases of living. Marvelous indeed are the changes wrought by the hand of history.

My father was born in the year 1820. I would not have the hardihood to attempt to set down and describe even in the simplest manner the transforming changes — inventions, discoveries, revelations — that have come about since 1820. The most casual contemplation of the innovations brings a sense of wonder, awe, and incredulity.

I am amazed at what has happened in my own lifetime, which as I write, has covered close to nine decades. At the time I was born in Sacramento the first transcontinental railroad was still uncompleted: there was no telephone, and of course no wireless or radio, no automobile, or airplane, not even a bicycle.

In our old family Bible, published in 1867, under the illuminated heading of "Births," appears this entry:

Rockwell D. Hunt
Feb. 3d 1868, Sacramento City, Cal.

Other entries on the same page include my father, Dennis R. Hunt; mother, Nancy A. Zumwalt; mother's first husband, Alexander R. Cotton, her children by Mr. Cotton, Albert T., Joel S., and Alta Irene (who died in infancy); and my brothers, respectively, Major C., Frank L., Mark T., and George G. I was fourth of the five Hunt brothers. Of all the persons mentioned in this paragraph, I am the only one living as these lines are written, in 1955. Furthermore, I attended the funeral of the last of my four brothers-in-law, Joseph F. Stuart, on the 3d day of January, 1955.

My birthplace was at our home on K Street, near Tenth, almost within a stone's throw of the then new Capitol building. But the period of my actual residence in Sacramento City was exceedingly brief, and personally, I know absolutely nothing about it; for in the matter of a very few months after my birth — perhaps even weeks — the family moved to the Hunt Ranch at Freeport, eight miles south, fronting on the Sacramento River and

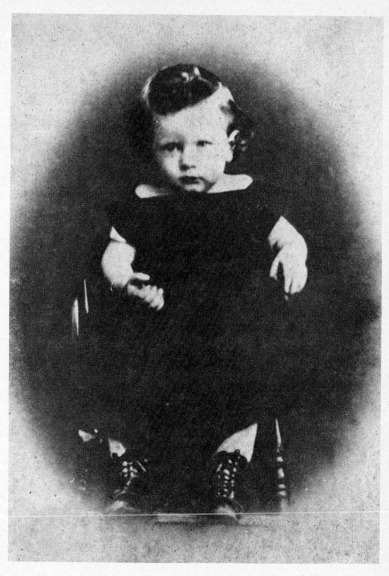

"ROCKY" HUNT, ABOUT TWO YEARS OLD

extending a mile to the east. The move was made — father, mother, four young boys including the baby (me), and the household effects — on a schooner, down the river, the exact date unknown to me.

For nine years my childhood home was at Freeport, and I seldom got farther away from the ranch than Sacramento, eight miles north. But that was a period in my life that means much to me now; and many a boy of today would envy me the experiences of those nine years on the banks of the Sacramento. For the benefit of my grandchildren, and their children, I must try to record something of that boyhood life.

My father, Dennis Rockwell Hunt, was born April 23, 1820, in Windhall Township, Bennington County, Vermont. His parents were Albinus Hunt and Hannah (Robbins) Hunt. His ancestry for several generations back was of New England stock. He was the oldest of a family of ten children, including, besides himself: Orilla Newcom, Jerusha Climena, Alanson Philander, Lydia Lucina, Cynthia Florinda, Albinus Adolphus, Charles Robbins, Allen Wood, and Major Leonard — quite an array of names, I think.

My father's grandfather, Charles Hunt, claimed to be able to trace all the Hunts in America of whom he could learn to three brothers who had emigrated from England to America several generations before his time. Albinus Hunt was born in New Hampshire about 1796, but moved to Vermont as a youth. While father was yet a young child the family moved from Vermont to Madison County, New York, not far from Hamilton, in Lebanon Township. There he grew up to young manhood. Being the oldest of the family and a man of spirit and adventure, he yielded to the lure of the gold of California. On the 13th of April, 1850, with a small party of friends he sailed as a steerage passenger from New York for San Francisco. Alonzo Hamilton, who became his partner, had already left on an earlier ship.

The incidents and experiences connected with the crossing of the Isthmus were among the most novel and interesting of father's entire life. He always recalled them with feelings of lively pleasure — the trip was like a continuous picnic under most fascinating conditions. There were the many varieties of tropical trees and other plant life, as well as parrots, monkeys, butterflies, and numerous varieties of gay-plumaged birds and strange animals.

But the experiences of crossing the Isthmus in the gold days are too well known to require telling in any detail here. After a long wait for a ship to take him to San Francisco, on account of the crowds of eager argonauts, he entered the Golden Gate on the 14th of July, 1850, glad indeed to be in California. To relate what he did during the next few years would be to add another narrative to the many of early pioneers. At this point it is sufficient to state that the tall, robust bachelor one day met an industrious young widow, as we shall see — and that's where I come in.

Leading farmers up and down the Sacramento River took particular pride in having at least one choice horse that was a good "stepper" on the road. In this my father was far from an exception. He always welcomed a "brush" with a neighbor when "traveling light" on the Sacramento road.

I must relate one such incident which involved Senator William Johnson, who lived some ten miles farther down river. The story must be substantially accurate — I used to hear it frequently in the family. It admirably illustrates a trait of my father's character. Being a well-to-do farmer and a member of the State Senate, Johnson was inclined to "high-hat" his more plebeian neighbors. As a matter of course he wished to drive a buggy horse that no one could pass on the road. When going to town he was immaculately dressed, wearing his fancy driving gloves, dressy suit.

On this particular morning, when father was starting for town, along came Senator Johnson from the south. Said he, somewhat condescendingly, "I think I'll be driving a little faster today than you care to travel." "Very well," replied father, as he fell slightly behind, but he was driving his best trotter that day and had no real intention of being beaten to Sacramento by Senator Johnson.

He drew up till they were driving side-by-side. Then the Senator urged his horse a little, but its rival, trained to perfection, kept right along with him. Very soon my honorable sire perceived that the Johnson horse had reached his peak, while his own had more speed held in reserve. Then, leaning over toward his neighbor, with his most ingratiating manner he said; "Well, Senator, I think I'll be going along now — I'm afraid I can't wait for you!" A good sport in defeat, the Senator responded, "Go right ahead, Rock; don't wait for me!"

And so father did. And afterward his southern neighbor confessed to him, "The only way I can beat you is with your permission—I won't ever pass you without your permission." If there was any one thing that gave father more keen enjoyment than driving a well trained horse that was king of the road, it was to handle the ribbons of a span of steppers, trained to work together in perfect rhythm, hitched to his light buggy; that, to him, as I have heard him express it more than once, was "a perpetual feast."

My mother's name was Nancy Ann Zumwalt. She was the oldest daughter of Jacob Zumwalt and Susanna Smith Zumwalt. Other members of the family included two sisters, Sarah and Elizabeth (we always called her Lizzie) and three brothers, John, Joseph, and Daniel. Her mother was twelfth in a family of thirteen children. Here are their names: Sally, John, Joel, Anna, Joseph, Phoebe, Reuben, Stephen, Mary Ann, Clarenda, Elizabeth, Susanna, and Cynthia.

The name Zumwalt is obviously German. One of my relatives spent a good deal of time in searching for its origin and meaning. He concluded that the Zumwalts originally, centuries ago, were German-speaking Swiss, who took the name from their occupa-

DENNIS ROCKWELL HUNT, NANCY ANN HUNT

tion, that is, "guardians of the forest." His conclusion may be correct. After some investigation my mother reported that a Jacob Zumwalt emigrated from Germany to America during colonial times and settled first in Pennsylvania, at the present site of Little York. It was said that the first hewed log house erected on the north side of the Missouri River was built by one of his sons, named Jacob. The maiden name of my mother's grandmother was Nancy Ann Spurgeon, whose parents had come from England and were relatives of the Spurgeons of that country.

Personally, while I readily admit there may be real fascination in the study of genealogy, I have never been sufficiently attracted by it to give the subject serious attention. Besides, I have not been convinced that a special investigation of my own ancestors would yield very enriching results.

Both of my mother's parents were born in Ohio, in a frontier farming community. But they soon moved to Indiana, and settled in a beech and maple timber, where they built a small one-room cabin. It was there that mother was born — she always felt a sense of pride in being a Hoosier. But when she was only three, the family moved again, farther west, to Troutman's Grove, near Joliet, Illinois, where they began pioneer life all over again.

The rigors of the early frontier are now well known. But no reading of history books, or even of personal diaries, can ever match the actual life my own mother knew as a girl, in the little clearing near Joliet. Neighbors were few and far between; school facilities were extremely limited; religious privileges were almost totally lacking. Yet no godlier people could be found anywhere than some of the staunch backwoodsmen of a century and more ago, out on the American frontier.

How mother, and the entire family, including her sick young husband, Alexander Cotton, and the two little boys, came to California by way of the covered wagon; how she lost her husband in the Sierra Nevada Mountains and tenderly buried him just inside the border of the new state; how she met the young bachelor Dennis Rockwell Hunt, and married him in 1855 — all this with its wealth of detail constitutes a human interest story in the history of the American West, a story, however, for which there is no space in this book.

The reader need not be concerned with the experiences and vicissitudes of the first years of my parents' life in California. Father seemed best suited to the farm: he spent much time seeking a satisfactory location, which proved trying to mother and the children. At length he decided to establish a home on a 500-acre tract at the little place called Freeport, south of Sacramento, on the bank of the river. And so it was that the family moved to the Hunt Ranch, shortly after my birth in Sacramento. It is around that home that my earliest memories cluster.

Nothing can better illustrate the daily life and toil of my mother during my early childhood than some of the pencilled entries in her old diaries, two or three of which are still in my possession. How she had the strength and the will-power to write down anything at all at the close of the toilsome day is strange to me now. Here are three entries for the year 1871 — I was three years old, my brother George a baby in arms:

> Friday, Feb. 17. Clear & verry pleasant, made Rockie pair drawers went to Mrs. McCrackens & Mrs. Swinnemans with all the children [five of us].
>
> Wednesday, May 31. Made Rockie a pair of Pants out of Father's old ones.
>
> Sunday July 30. Went to work & worked all day verry hard getting John [her brother] ready to go home the children all went to Sunday School. I was sick all day but kept to work till it was done.

Next I insert some entries for 1872:

> Monday, March 4. Washed a little for myself and a little for Mrs.

Greer. Went over twice to see her   fixed the boys' shirts & Frank
a waist. Frank & Mark not well   stayed home.

Sunday, April 14. I went to Sunday school with the children
went on foot & carried the baby [one mile]   we made arrangements for a picnic the first of May.

Saturday, April 20. went to town   took Major & baby.   got
Major a suit of coat & pants   necktie   got myself a calico
dress & one for baby & hat for him for six bits.

Wednesday, April 24. Sewed for dear life.

Thursday, April 25. Sewed all day.   finished baby's dress   made
cookies and pies.

Friday, May 3. Cut out a waist and sun-bonnet for Frank &
Georgie out of my old dress & made them.

Saturday, May 4. I cut and made Rockie a waist out of a rem-
nant of my dress.

Tuesday, July 9. So busy no time to write   the doctor came
down.

Monday, September 16. Hurry and working verry hard all the
time for the fair.

Here I am constrained to say of my mother—as has been said
of Helen Keller, "she made so much out of so little."

As a single indication of mother's activity at quilting, I found
a scribbled item by her in an old "Ladies' Note Book and Calendar" for the year 1901, which states, after noting that three quilts
had been made for each son, "43 quilts I've made." She was then
living in Napa. On a soiled scrap of paper I found a list of names,
in excess of 100, with the notation, "My Napa friends that I
called to see in two weeks." She never lacked for good friends,
especially in relation to her activity in the church, of which she
was very fond.

In one of my little books, *California Vignettes*, I paid a brief
tribute to my mother. In the story of my own life—she has
meant so much to me all through the years—I wish to include
portions of the tribute written long ago:

"The simple story of my mother's life would make a human

interest document. She embodied much that is universal in womanhood. The days of her years typify the onflowing stream of American history — with thousands of others she became a significant part of the great Westward Movement . . .

"I know of no nobler calling than that of a good mother. The good mother 'looketh well to the ways of her household, and eateth not the bread of idleness.'

"Thrice blessed am I as I recount the virtues of my own sainted mother, whose devotion to her family knew no bounds but suggested the breadth and depth of the infinite. That she was industrious, likewise thrifty, no son of pioneer mother need be told; totally ignorant of calories and vitamins, she was, nevertheless, an excellent cook, and notwithstanding the constant cares of a large household she managed to do an amazing amount and variety of quilting and fancy work; was a sincere lover of the beautiful, whether seen in her everbright flower garden or in the realm of natural history; she exemplified in herself and inculcated in her children puritanical habits and strict integrity; in times of trial and strain she was sustained by a simple religious faith that triumphed over every form of besetment.

"My mother was but one of countless thousands of devoted mothers of her generation. We of today are blessed anew by their hallowed influence. But I am thinking reverently of *my mother* as in fancy I pass from flower to beautiful flower in my own memory garden. And I am constrained to say of her who gave me birth and nurtured me, 'Many mothers have done virtuously, but she hath excelled them all.'"

The Hunt ranch, or farm, of 500 acres bordered on the east bank of the Sacramento River for about half a mile, extending eastward toward the Lower Stockton Road (now Franklin Boulevard) slightly more than a mile. On the north was the Erskine Greer (later O'Toole) ranch; bordering on the south that of George Hack, an early pioneer.

The different fields, enclosed by fences, were known to us by their special names. Just beyond the big barn and cow corral, were the "North Meadow" and "South Meadow," of about sixty acres each, separated by an east-west lane. Next came the "Race-track Field," extending the full width of the ranch, bordering on the east the canal that bisected the whole area from north to south. It was given that name because for years it contained a mile-track where horse races were frequently held during the time of my earliest childhood. Crossing the canal bridge, on the north was the "Windmill Field" (for years a windmill stood there); to the south was the "Willow Field," a large part of which was low land covered by a dense growth of native willow trees. The best place for mushrooms was the upper part of the Willow Field. But the biggest mushroom I ever found was in the south-east corner of the Race-track Field. Still farther east was the "Lake Field," with its more than 100 acres, much of which was a wide tule lake during the winter. A great deal of our boyhood sport centered about the "Lake Field," where wild ducks and geese came by the thousands, and swans and pelicans were no uncommon sight.

Between the Freeport Road and the levee that bordered the river was a narrow strip of valuable land. On this was located our house and yard, the horse stable, hogpen, and the small family orchard and vegetable garden. As I recall that little orchard, only a few steps from the house, I think it worthy of a special note because of its unusual selection. There were four apple trees, all different, with fruit ripening at different times. At the base of the levee were four pear trees, beginning with the early sugar pear, ending with a late winter pear. The only peach tree we called Indian Blood Cling, whose rich juicy fruit was blood red — I have never seen any other peaches like them. Next to the road was a row of four large mission fig trees, the last one of which was removed in 1954. There were two plum trees and one quince. Between the trees was space for vegetable gardens; alongside were gooseberries and blackberries. It's pleasant to remember the little family orchard of my childhood days. To the south of the house was "The Grove," with its fine growth of dozens of sturdy young oak trees. "The Little Grove," also of fine young oaks, was east of the road, at the southern end of the ranch.

Immediately to the south of the cow corral, during those early days, was the ranch orchard, including pear, apple, cherry and some other fruit trees. The astrachan apple and sugar pear trees were favorites. But long since, the oaks of our lovely groves, as well as the fruit trees of both orchards, have disappeared — with the exception of a few spreading oaks, now grown large, about the more recently built houses, a faithful reminder of the past.

No part or feature of the entire ranch meant more to us boys than the grand river itself. No description can picture our home as it was to us unless it tells of the great oaks and sycamores, and the buckeyes and the willows and cottonwoods, with the graceful wild grape vines reaching to the very tree-tops. The river bank was a fascinating stretch of wilderness to us.

At the base of a great oak, not far from the house, we could fish for perch. A few rods to the south was a tall sycamore tree, one of whose lower limbs grew parallel to the surface of the river, affording a handy ready-made spring-board for the young diver, at our favorite swimming place. But chief of all trees at that popular rendezvous was the venerable leaning buckeye tree, which was climbed again and again by every able-bodied boy of the neighborhood. Dozens of youngsters carved their initials on its trunk and branches, often with the initials of girl friends; and the hearts carved on that old buckeye tree left no doubt of the budding romanticism of the carvers!

It was a great day when the boy first ventured to swim clear across the river — another would accompany him in a row boat for any needed protection. There were no fancy or highly-skilled swimmers among us, but we learned to paddle at a very early age. And of course we learned to handle a row-boat quite naturally, though the narrow flat-bottomed duck-boat seemed tricky to the beginner.

Such is a quick glimpse of the Hunt Ranch at Freeport, as it was at the time of my earliest recollections. The land is still there, its value multiplied many fold. But what a change! Gone is the lake "out-back," with its acres of tall tules; gone are the old willow trees, and the groves of young oaks; gone is my childhood home, to make way for the railroad that now tops the levee. The Sacramento River is still there; but the river bank, with its thousands of tons of rock-fill, with not one tree, bears not the slightest resemblance to the scene of my childhood.

My father was not what you would call a scientific farmer; he never made much money — was never a rich man. But he was a man of true pioneer spirit, who took time now and then to "gas" with a like-minded neighbor — maybe whittling a stick with his sharp-bladed jack-knife — who loved good horses, and who gave his five boys a chance to live a life on the ranch that imbued them, also, with something of the spirit of the true California pioneer. I am grateful for the opportunity that was mine, back in the eighteen-seventies, to spend my early boyhood years under conditions that — unconsciously at the time — helped to lay foundations for a broader, more fruitful life in years that were to come.

Besides the milk-cellar underneath, and the dark, unfinished attic, there were in all eight rooms in our house. These were the rather large kitchen, opening onto the south porch on one side and into the sitting (living) room on the north, four family bedrooms in all, the spare room, and the parlor. There was no separate bathroom, no built-in closets, no hot-and-cold water fixtures, and of course no gas or electric appliances, such as are

BOYHOOD HOME AT FREEPORT

now so commonplace. For lights we depended on kerosene
lamps, supplemented by white tallow candles.

Each of the rooms has its own associations and memories. Next
to the kitchen the sitting room was most used. We seldom saw
the inside of the spare room: it was reserved for visitors, and
visits were infrequent. Of all the rooms in the house, however,
the parlor was the "holy of holies." In my *California Vignettes*
I tried to describe our parlor: I shall give here a condensed
statement of my recollections:

> On the floor was a scrupulously clean old-fashioned carpet —
> the only Brussels carpet in the house — with a pattern of artificial-
> looking flowers, blocks well suited for playing marbles — but of
> course we were not permitted to play marbles in the parlor! On
> the walls hung a number of family portraits in quaint frames, and
> two or three framed mottoes worked in bright-colored worsted
> yarn in perforated cardboard. One hanging over the front door
> proclaimed "HOME SWEET HOME"; another bore the legend
> "PRAISE THE LORD."
>
> Over in the northwest corner stood the "what-not," its half dozen
> bracket shelves literally covered with seashells, mineral specimens,
> and bric-a-brac, some pieces resting on dainty doilies or hand-
> wrought mats. The furniture included a big sofa and set of stiff
> looking chairs, upholstered with shiny black horsehair that was
> so slick and springy that a small boy was in danger of sliding
> off onto the floor!
>
> The center table was very heavy and quite impressive. It had
> a great marble top resting on a support of bronzed cast-iron grill
> work. On the table were a variety of mats and tidies, or doilies —
> samples of mother's tatting and crocheting and Aunt Sarah's knitting.
> On these rested the family photograph album, an assortment of old
> daguerreotypes, a collection of old Mexican dollars, and other me-
> mentoes and keepsakes. There was a big vase with a beautiful
> display of everlasting flowers and exquisitely arranged dried grasses.
> Exactly at the center was the stately parlor lamp, all trimmed and
> ready, but seldom lighted.
>
> The huge family Bible occupied a place of honor all its own on

a prim little stand to the right of the front door as you entered. It was covered with a fluffy tidy lovingly made for that very purpose. The Chickering square piano stood next to the wall adjacent to the sitting room.

Into that dear old parlor mother took her boys, on Sunday evening, for religious instruction and prayers. The great Bible was in her lap. We looked at the colored picture of Moses in the Mountain, Daniel in the Lion's Den, and Jesus at the Last Supper. Mother offered a simple prayer, asking God's blessing for each of her boys, and ending with the Lord's Prayer, repeated by all of us together. Who could ever forget such an experience?

CHAPTER TWO

BOYHOOD DAYS

When I was a lad at Freeport there was no lack of games to be played, either at school or at home. In fact, I hadn't imagined there were so many until I began to recount them in memory.

I suppose that "playing horse" was common to all farmer boys almost from babyhood, where the simplest kind of harness made out of baling rope or string was used, but the driver always had a whip of some kind. Every boy wanted a whip of his own: a good leather lash with a buckskin snapper was most highly prized; but few of us were lucky enough to own one. Of course everybody also played "hide-and-seek," a more complicated form of which we called "picket." Such games as marbles, tops, and kite-flying came in regular seasonal rotation. "Blackman" was played by boys and girls together, usually at school or picnics; same with "drop-the-handkerchief." The final test of our prowess in walking on stilts at our home came at the huge manure pile just outside the window of the horse stable — it was rather ignominious to fail there! Simple yard games included pee-wee, horse-shoes, and tag — sometimes leap-frog, follow-the-leader, and crack-the-whip. Different forms of ball playing included "one-old-cat," "sky-ball," "three-in-and-nine-out," and regular "tom-ball" — even two or three persons could play "catch." But there was nothing distinctive about these games at Freeport.

The bow-and-arrow took the boys out into the fields. A fine

bow made of hickory was unusual. We developed skill in making sharp-pointed arrowheads from pieces of tin. In all our hunting expeditions as small boys I have never known of any bird or animal to be killed; but what of that! It was great fun. One of the cheapest of all our playthings was a slim, tough willow branch, on whose small end we molded a gob of moist 'dobe with our hands: in a wide circling swing the 'dobe was released, almost like the cracking of a whip, and it went sailing through the air for a long distance.

But we played games in the house, too, checkers being the most popular, after marbles. Dominoes probably came next. In case of some small dispute, the contestants might have to "draw cuts" to determine the winner. Among the Hunt boys there was sometimes a good deal of "tall talk," but very seldom any serious quarrel.

The people roundabout were of the pioneer type; most of them had spent but little time in the schoolroom. They knew little of grammar, had never heard of rhetoric. The common vernacular of some of the neighbors would be an interesting subject in local folk-lore, as illustrated by such expressions as, "I seen it," "he done it," "that dog wouldn't bite nobody," and others. Almost everybody dropped the final "g" in words like fishin', workin'; one might be heard saying, "He come a-runnin'; them cows was after him." Some would claim the knife was "hisn"; others claimed it was "hern."

Slang expressions, as now, were plentiful — some of them decidedly picturesque. Let me recall a few. "You make me sick," "Oh, give us a rest," "Anybody that'll take a dare'll suck eggs," "Chewin' the rag," "In a pig's eye," "Goin' like sixty," "He's one o' them blowhards," "You go shoot yourself."

My mother set a high standard for her boys in matters of honesty and moral responsibility. Even "white lies" or "storying" was severely frowned upon. I took quite literally the scriptural verse, "Thou God seest me." I believed He saw everything and judged accordingly.

It would not be accurate to say that our life on the farm, even as young boys, was all play and no work. I can't remember just when I began to do things that might be called work — they came about as naturally as learning to dress myself, tie my own shoestrings with double bow knot, or washing my hands and face before dinner.

I helped with "doing the chores," morning and evening, about as far back as I can remember anything. If I was too little to milk cows, I could hold the cow's tail, sometimes filled with cockleburs, and thus protect the older brother who was milking; if too young to bed the horses or curry them in the evening, I could hold the lantern while another did the work. I could lead the tame horses to the water trough: even the big bull was easy to handle if he had a ring in his nose.

Feeding the young calves was a chore of great regularity. I was pretty small when I began teaching them to drink milk, by coaxing them to suck my fingers that had been dipped into the warm milk, then gradually removing my fingers from the bucket.

But the big chore, morning and evening, was milking the cows — that was expected of us, of course very gradually, just as certainly as morning and evening came. It never seemed wholly mandatory — it was simply expected. Every cow had a name; as "Lucy," "Old Roany," "White Kicker," and all the rest.

Beginning quite young, we all had a part in milking, churning, and butter making. There was not always a clear-cut line between work and play; but the very regularity of some of the chores left no doubt — that was work. And turning the grindstone while father sharpened the sickle of the mowing machine, or the axe — that was work; though I really think father got some fun out of "bearing down" on the sickle harder than necessary, to test our muscles!

One chore was to carry wood upstairs and into the kitchen, to keep the big wood-box filled — and it took a lot of wood! As an economy measure we devised a method of using a gunny-sack, laying it flat on the ground, loading it with sticks of stove wood, then with a shorter boy in front and the taller boy behind, two of us to carry a large load up the stairs with even balance. Cleaning out the wood-box was an exciting event for us children; for we would find lost marbles, a top, a ball, or a piece of string, and sometimes — most exciting of all — a mouse nest filled with baby mice. After a thorough cleaning, the huge box was ready to be filled again.

The first period of my home life on the ranch ended when I was only nine years old; so I cannot say that I had much real work to do — there were three older brothers and the hired men: they did the heavy work. Still, I learned how to do a good many things, for between times there was always something useful to be done. Those nine years, were, on the whole, a very important part of my life, not because of any actual work I did, but because of the useful habits I acquired, the freedom of outdoor life I enjoyed, and the many things I learned as a farmer boy in a perfectly natural way.

My first school, called the West Union, was located a mile north of our home. It was a little one-room wooden building, with capacity for maybe thirty-six pupils. I started going to school when I was only five years old — that was because the teacher, Mary McCann, lived at our house, and she persuaded my mother to let me go.

Of course we walked: such a thing as a school bus had never been thought of. On the way to the schoolhouse we had to pass through Freeport, with its shoemaker's shop, owned by Andy Greer, its blacksmith shop, owned and operated by Tom Kirtlan, its combined post office, general store, and saloon, run by George Webber, and later by Phil Reihl, then on by the O'Toole place, and the Kelly farm. At the O'Toole place they had some geese that sometimes frightened us little folk with their audacity; at Kelly's there were two or three dogs that were inclined to be vicious.

The pupils of that school (usually called scholars) were of all grades, in one room, taught by one teacher. For a little while all five of the Hunt brothers were there at one time. My oldest brother, Major, was a youth of fourteen or fifteen when I began, at five.

One of my first tasks was to learn the alphabet. Then there were large charts with pictures and simple words like C A T, D O G, B O Y, with the word spelled out in big letters. The beginner would tell the letters, then the picture would help him to say what they spelled. A few years later it came my younger brother George's turn: he read off the letters correctly, "MOUSE," then, glancing at the picture, he boldly said "little rat" — not a bad guess from what the chart showed!

Memory played a large part in my early schooling. I memorized the name of California's counties in alphabetical arrangement; later I memorized the capitals and their locations in all the states in the Union; as "Maine, Augusta, on the Kennebec River; New Hampshire, Concord, on the Merrimac River," and on through the entire list. Of course I learned the names of the presidents in order, beginning with George Washington. But also we had to memorize certain poetic and prose selections. All of which might have been bad pedagogy, but to me not without some permanent value. Isn't it still necessary to memorize the multiplication table, and the order of the letters of the alphabet?

As an inducement to good conduct and to study, the teacher had a system of colored picture cards, called "Reward of Merit," signed by herself, a certain number of which would entitle the pupil to a much larger card.

One day in school I had a strange little accident that never happened to any other boy I ever heard of. My sharpened slate pencil, about two and a half inches long, was the cause of it. I put it into my mouth and found it was just long enough to reach from the roof of my mouth to the bottom when I held it in a vertical position with my mouth wide open. But it got stuck tight in that position and I couldn't take it out — it hurt so! Finally the teacher, seeing my distress, called my oldest brother Major over, and he got it out for me. Really, my embarrassment was greater than the actual pain.

I had four different teachers at the West Union School. Besides Miss McCann there were George H. Tuck, B. F. Howard, and Albert Leimbach. I remember Mr. Tuck, after all these years, chiefly because while he was my teacher I won two prizes, open to the whole school. I was only about seven years old, and was so surprised when the announcement was made that I couldn't forget it even if I tried. The first prize was for deportment — I had gone through the whole term without being seen whispering once, and there were no other black marks against me. I was presented with a bright $2.50 gold piece! I had been simply a bashful little boy, too timid to do anything to disturb the teacher.

The other prize was for improvement in penmanship. That was amazing; for I had scarcely learned to write at the beginning of the term: but it was for *improvement* in penmanship, not penmanship. My prize was a fine copy of the *Compendium of Spencerian or Semi-Angular Penmanship*. The fly-leaf bears the inscription:

From George H. Tuck

to

Rockie D. Hunt

as a Reward for Industry

For eighty years I have treasured this book: it was a stimulus to me to be a good penman. I hold it in my left hand as I write these words. As to the $2.50 piece, I deposited it in a savings bank in Sacramento, which later became bankrupt — and that was the end of my prize money!

My principal reason for remembering Mr. Howard is that he would play ball with the boys at recess time — we liked that. The ball we used was of solid rubber, and the playground was not very large; so we had a rule that "over the fence is out." In spite of the rule, occasionally the ball soared over the fence and into Mr. Kelly's alfalfa field. More than once he saw some boys there looking for the ball, and he came tramping over, berating them savagely as they scampered out of the field — we didn't like that! Someone devised the inelegant slogan, "Tom Kelly, with a buckskin belly." However, no boy suffered any actual physical harm at the hand of Mr. Kelly.

Albert Leimbach was my last teacher at the old West Union School. He was a good teacher, not at all the blustering type. As usual I got along well in my studies and liked my teacher. After our family moved to Napa in the summer of 1877, I wrote Mr. Leimbach a letter, the first I ever wrote, so I took a good deal of pains in writing it. I was nine years old. It made me happy to have a reply from my teacher.

One sport the boys enjoyed after a rain, when the ground was wet and slippery was that of sliding on a selected spot on the adobe from a running start. There was no snow or ice to skate or slide on, but we developed considerable skill in sliding on the slippery mud, going on one foot, sometimes a distance of fifteen to twenty feet. When a boy lost his balance and took a tumble and got mud on his pants, we said he "caught a cod-fish."

Naturally, there was an occasional school-boy fight, but that usually occurred after school. I was a very peaceful child — never got into a school fight. Sometimes, in the spring, the boys walked over to the river on the way home and went swimming.

On at least one occasion some of the girls went over and hid the boys' clothes or tied them into knots.

Now and then some little childish romance came to light, as when a boy would scribble a note and furtively throw it across the aisle to a special girl: when she opened the note it read:

> Roses are red,
> Violets are blue,
> Sugar is sweet
> And so are you.

Singing by the entire school was usually a part of the day's program — of course without benefit of piano or organ. But some of the teachers were not very musically inclined. The "Multiplication Song" and the "Geography Song" were going out of use — like the "dunce cap" — in my early childhood. But I used to hear older boys and girls sing such songs as that beginning —

> Oh, have you heard Geography sung —
> For if you've not it's on my tongue.

Some of the songs were intended to convey moral lessons: as —

> Speak gently, it is better far
> To rule by love than fear;
> Speak gently, let no harsh word mar
> The good we may do here.

Here's another of the same sort:

> Little drops of water,
> Little grains of sand,
> Make the mighty ocean
> And the pleasant land.

Later, in college, a member of the Temperance Society, when called on for his quotation, presented this parody:

> Little drops of water,
> Little sips of gin,
> Make the red proboscis
> And consume the tin.

The older pupils enjoyed such songs as "My Old Virginny Home," "Moonlight on the Lake," "Golden Slippers," "Old Black Joe," and "Maggie May." When I was fourteen years old, and Mrs. Breck in the Freeport School, the teacher, tried to get me to sing with the others some of the little songs suited to mere kindergartners, I stubbornly balked. I still remember one of those songs whose first lines were:

> Oh, I'll be as good a child as ever I can be;
> I'll mind what my teacher says to me.
> When wicked children tempt me to play
> I'll ask my teacher to send them away.

Imagine a big fourteen-year-old farmer boy being asked to sing a song like that!

Outside of school I learned some songs, often from the hired man, that would not pass muster in any Sunday School, or even day school, as one or two sample quotations will reveal:

> Where, O where, has my little dog gone?
> Where, O where, can he be?
> With his tail cut short and his ears cut long —
> Where, O where, can he be?

Another, taken from a convivial song:

> If I had a cow that'd give such milk,
> I'd dress her in the finest silk;
> I'd feed her on the choicest hay,
> And milk her forty times a day.

Other popular songs were "Little Brown Jug," "Old Dan Tucker," and "Pop! Goes the Weasel."

During my childhood days I learned more songs in church and Sunday School than all other places combined. Naturally, one of the very first was "Jesus Loves Me, This I Know." Among the most popular were, "The Sweet By-and-By," "Gather at the River," and "Stand up for Jesus." Among the church hymns some favorites were: "Rock of Ages," "Come, Thou Fount," "Sweet Hour of Prayer," and "Nearer, My God, to Thee."

Those first years of school, in the little country schoolhouse, were good for me. My teachers showed genuine interest in my personal progress, and I acquired the habit of being thorough in my studies. I doubt whether I could have made much more substantial progress in the luxurious, graded schools, with all their modern equipment, of the present day. I really studied the McGuffey readers, and my teachers saw to it that I learned my lessons.

The church of my childhood was really no church at all, but only the little West Union schoolhouse, where I went to school. Freeport was one of the stations on the circuit of a Methodist itinerant preacher. Preaching service was held fortnightly; Sunday School every Sunday morning. There were probably not more than a dozen grown-up members: the congregations sometimes consisted of from six to ten persons, though usually the little schoolroom was comfortably filled with the country folk living round-about.

On Sunday we were not permitted to work — except to do the regular chores, of course. The wood and kindling must be brought in on Saturday; likewise our shoes must be blacked. We were not to go hunting or fishing, nor play the regular games, nor go to parties on Sunday. Sunday School and church were the regular order for the forenoon. For that we must be scrubbed clean, then we put on our "Sunday-go-to-meetin'" clothes.

This scrubbing was serious business. Here's how mother handled it when we were little — take my own case; and don't imagine I have forgotten it! It was in the kitchen, where a wash basin filled with warm water was ready on the table. She used a big cake of the hard mottled soap, the kind father always used in washing harness. She began with my head and scrubbed it thoroughly, some of the suds getting into my eyes — and they did smart! Then she came to my ears, and the place behind my ears, and all around my ears — the dirt didn't have a chance! And so it was with my eyes, mouth, chin, and neck. But finally we were ready for Sunday School; father gave us a dime for collection; and off we went in the spring wagon.

In the afternoon, after dinner and before chore time, we usually stayed in the house or about the yard. Mother would read to us from the Sunday School paper or a book. She knew that healthy young boys like to be active; but considering her puritanical principles, she managed her brood remarkably well during those sometimes difficult Sunday afternoons.

The preacher that I remember best was Rev. H. J. Bland, who had come to California in 1857, and was a brother of Rev. Adam Bland, who had reached San Francisco a half-dozen years earlier. Our Freeport preacher was not a great scholar; he had never heard of rural sociology; he was not an eloquent speaker, never served a large city church. But he was a faithful minister of the gospel, was sure of his message, bold to denounce sin and exhort to Christian duty. He courageously held forth for the church at the Freeport station. His son Henry Meade Bland, later a teacher in the San José State Normal School and the University of the Pacific, became second Poet Laureate of California, following the death of Ina Coolbrith, who was the first to enjoy that distinction.

Among the members of the Freeport church there was no more devoted member than my mother. The congregation was never complete without her and her children. But she was also a regular teacher in the Sunday School. Many a Sunday morning my father's stoutly built spring wagon carried a dozen or more of the neighborhood children, including the Hunt boys, bound for the West Union schoolhouse. The preacher always found a welcome in our home: a well prepared chicken dinner awaited him whenever he could call. All in all, my mother was more than a pillar to that little church; but it served to help her to stand true to her high purpose and to rear her sons in sobriety and integrity.

Hog-killing time on the Hunt Ranch came annually, after the first frosts, usually between Thanksgiving and Christmas. Ordinarily two hogs of the proper weight and in good condition were selected for the slaughter. Father was the executioner, sometimes using a sharp butcher-knife to cut the hog's throat, sometimes employing the axe for a heavy blow on the head — though in later years the rifle was deemed more satisfactory.

After bleeding, the carcass was doused in a caldron of boiling-hot water; then we all had a hand in scraping the hide clean of hairs, with knives little and big. We boys were eager to get the bladder, in order to blow it up to full capacity, tie the tube tightly, after putting two or three dry beans or peas inside. When the bladder had become thoroughly dry we had a good make-believe balloon, also an excellent rattle, which would keep for a good many days.

The clean carcasses were hung, heads-down, from a limb of the oak tree near the pump, out of reach of the cats and dogs, and exposed overnight in the cold crisp air. After that they were ready for the dissecting process.

Then, as I remember it, we had several days of feasting on the choicest of head-cheese, spare-ribs, fresh sausage and pigs' feet — though personally I cared little for the feet. I could scarcely conceive of better head-cheese than that prepared and served by my mother on the Freeport Ranch.

At the base of the levee we had a small smokehouse in which, over a period of a few years, hams and bacon were cured. But a large part of the meat was salted down: then for months salt-pork was an important article in the family diet. In fact, we had so much pork-and-beans that we sometimes got heartily tired of it, and were ready to welcome a change to wild ducks and geese, or beef-steak.

Hog-killing might be called a family event, the family including the hired man. As boys we used to hear a good deal about making whistles out of pigs' tails and a purse out of a sow's ears: but I soon came to regard all such talk as pure myth.

My childhood reading was rather limited in scope; but we had access to some good books, from the Sunday School library, and a few belonging to the home. For example, we had a beautiful copy of *The Annals of San Francisco*, which father had presented to his brother; and Richardson's *Beyond the Mississippi* was a book which we thumbed through many times; although the text was too advanced for us, we looked at the pictures again and again. These two favorites are now among my choicest items of Californiana. In addition to our schoolbooks we had such books as *Swiss Family Robinson* and *Thaddeus of Warsaw;* then, a little later, *Log Cabin to White House, Tom Sawyer, Memoirs of U. S. Grant,* and an increasing number of others. As I became older I read *Plutarch's Lives,* and at seventeen made bold to read Bowne's *Philosophy of Herbert Spencer.*

The Youth's Companion was the number one paper; its weekly visit was always eagerly awaited. Second to it was the *Classmate,* leading Sunday School paper. The newspaper most depended on was the Sacramento *Record-Union* — but that was for the old folks.

We never had the habit of reading in bed, partly because there was no lamp for our bed. Bed-time usually came pretty early; but we did not always go to sleep right away: sometimes we boys took some dried apples or figs with us and put them under the pillows. And when I was very small my brother Mark and

I slept in a little trundle bed, in the same room with father and mother. We discovered that the box of ginger-snaps had been placed on top of the wardrobe at the foot of our bed. By standing on the bed-rail Mark was just able to reach into the box — I was too small. So, for I don't know how long, after we were safely in bed, alone, Mark quietly reached up each night and took out three ginger snaps, giving me one and eating two himself!

Here are a few of the standing orders in our home while I was a child:

"Clean your feet" — meaning boots or shoes — before coming into the house. An order that was much needed.

"Take off your hat!" It was not right to wear a hat in the house.

"Comb your hair," before meals: this in addition to washing hands and face.

"Keep your shirt-tail in." One was not well-dressed otherwise: it was a serious criticism to hear the words, "Your shirt-tail's out."

"Keep your pants buttoned" was an order that every boy had better pay strict heed to.

"Always say 'Mister' when speaking of a man; it's improper to call him by his first name."

"Never walk pigeon-toed": toeing-in is considered very bad form.

"Keep your nose clean," was not always easy when one had a handkerchief only on Sundays.

"In company children should be seen, not heard."

Of course we were carefully taught to tell the truth and use only good words. Mother said: "I'll have to wash out your mouth with soap if you tell a lie or say bad words."

One or two other bits of the folklore of childhood may at least be mentioned. One pertained to apple seeds. While eating an apple we often carefully counted the seeds, reciting a little jingle, as we checked them off, something like this:

> One I love, two I love,
> Three I love, I say;
> Four I love with all my heart,
> Five I cast away:
> Six he loves, seven she loves,
> Eight they both love.
> Nine they court,
> Ten they marry.

Any count above ten was purely impromptu.

Then there was the "love vine," or "love-entangle," as we called it — in reality a bright yellow parasite properly known as dodder, whose long thread-like tendrils twine about clover, or wayside bushes. When a boy came upon a growth of "love vine," he was likely to pluck a handful, swing it three times around his head, then throw it into the tall grass or shrubbery. If it grew, that was proof she loved him; if it died she loved him not. But to the farmer it was dodder, a pesky parasite — good for nothing.

As farmer boys back in the 1870's we always looked forward to certain special days of the year — Christmas, Easter, May Day, and Fourth of July. There were also Thanksgiving Day and birthdays; but they did not mean quite so much to us.

Although the Christmas entertainment was primarily for the children, most of the grownups of the community were there, too, on Christmas eve, in the schoolhouse. The Christmas tree was lighted up with many little candles; there was always plenty of candy and nuts. Joe Gosling, Sunday School superintendent, was usually in charge. For the children the religious setting for the program was overshadowed by the appearance of Santa Claus — one of our neighbors, whose identity some one was sure to discover and pass the word around.

Giving out the gifts was the most interesting part. When the recipient's name was called he marched to the front for his package, which he opened so all could see: if it was a horn he gave it a toot; if it was a mouth-organ he played a few notes. There was plenty of hilarity and innocent fun. Then, after singing "Joy to the World, the Lord is Come," everybody went home happy. Each wished to be ready early the next morning to greet the others with "Merry Christmas!" No child had been forgotten — it was one of the happiest times of the year for us.

Each year we boys looked forward to the coming of Easter Sunday. Beginning weeks ahead, each of us would hide away some eggs, which we found in the hens' nests, to be sure of a good supply for coloring. Before we had heard about Diamond Dyes we learned what to use to bring out certain colors, from bright yellow to dark brown. Black walnut hulls and coffee would produce different shades of brown; onion skins and saffron made the eggs yellow; dipping them in red ink gave a bright pink. Also, with mother's help we learned how to sew a bright piece of calico print tightly around the egg so that the colored pattern would be neatly transferred to the egg. Of course each boy had all the eggs he wished. One Easter Sunday — I think I must have been a pretty big boy — I ate, in all, fifteen eggs; that was my record.

For many years it was a regular custom to have the Grangers' Picnic in Beach's Grove on May Day. Farmers from far and near came with their families, in wagons, carriages, and buggies, and made a day of it. It was a lively time for us boys: the older folks enjoyed it, too, for friends and neighbors who did not get to see each other often had the best kind of time in their group reunions. Families united for the picnic dinner: the tables were loaded with good things. I remember that one of mother's frequent contributions to the dinner was a huge chicken pie, baked in the kitchen wash-pan. One morning mother placed the big pie, hot from the stove and covered with heavy cloth, under the front seat of the wagon, all ready to go, but unknown to me. Boy-like I was climbing around in the wagon when all at once I put my foot right into that pie! But it was well protected by the cloth cover, the chicken pie suffered no damage, and nobody told anybody what had happened. I may safely confess after all these years!

There was dancing to the music of a small orchestra, and there was the merry-go-round for the children. Ice-cream and lemonade were a special treat to us boys. In the afternoon a program of foot races and other contests had the right of way. Sometimes they had a greased pole, with a prize for the boy who could reach the top. But most exciting of all was the chase for the greased pig — as the frightened pig dashed wildly through the crowd the scampering of the people can only be imagined.

Picnic Day saw more horse-drawn vehicles on the dirt road than any other day, many of them from Sacramento, ten miles north of the grove. It seems remarkable there were so few accidents or runaways. There were no traffic laws like we now have; and there were a good many friendly "brushes" on the road.

For us boys on the Freeport ranch the Fourth of July was the greatest day of the calendar. For weeks we eagerly looked forward to it. "Are you going to the Fourth?" every boy was asking his neighbors — which meant, going to Sacramento to celebrate. Everybody who possibly could "went to town." The day was ushered in with shot-gun salutes by the older boys and men at the midnight hour, also with explosion of giant firecrackers and the bang! bang! bang! of the six-shooters. But all that was not enough. A group of men had arranged to "fire off the anvils" — that was real cannonading! One of their number used a long iron rod, heated red-hot, to touch off the heavy charge of powder, and the explosion could be heard for miles.

The beautiful flag was hoisted to the top of the flag-pole in honor of the day. But the real celebration was in Sacramento: of course each of us had to have a little money to buy fireworks. We had been saving up the dimes received from the "rag man," and this was supplemented by father, who enjoyed seeing his boys have a good time.

Once in town, we lost no time in hastening over to Chinatown, on I Street, where we mentally figured out what fireworks we could buy with the money we had — how many bunches of small firecrackers, and giants, how many Roman candles, sky-rockets, pin-wheels, volcanoes, and torpedoes. By working together we managed to get a good assortment.

A big event was the "Procession," a truly wonderful sight for us. I remember the great procession of July 4, 1876, the Centennial Year. There was a big ship, on wheels, representing Columbia, the Ship of State. It was impressive to watch it as it moved majestically down K Street.

Best of the whole Fourth was the grand display of evening fireworks in Capitol Park. We went early, to obtain a good spot where we could see everything. When it was all over we were sleepy and tired, ready for the ride home. For the first mile or two we kept looking fondly back to watch the shooting sky-rockets as they exploded high in air. But in a little while, after the horses had settled into a steady trot on the open roadway, we slipped down, one after another, into the bed of the wagon, and soon were fast asleep. Our Fourth of July celebration faded quietly away, blended into happy dreams of boyhood.

The move to Napa in 1877 was a real occasion for the D. R. Hunt family — the most significant occasion, I think, in the history of the family to that time, since the birth of the youngest of the five sons, my brother George, in 1870. Major, my oldest brother, was almost nineteen: I was nine and a half.

We called it sixty miles from Freeport to Napa, crossing the

Sacramento River on the ferry boat, then proceeding on the Yolo side by the cut-off through the Glide tules to Dixon, then on to Elmira, Suisun, and Cordelia, when we came into the beautiful hills as you enter the charming Napa Valley at the little Suscol settlement, where Mr. True had his tavern. Then it was almost due north to Napa City, county seat of Napa County.

But there was no great van for the transport of our household goods — nor did we ship them by freight car. We carried our possessions in our sturdily built wagon, drawn by my father's strong horses. And it required more than one trip to complete the job.

Three little incidents *en route* so impressed my childish mind that I can recall them now with vividness. The first was at the end of the first day of the two-day trip. We stopped for the night at the Eibe Ranch, not far from Elmira. Mrs. Emily Eibe West was a distant relative of our family, whom we boys always referred to as "Aunt Emily," and her son Tom Eibe is still well remembered in that farming community. But what impressed us boys was the hills to the west of us — they seemed so near that we could easily walk to them after supper, and were inclined to start out. We had not been used to seeing big hills at Freeport. On being told they were so many miles away, the thought of such a walk had to be abandoned; we contented ourselves by going over to the nearby railroad track and laying on the rails a few pins whose heads were carefully placed upon metal buttons so that when the cars ran over them we might find some odd little stick-pins.

The second incident was our stop for lunch in the hills west of Cordelia. We boys reveled in the hills — they were a real treat to us! I could now come close to identifying the exact spot on the road where we stopped. We climbed up and around on the hillside, to the right of us, then down into the canyon, to the left, where the live oaks and buckeyes were.

Then, after crossing the boundary into Napa County, and fairly headed to the north, all at once we caught a glimpse of the castle-like towers of Napa State Insane Asylum in the distance. I thought, "with all those towers and steeples, what a beautiful city Napa must be!" Alas, it was the impressive home for those who had been declared insane, or mentally ill, whose imposing central tower was later laid low by an earthquake; and the entire structure, more recently, has been completely supplanted and transformed from the appearance of a great medieval castle to the more scientific arrangement of the cottage system — no longer the "Insane Asylum" but now the "Napa State Hospital."

With profound gratitude in my heart, I wish here to record the fact that the move from the Freeport ranch to Napa was brought about chiefly by the loving devotion and initiative of my mother. She was deeply religious, and she had in childhood enjoyed only very meager opportunities for an education. There was no church in Freeport, which was an outlying station on the circuit of a Methodist preacher, service being held weekly, sometimes only bi-weekly, in the little West Union schoolhouse, a mile from our home. There were no school facilities beyond the elementary grades, and Sacramento was eight miles distant — such a thing as a school bus was unknown. The move to Napa was motivated by the superior educational and religious facilities offered there; mother was determined that her boys should have better opportunities. So far as I ever knew, father never actively opposed the move — a major change for him as a farmer — but he was less aggressive in the matter, though it became apparent enough that he too wished his sons to enjoy better opportunities.

At Napa not only were there good public schools, but also, and chiefly, there was Napa Collegiate Institute, controlled by the Methodist Episcopal Church, which later became the four-year Napa College. My oldest brother Major had been a boarding student there and had graduated from the Commercial Department even before the family move. Each one of the five brothers, for varying periods of time, attended Napa Collegiate Institute.

Our first home in Napa was on north Main Street; but that proved to be purely temporary. Then we lived at the Eaton place in the southern part of town, on Elm Street. While there, father purchased the Fancher home, corner of Franklin and Elm Streets, and small acreage; and that proved to be my home with the exception of three years, until 1896, by which time all the Hunt brothers were on their own, and our parents then moved back to Sacramento.

But in the meantime, after three years in Napa, the family had returned to the Freeport ranch because of its unsatisfactory management by the tenant. It was during that period, 1880 to 1883, that I really learned the work as well as the play of the farmer boy; also received my last public schooling. More about that period on subsequent pages.

The Franklin Public School, my first in Napa, was very conveniently located for me. It was a two-room school, and my teacher's name was Mr. Tinning. My brothers Frank and Mark went to the Central Public School, half a mile from home, for the higher grades; and in the course of time I was transferred to Central, which was a fairly large school, including the upper grades. The principal at the time was a very tall young man, Frank H. Darling — though he didn't seem young to me then — and I think he had red hair.

It was while in that school that I had what to me was an experience of a lifetime. I had never given offense in school; my "deportment" grade was always high: but in that Central Public School I came within an ace — whatever that means! — of receiving a flogging by the big principal. Here's how it happened, as nearly as I can now remember — it is still quite vivid.

In our arithmetic book there was a note in small type in which the word "uniformly" was used. This I did not understand. My teacher, Miss Gregory, asked me to remain after school. I either forgot her order, or failed to take it seriously. Anyway, the next day, to my amazement, with four or five other boys charged with various kinds of misconduct, I was sent upstairs to the principal's room for discipline. Mr. Darling lined us up along the blackboard near the front, on the right side as you enter, I being the last one in the line.

Then the principal went to work on us, one after the other, in the presence, of course, of his room-full of older pupils, including my two older brothers. Each boy was catechized, as to his age, his weight, etc., the final question being, "How long has it been since you had a whipping in school before?" Then he took his ruler, or strap, and laid it on — each one till he came to me! By that time, painfully conscious that my own brothers sat there grinning at me, feeling terribly humiliated, and whimpering a little, Mr. Darling quizzed me. He came to his final question: "How long since you got a whipping at school?" It must have been close to a sob as I replied, "I never had one." "Then I'm not going to give you one now," he said — and he didn't! But that was the nearest to receiving a flogging in school I ever came — it was near enough!

My brothers graduated from the school under the new principal J. L. Shearer; but before my turn came to graduate the family moved back to Freeport, where I attended my last public school.

When I report that the family moved back to the ranch in 1880, that does not include one member, my oldest brother Major — he had married his Napa sweetheart Anna Thorne, and was on his own. But four of the five were there — two were too old for the public school; all of us were old enough to work. And there was plenty to do — more than plenty during the summer months.

It was chiefly a dairy farm — and there is something very steady and exacting about dairying. "Cow time" comes with painful regularity. Whether playing a game of ball, or in swimming in the river, or in the watermelon patch in the back field, whenever we heard the ominous words "Cow time," the sport was suddenly ended, one of us saddled his horse to go out and bring in the cows, another threw down the hay from the barn loft, while the third spread it before the stanchions, and the cows filed into their regular places. Then all hands literally became busy with the milking — no electric milking machines in those days! As a youth I got to the point where for a while I milked as high as twenty-five cows night and morning, as my regular chore, though that was a maximum.

Naturally, when three or four of us were at work in the cow barn, our chores were taken as a matter of course; sometimes there was even an element of fun. One year, when I was about fourteen or fifteen, I played a trick on our Chinese house boy (about my age) that I have been just the least bit ashamed of ever since. At the time a part of his work was to help with the milking. We had one white cow that we all knew was a kicker: she was high strung and irritable — needed to be handled with punctilious care, or there was danger she might kick over the bucket of milk and perhaps the milker, too.

One day the Chinaboy was about to milk the cow standing next in line, so his back would be to "Kicker." As a precaution, he "heisted" her over as far as he could, to leave ample space between the two cows.

I observed his timid action, and decided on the trick. Slipping in between the two cows standing next beyond "Kicker," I quietly reached over the one next to her and just slightly tickled her on the back. That was enough! It was like pulling the trigger! She blazed away with her left hind foot, which found the middle of the young Oriental's back and "scared him out of a year's growth!" He jumped to the middle of the barn floor and groaned as if he had been nearly killed. The trick was only too successful! I don't suppose that lad ever did know why the white cow kicked him in the back!

While I did a good many kinds of farm work, there were a few jobs I was not called on to do, because there were my older brothers, or the hired man. For example, I did not run the mowing machine, I never plowed with the gang plow (though I could follow the harrow for hours), or drove the four-horse team. But I could rake the hay into windrows and had plenty of experience putting up the cocks, then loading the hay onto the wagon to be hauled to the barn.

Some of the hardest work I ever did was in the mowing season in the dusty hay away in the wings of the big barn loft, standing knee-deep in the hay dumped from the derrick fork, with the hot roof only two or three feet above my head. That was what I called *work!*

I recall one other spasmodic piece of work that was a fair match for the hay-mowing. The threshing crew were in the back field threshing the barley crop: one man was hauling the filled sacks to the granary, where I was engaged in emptying the sacks. Then they ran short of sacks in the field, and it was my job to furnish empty sacks for the crew — otherwise valuable time would be wasted. There I was, standing in the loose barley on the granary floor, racing with the threshing machine out back, trying to empty those 100-pound sacks of grain fast enough to keep the threshing machine running! It didn't last long, but while it did last, I think it was as strenuous as any effort I ever put forth on the farm — or anywhere else!

Making good butter was a meticulous job. Our milk cellar was the basement floor of the house, the west wall being directly against the extended levee along the river. When the doors were closed it was almost totally dark inside, not far from being sub-

terranean, which made it easy to maintain an even, cool temperature the year round. On the hard ground floor stood the well-
built milk racks; near the center was the large box churn, and
alongside was the butter-maker. After suitable working and
salting, the butter was molded into two-pound rolls and each
round roll stamped with the "H" on one end. The Hunt butter
became well known to the Sacramento grocers. Later on my
brother Mark, who was a farmer most of his life, became one
of the best butter makers in the county.

The fresh milk was brought in from the cow barn, strained
into milk-pans that filled the racks. After the proper amount of
time skimming the milk was a regular chore, the cream being
accumulated for churning and the sour milk carried out to the
hog-pen and poured into the swill barrel.

Washing the pans was done systematically, putting each pan
through three processes — three boys could work at this to good
advantage, each for a single process. First, there was the quick
rinsing; second, the thorough washing in hot water; third, the
scalding, in water near the boiling point. Then the piles of pans
were carried outside to the long table and spread in such a way,
each resting upon those beneath, as to dry perfectly in the sunshine.

The last public school I attended was the Freeport School,
located at the southern end of the Hunt Ranch, almost against the
levee. My last teacher was Mrs. Mary Breck. I had come up to
the highest grade in the one-room school — then called the first
grade — a tall, awkward, gangling boy of fourteen. But I was
a good student, that is, if report cards are any criterion!

Most amazing of all is the report card for the month beginning
February 5, 1883, duly signed by my teacher and approved by
my father, recently found among my old belongings, that shows
an average of 100⅜%! Eight subjects, including Deportment
(in which I received 100) were graded; but in Philosophy

(elementary physics) my grade, *recorded in ink*, was 106, and Physiology 105½ — allowed, as nearly as I can remember, for certain extra work. For that month I amassed the astounding total of 803 points: average, 100⅜%! Any wonder I look upon that report as a treasured souvenir!

I had become proficient in diagramming sentences as a method of studying grammar, showing the relations of subject, predicate, and all modifying words and clauses properly arranged in what might be called a neat little organization chart. The teacher thought I wrote a good Spencerian hand. It amuses me now to recall that, for the special day the trustees visited the school, Mrs. Breck had me diagram some complex sentences in my best style on the front blackboard, imagining that such an exhibition would favorably impress the farmer-trustees, who had never heard of a diagrammed sentence, when they came to inspect the school!

My classes were very small, the only other pupil who was in almost all my classes was Flora Beach: Flora and I were rivals in a way — both of us made high grades. And I here confess we thought a good deal of each other — just as schoolmates, of course. Of all the girls of my acquaintance in that entire community I would have singled her out as the most attractive and most promising.

One day — maybe more than one! — since our desks were not far apart, we took to writing notes on our slates and holding them up rather shyly for each other to read. One note she wrote I can remember almost literally today. It read something like this: "When I go to Harvard I'm going to study Philology, Archaeology, and Anthropology." Then I wrote on my slate, and held it up, not quite so shyly, for her to read: "When I go to Yale I'll study Philosophy, Geology, and Ethnology."

But Flora never went to college. Yet if she were living today I think she would remember our exchange of fanciful notes, with the big words we knew so little about, written on our slates in the

ROCK HUNT, AT FOURTEEN

little green Freeport schoolhouse, three-quarters of a century ago.

Mrs. Breck was a good teacher — it's pleasant to remember her now, and I still prize the scrapbook she gave me in 1882. I responded to all her instruction heartily and with alacrity — with one exception: that was her vain attempt to get me to sing with the others when the song was some simple little ditty intended for tots of six and seven, and I a gawking youth nearly six feet tall! Even when she tapped me gently on the head with the drumstick she used as a baton I failed to respond! But far be it from me to hold that against her now!

Never in my life have I, even in the slightest degree, acquired the habit of using profane or vulgar language. The early instruction by my mother has been adhered to throughout. As a mere youth I once offered my brothers and neighbor boys a dollar for every time they heard me use a swear word if they would give me a dime for every time I heard them. Not one of them ever took me up!

This probably seems strange for one growing up in California where swearing was so common among men. Many young men who had never uttered an oath back in the states, quickly acquired the habit in early days in California, and — as one writer expressed it — "clothe themselves with curses as with a garment." In the famous Shirley Letters the writer said, "...during the short time that I have been at Rich Bar, I have heard more of it than in all my life before."

I have been, though not frequently, in the company of a small group of men where the use of profanity was virtually unanimous. This was particularly true in the mountain camp, where every other man swore as naturally as the water of the creek came tumbling down the cascade — they even seemed to vie with each other in the profuse use of profanity: I was not tempted to indulge in any degree.

While the habit with some has become so fixed as to be almost second nature, and they may attach no evil to it, to me it is revolting, wholly unnecessary, and reveals a paucity of vocabulary that is deplorable. Instead of adding weight to simple statement of fact or opinion, from my standpoint it has precisely the opposite effect — it reveals weakness and limitation.

It is a matter of regret that most recent works of fiction, even novels of high literary rank, contain a greater or lesser degree of profanity and vulgarity. My spirit rebels against it. If, as one argues, this is but a reflection of real life, then, I ask, is it essential to good writing to be so realistic as to descend into the filth and slime of cheap vulgarity? Personally, I resent such writing.

My extreme bashfulness as a child and youth often amounted to a real personal affliction. I seemed incapable of shaking it off. Many and many a time it made me suffer poignantly. Even as a young boy I was backward when it came to standing up for my own rights; I'm sure I was needlessly imposed upon by others sometimes — or even by my own brothers — on a good many occasions.

My bashfulness became more acute when I reached my early teens. It was particularly trying in relation to the girls. I had no sister, not even a girl cousin who lived with us for any length of time. Yet I was — quite normally, I suppose — very curious about girls. Other boys could enter heartily into the common games, like black-man, blindman's buff, and drop-the-handkerchief, with the girls; but my bashfulness brought a self-consciousness that caused me to hesitate, or stand aloof. And I hated myself for it.

What made matters worse was the fact that my teeth became defective while I was still quite young, and I had become painfully conscious of this; so I restrained myself in smiling and seldom laughed heartily. We were permitted to grow up with scarcely any dental service; our parents did not require any special attention to our teeth. In our country neighborhood about the only occasion for going to a dentist was to have a tooth pulled! And our diet was not selected with reference to producing good sound teeth. All this has always been a matter of keen regret to me. In my case it greatly emphasized my natural bashfulness, besides bringing many an hour of painful toothache and depriving me of a fine part of my normal heritage.

A climax in my awkward bashfulness was reached one evening when I was about fourteen, at a party of boys and girls, gathered from the neighborhood. At least one of the games was of the kind they used to call "kissing games." Some one would spin a pie-tin on the floor in the center of the circle. Forfeits were to be paid, according to the judgment meted out by the blindfolded leader, who would solemnly say; "Heavy, heavy, hangs over your head — what shall the owner do to redeem it?" Then blind justice would announce the penalty and the culprit proceeded to carry out the decree. My turn came: "What shall the owner [myself] do to redeem it?" In solemn tones came the (to me) terrifying reply, "Go to Jerusalem with Flora Beach." "Going to Jerusalem" with a girl meant that the boy must go all around the circle and kiss every girl, and the girl named must accompany him and kiss every boy! Great horrors! I had never done such a thing as that! I couldn't do it then! I flatly disobeyed the judicial decree at my peril and almost broke up the party! I never found out just what Flora did; but many a time I've thought, what a gawking, clumsy, bashful youth I was, and what an opportunity I missed forever — and there wasn't a girl in the party I liked better than Flora!

I don't suppose Freeport proper ever had a total population in excess of 150 souls, including children — usually it was more likely to be under 100. But to me as a small boy each man living there was a real character. Let me mention the men I remember best.

In retrospect I would not give greater prominence to any man there than to my own father. But omitting him, probably best known among those living there during my boyhood years was Tom Kirtlan, the blacksmith, head of a family of sons and daughters. He and my father were great cronies. Many a time in fascination I watched him at his work at the anvil, making the sparks fly as his hammer descended upon the red-hot iron, blow on blow, then listened to its "fizz" as he plunged it into the water trough. He never seemed to mind my presence. He did the blacksmithing for farmers up and down the Sacramento River for several miles. His son Fred was my most constant playmate and schoolmate among the boys of the neighborhood.

In partnership with Mr. Kirtlan was Jim Lee, who might be called a carriage maker and painter. He was an old bachelor, with rather bald head and full reddish-brown beard. When he dressed up in his Sunday best he was, I think, the nearest of any of the men, the dude of the village — his boots were well polished, his suit spotless. During high water he was called upon more than once to build a row-boat for some farmer whose land was flooded. We boys were always proud to have a bow made by him out of a hickory stick. He seemed to be well liked by everybody.

Across the road from the blacksmith shop was a comical-looking little building, the boot-and-shoemaker shop, where Andy Greer could always be found "pegging away." He was perhaps the most unique character in Freeport, small in stature, with prominent red nose and brick-red beard. There he sat, in his close-fitting concave leather seat, working long hours at his trade and taking real pride in what he did. Often one or two boys would be found there, and they were made welcome: they liked to watch him make "wax-ends," or listen to his queer little songs. A fragment from one of his songs, far from elegant, ran something like this:

> Punkin pie and a bottle of gin
> Got so hot the head fell in.

Sometimes he would give the boys little pieces of his black shoe-maker's wax, which they promptly turned into chewing gum. Most happy of all was the boy for whom he would cut with his sharp knife a fine leather whip-lash—that was a real prize.

Undoubtedly the most pompous personage of Freeport was the store-keeper and postmaster, Phil G. Rheil. His predecessor, Mr. Webber, had moved to the new village of Clarksburg when I was very small. Mr. Rheil was heavy-set, with rather prominent paunch and a closely cropped black chin beard. He was probably the only man for miles around that regularly wore a white shirt on week days. The general store was the chief institution of the village, with its pot-bellied stove in the middle, glass jars of candy on the counter, kitchen utensils hanging on the south wall, and drygoods neatly arranged on shelves on the other side. At the front was the post office, where eager inquirers had to wait while on the papers were written the subscribers' names, and the mail distributed. In the rear was the saloon, from which an occasional customer emerged, sometimes with unsteady step. On the porch was a wooden bench, for the accommodation of visitors—Mr. Rheil was intolerant of the boys who liked to sit and sit. It seemed to me that he regarded himself as a kind of mayor, or magistrate; but I found he was far from being universally liked, especially because of the evil influence of the saloon. Such places, up and down the road, used to be called "dead-falls."

I must mention one other man, though he was not an actual resident of Freeport. That was Joe Gosling, a farmer who lived in what was called the "Pocket," a mile and a half or two miles to the north and west. Mr. Gosling was for years the most active religious leader of the community. He was Sunday School superintendent, chorister, and teacher all combined. In his church work he was faithfulness personified. He was rather deaf, which was sometimes embarrassing. When he suffered a broken leg, during flood time on his farm, he was still happy in his religion, undaunted by physical suffering or financial loss. He was unremitting in his prohibition principles in season and out of season. Despite all his limitations and handicaps, Joseph Gosling was a true benefactor to the entire community in the days of my childhood. For his steadfast devotion, his never-failing geniality, and his unceasing toil he is richly deserving of high tribute.

I have just been recalling my early impressions of Joe Gosling, Tom Kirtlan, Jim Lee, Andy Greer, and Phil Rheil. Out of respect to my father I must now add this note: he carefully instructed his boys not to say "Joe" Gosling, "Tom" Kirtlan, and so on; we were always to refer to them as "Mister Gosling" and "Mister Kirtlan." But when we heard these neighbors called "Joe" and "Tom" every day by all the other neighbors, what was more natural than for the boys to follow in the footsteps of their elders and call them by the names they universally went by? This note is added simply to keep the record straight.

The beautiful straight flagpole, said to be 130 feet high, was the distinctive, dominating physical feature of Freeport. As I recall it, the perfectly rounded, gradually tapering pole was nearly two feet in diameter at the base, composed of three sections, or parts, neatly spliced together, thus presenting to the eye the appearance of a single unbroken pole made from an extraordinary tree. The splicing of parts had been splendidly and securely done by the use of encircling iron bands — these we boys called the "first irons" and the "second irons": we used them in measuring our throwing ability.

The pole had been raised and set in place by the use of oxen, earlier than I can remember — to me the flagpole had always been there. On its top was a large weather-vane in the form of a big red rooster: on special occasions, such as the Fourth of July, a large hand-made American flag was raised, where it waved proudly, to our delight.

The flagpole stood just outside the northeast corner of our family orchard, by the side of the road, at the entrance to the ferry landing. It was a landmark for miles around: we looked back at it with pride from different angles while riding along the many curves of the road, which followed the winding river-bank — now it appeared directly behind us, then far over to the right, and again sharply to the left.

It was a neighborhood event when the flagpole was painted by a skillful steeplejack, called "Skeezle-jack," the pole climber. This occurred several times during my boyhood years. The Freeport flagpole belonged to the entire community, and every-body was proud of it. Its removal, after many years, was a severe blow to the prestige of Freeport.

Freeport is just a tiny bit of a place — always has been little — scarcely large enough to be called a village, established in 1862 by the Freeport Railroad Company, to be a shipping center. It is located eight miles south of Sacramento (at least ten miles by river) on the east side of the Sacramento River. It was to be really a "free port" as compared to Sacramento, which then levied a tax on "all transit across the levee."

The Sacramento Valley Railroad Company (or Sacramento and Folsom) persisted in maintaining a desperate opposition against the powerful Central Pacific. Failing to effect an advan-tageous sale or to prevent the continued progress of the C.P., the company attempted the building of a road from its Brighton station, half-a-dozen miles to the southwest of Sacramento, direct to Freeport, regarded as the head of the tide water navigation on the river. The project was to include the construction of a road to Placerville, ultimately to serve as a link in a great transcontinental road crossing over Johnson's Pass and continuing by way of Carson Valley, Nevada.

All this, however, came to naught: the Central Pacific was too powerful. To be sure, piles were driven into the river, above the Erskine Greer place, for a wharf; grading for the proposed road was done, tons of gravel were spread along the right-of-way; but no railroad was ever completed out of Freeport — Freeport never became a shipping point to rival Sacramento, nor even an incorporated city.

One of my earliest recollections was that of going north half a mile on the county wagon road to what we called the "First Hill" — nothing but the slight elevation for the railroad crossing. For there we could fill our little soap-box with rocks and pebbles for our slings and to throw at birds.

Yes, Freeport has always been a little bit of a place. But it has meant a big lot to me.

It's where the Hunt Ranch has been since before I was born.

It's where I first went to school.

It's where my mother's flower garden was, between our house and the Sacramento River.

It's where I learned swimming, wading, fishing, and boating.

It's where I learned to milk cows and ride a horse.

It's where I watched for the big steamboats, schooners, loaded barges, and flood-time driftwood.

It's where I saw the professional fishermen in their boats handling their long nets, catching a salmon now and then.

It's where I saw overhead, in beautiful flight formation, great flocks of geese—honkers, brant, gray geese—migrating northward, with occasionally a high-circling flock of pelicans, or swans, or sand-hill cranes.

It's where I learned about the Sacramento, "River of Gold," sometimes gentle as a little lamb on a quiet summer evening, sometimes angry when ruffled by a so'-wester, or a heavy norther, sometimes ferocious in flood time, tumultuously rushing on, seeking a vulnerable spot in the obstinate levee.

Freeport is where I spent the first nine years of my life, then other years later on, then where golden memories of many and many a year enable me now to live again the days of early childhood, those days when the riverbank was filled with great oaks, and sycamores, and buckeyes, and cottonwoods, many of them covered with gracefully festooned wild grape vines, with different kinds of willows everywhere in between.

I have no artifice to recite all the things I saw and heard and learned at Freeport; but I can sum it all up in saying the first HOME of my childhood was there. It's a little bit of a place, but it means a lot to me.

CHAPTER THREE

WELL-SPRINGS
OF YOUTH

I cannot write of my student days at Napa Collegiate Institute, and later at Napa College, without the stirring of deep emotion. It was never a large institution, nor was it strong financially. Its continued operation meant constant struggle on the part of the trustees; and the sacrifice involved in its maintenance was heroically shared by the devoted faculty.

But I have no words to express what it did for me — hallowed now are the blessed memories. Fortunate beyond telling was I in being a privileged student in the dear little College, in the days of my youth. Thrice blessed am I with the golden memories that glow and glow. Many and many a time in more recent years have I entered enchanting Napa Valley and passed through the streets of its county seat: but never a time without a rapturous feeling deep in my soul, a feeling of tenderness and affection for Old Napa College, which is no longer there — except in sacred memory. I live over and over again the days of yore, and my spirit is thereby refreshed.

The College, which was controlled by the Methodist Episcopal Church, drew our family to Napa; and to my noble mother must go the chief guerdon. She was determined that her boys should enjoy better opportunities than had been her own. Each one of the five Hunt brothers, for longer or shorter period, was a student at the school, commonly called, during its earlier years, the "N. C. I."

Not until the winter of 1883-84 did I enter upon my studies; for during several months I was a victim of persistent malaria, brought on because of the swampy conditions bordering the Freeport farm. I was not sick enough to be kept in bed, but not well enough to maintain a regular school program. It was during this period that I took piano lessons for one month! The time spent in practicing was by no means wasted.

For me registration at what was called the College was the beginning of a new life. The principal was Professor Abner E. Lasher, a heavy-set, broad-shouldered man of about forty, with auburn hair and reddish-brown beard. His countenance seemed stern, he seldom revealed any sense of humor, his mastery of himself and of the situation was apparently perfect. If the students did not love him, they certainly respected him. He was known as a strict disciplinarian. Professor Lasher was succeeded in 1886 by Dr. J. N. Beard, as president of Napa College.

Unquestionably the most lovable member of the faculty was Professor William C. Damon, who taught history and the classics. He owned a small farm in nearby Brown's Valley. I remember picking cherries for him one spring: almost as many went into my mouth as went into the bucket, the first day: after that my appetite for cherries failed! Students soon learned of Professor Damon's prohibition principles, amounting almost to an obsession; some who were unprepared with the day's lesson were able to get him talking on his favorite subject before it came time for them to recite! Then the bell ended the hour! He seemed to know just where young people lived — there appeared to be no social distance between him and his students. Now and then he would come up with something a bit startling; as, one day, in history class, he turned to me with the question, "Hunt, would you consent to get married on Friday?" My reply was, "Certainly

— if I could find anybody that would have me!" I recalled having read that Queen Victoria was married on Friday.

I had two or three teachers in mathematics; but it was Professor Charles B. Ridgaway, who came a little later, that taught the more advanced courses and with whom I formed a close friendship that lasted through many years and enriched my own life. We were active together in church work; we were together on a delightful camping trip in Lake County; long after his retirement from the University of Wyoming, I enjoyed visits with him at his home in San Diego. It amuses me now to recall how, as a boy, I had become "miffed" at him one day in geometry class because he "sprung" an examination without previous notice. I got on a "high horse" and refused to hand in my paper. The professor said nothing; but my next report showed a grade of 61 — an unheard of record for me! Simply explained by the fact that the test was weighted at one-third, and mine (being zero) was quietly deducted — the other two-thirds was not so bad!

When I was near to the point of graduation from N. C. I. (I did graduate from the Commercial Department in 1887) the school was changed, by trustee action, from a collegiate institute to Napa College, with its four-year curriculum. This meant that I must continue three more years in order to graduate and receive a degree.

For the moment the change was sharply disappointing. But, viewed in retrospect, it proved a great boon to me; for had the change not come, there is very little likelihood that I ever would have completed a college course.

I liked my studies and usually did very well in them. The classes were all small, some very small. It was thus clearly obvious when a student failed to prepare the day's work. I studied diligently but not excessively. Friends are much surprised now when I tell them I never studied later than 10:30 o'clock at night: but I held tenaciously to my hours of study; and I could always depend on the protection of my mother against outside annoyance or distraction. There was no radio or television, and social events were confined rather strictly to Friday and Saturday evenings.

An extremely valuable feature in my college education was my extracurricular relation to the debating society, known as the Orophilean Lyceum. The word "Orophilean", derived from the Latin and the Greek, had been freely translated into "A lover of eloquence." My membership extended over a period of six years, including three semester terms when I was president. I can remember yet with what care I prepared my boyish argument for my first debate, "Resolved, that capital punishment should be abolished." My industry was rewarded: my affirmative side won the decision of the judges! The only difficulty is that capital punishment is still practiced after seventy years!

Experience in the Lyceum, in essay and oration, in debate and as critic or editor, in parliamentary practice, and in presiding —all proved invaluable to me. Many a time have I had occasion to recall the motto of the society, *"Ad Astra per Aspera."* What it did for me it did for hundreds of others.

Being a church-related school, there was compulsory daily chapel, and the boarding students were required to attend regular church services on Sunday, though not necessarily the Methodist Church. The two pastors of my student days were Rev. John Coyle and Rev. Martin C. Briggs, both of them able preachers and esteemed personal friends. Dr. Coyle was a speaker of rare eloquence: he was pastor from 1882 to 1884, and again from 1887 to 1892. Dr. Briggs, who had served the church and the state well through many years, from pioneer times, and as a founder of the University of the Pacific, was still a forceful and devoted minister. It was while he was pastor that I, then a youth of seventeen, joined the church. That was my beginning as a lifelong layman. During my first regular teaching in the College, Dr. Doremus A. Hayes, a scholarly young minister, had become pastor: he proved himself very popular with the more intellectual class of teachers and students. Later he was called to a professorship in Garrett Biblical Institute of Northwestern University, where he won eminence as a biblical scholar.

Among the trustees of the College, some of the best known, with whom I had personal acquaintance — men of devotion and sacrificial spirit, included Abram W. Norton, Chancellor Hartson, S. E. Holden, Joseph F. Lamdin, S. M. Tool, and Lewis J. Norton.

It was in 1886, I think, that John R. Mott, himself quite a young man, visited the College and organized its Young Men's Christian Association. This was a memorable event in the history of the institution, which was then in process of transition from Institute to College. In addition to the Y. M. C. A. activities, religious meetings of deep spiritual interest were held, under President Beard's guidance, on Sunday afternoons in the parlor of the Ladies' Hall.

It was something of a surprise to me recently to find that I had kept a diary of my summer vacation of 1887 and that this simple diary had been preserved all these years. Since the experience of that summer was memorable in my young life, I have concluded, with this diary to aid my happy memory, to give a brief account of what happened.

May 26, 1887 was Commencement Day at Napa College. I called it "a day of joy and feasting." I was a member of the graduating class of the Commercial Department, at the head of which was Professor Harry L. Gunn, the class numbered twelve boys and one girl. Professor Gunn was an excellent penman, and a very successful, painstaking teacher. I was naturally elated to read on my diploma "With Highest Honors." My student oration, as part of the program presented at Napa Opera House, was on the topic "Integrity versus Ability" — my first on a commencement program. In the early afternoon came the Alumni Banquet, following which a ride with congenial friends to Napa Soda Springs, with dinner there, brought to a close one of my happiest, most eventful days for me up to that time.

During that year my closest chum had been Fred Wetmore, a student from Siskiyou County, near the Oregon boundary. I had accepted Fred's invitation to spend the summer vacation with him at the Wetmore farm.

I had never been so far away from my own home. And such a ride on the railroad! The scenery of the northern mountains — crossing and recrossing the upper Sacramento River, the fairy-land at Shasta Springs, the splendid views of Castle Peaks, the rushing cascades, snow-covered majestic Mt. Shasta — I was enthralled and fascinated. Mt. Shasta has been my favorite California mountain since that time.

Fred's father met us at Yreka, and took us to the pleasant home in pretty Scott Valley, with its lovely Crystal Creek, some twenty-five miles to the south. Cheese making was Mr. Wetmore's chief occupation; so I was able to help with milking the cows. Once or twice I lent a hand in the hayfield, or at some other task; but, the record clearly shows, work was purely secondary with me during that summer vacation of 1887.

Considerable time was spent at hunting. I saw two wild cats, shot at one without success. An eagle fell before my rifle, and a weasel before the shot-gun; I had no encounter with a bear or mountain lion, and none with a buck deer. The hare, squirrel, grouse, quail, dove — such were the more common kinds of game. There was a small amount of fishing, without any sensational results.

The small Methodist Church was situated about two miles from the home — the Wetmores were among the leading supporters; Fred's father was Sunday School superintendent. I participated in the religious activities, including the Young Peoples' Prayer Meeting. Also I was initiated into the order of the Sons of Temperance, which took the place largely of a community social club.

But probably the experience that for me proved to be the greatest innovation was in association with the young ladies. Up to that spring I had been very shy — my innate bashfulness even from early childhood had by no means been overcome. That summer, however, for some reason obvious enough to a normal young man, my native shyness almost completely vanished. I suppose the easier manner of my chum and their hired young man had something to do with it. At any rate, I was with the girls more that summer, I am certain, than I had been before in all my life! It seemed the most natural thing in the world to escort Nettie or Nellie home, and the homes were some distance from the church or other meeting place. More than once it was past midnight when I arrived at the Wetmore home—an unheard-of thing for me!

The special occasion now best remembered was the Fourth of July. About twenty young people of Crystal Creek went in a four-horse wagon up Kidder Creek on a combined picnic-fishing excursion. The picnic lasted several hours, but no fish were caught! I should add, we reached home early, about seven o'clock in the evening, tired and happy. I had enjoyed the company of Nellie. Perhaps it may not be out of place to remark here that the girls I met that summer in Scott Valley were wholesome young ladies, without affectation, in striking contrast to many who have never enjoyed the healthy conditions of country life. From Scott Jones, Mr. Wetmore's hired man, who talked incessantly about girls, I learned a superlative expression that might well be regarded a classic by the folk-lorist. Scott's paragon of perfection he thus described: "She's as pretty as a painted wagon! Sweet as honey on a bear's paw — and just seventeen!"

The Siskiyou vacation came to an end in late July — I was again at home in Napa. I had gained in weight and physical vigor; and in other ways was benefited by the summer at Crystal Creek. The one regret I have felt ever since is that I failed to take advantage of the opportunity to climb to the summit of Mt. Shasta, my favorite mountain.

In that glorious spring of 1890 the senior class (Lorenzo Scranton, Henry Tillman, and myself), pioneer graduating class of the budding young College, enjoyed special privileges, which made some of the lower classmen a bit jealous. For example, the old rules about the limited number of picnics and social events, and of being restricted to a single date during a semester with an individual girl friend, were virtually rescinded and completely ignored in our case. And my father's three-seater spring wagon, with span of good horses, was put to good use on more than one Friday or Saturday for three privileged couples.

Most wonderful of all, our formal studies were completed, examinations and all, a full month before commencement! We enjoyed ample opportunity for our numerous class meetings, for planning our Class Day exercises, and preparing our graduating orations. All through our previous collegiate life no such freedom had been enjoyed. To cap it all, I am particularly proud of my final monthly report card, which contains the single entry, "Conduct, 100." At the bottom appears the name, "J. N. Beard, President." To look at this card today, which was issued for May, 1890, gives me a feeling of exhilaration even now!

Commencement Day came in the forenoon of Thursday, May 29, 1890. Our class motto, appearing at the top of the printed program, was *"Numquam Retrorsum."* The exercises were held in the Napa Methodist Church. Besides several musical selections the program included an oration by each of the three graduating seniors. I led off, my topic being "The Heritage of Culture";

Henry Tillman was next, speaking on "The Prospect of Universal Peace"; last came Lorenzo B. Scranton, whose subject was "America on the Seas." The address to the class was delivered by Dr. E. R. Dille, who was perhaps the leading member of the California Methodist Conference.

Each one of us received a different degree: Scranton, completing the Classical Course, received the A. B.; Tillman, a student of the sciences, the B. S.; mine, I had completed the Latin-Philosophical Course, was Ph. B. Those were the first degrees conferred by Napa College, with a single exception — in 1889 the degree of Bachelor of Painting had been conferred upon Corinne Damon, oldest daughter of Professor Damon, on completing her studies in the Art Department.

On the afternoon of Commencement Day, on the college campus in front of the Ladies' Hall, the Class Day Exercises of '90 were held. With simple ceremony we planted the class tree, which, like the College itself, proved to be short-lived. My main function on the program was to serve as class historian. I took occasion to indulge in a little by-play on our being a class of three. I said:

We are three: '90 has been an unbroken class for three years. ... We have completed three courses of study — the classical, philosophical, and scientific. On three occasions during the last session, at three places we have enjoyed class picnics; and on these three occasions our class has been graced by the presence and beauty of three companies of young ladies of three each. There are three states of matter, solid, liquid, and gaseous, '90 being always solid—and three conditions— atom, molecule, and mass, '90 being a vast concourse of atoms while in mass meeting. There are three dimensions, and three is the smallest number of lines that may enclose surface.... When man came into being, there were soul, body, and spirit; likewise again, the highest attributes of the spiritual nature may be summed up in faith, hope, and love. ...

Some of my concluding words were:

> We write our history on tablets more enduring than clay or marble; our deeds of life are engraven deeper than the markings of the sculptor's chisel; we trust that we leave influences more permanent than Egyptian pyramids. We build character; character is eternal.

The Class Prophecy was read by Scranton; the Class Day Address was presented by Tillman. The exercises were brought to a close by the giving of the class yell by "the three":

> Sixty times thirty,
> Thirty times three;
> N. C., Ninety we!
> Hurrah for just us three ! ! !

Two years later, in May 1892, at the conclusion of my first year of regular teaching, I was awarded the Master of Arts degree. While I had been industrious since graduation, I had not pursued class work in the College as a student; but as part of the Commencement program I presented a more pretentious Master's Oration, my topic being "Demands on the Modern Scholar." In the meantime, also I had graduated from the California School of Elocution and Oratory, in San Francisco.

While living in Napa, during college and post-college days, I derived much pleasure in chorus and male quartet singing. With a very limited amount of instruction and practice in reading music, I was for several years a member of the Orophilean Lyceum male quartet, singing the low bass part.

Through a good many years, beginning when I was a college boy, I enjoyed singing in the church choir, under the competent direction of Professor Frank A. Bacon, which necessitated acquaintance with many hymns and anthems. I wish to record here my great love for certain hymns found in the Methodist Hymnal, and elsewhere. As an author, who could equal Whittier in his thought on the Christian Life — as in the lines:

> Drop thy still dews of quietness,
> Till all our strivings cease;
> Take from our souls the strain and stress,
> And let our ordered lives confess
> The beauty of Thy peace.

And what more inspiring challenge to discipleship can be found than the words of Washington Gladden:

> In hope that sends a shining ray
> Far down the future's broadening way,
> In peace that only Thou canst give,
> With Thee, O Master, let me live.

As a song for the militant Christian in a modern age, I have found none quite equal to Maltbie Babcock's "Fortitude," which begins —

> Be strong! We are not here to play, to dream, to drift;
> We have hard work to do and loads to lift;
> Shun not the struggle; face it — 'tis God's gift.
> Be strong, be strong!

I had the grateful privilege of hearing Babcock speak while l was a student in Baltimore. Finally, I must add that the stirring hymn by Martin Luther, *"Ein Feste Burg,"* has had for me a special appeal through many years:

> A might fortress is our God,
> A Bulwark never failing . . .

Of all the anthems, composed by Mozart, Haydn, Handel, Gounod, Barnby, Mendelssohn, and others, if I were to select a single one that to me seems the very acme of tenderness and loveliness, it would be Mendelssohn's "Oh for the Wings of a

Dove." The obligato part was sung by Gertrude Carly who later, as Mme. Auldt, achieved eminence in this country and in Europe.

My experience as a member of the Napa Male Choir afforded me much enjoyment. This was a feature of the city Y.M.C.A., and was likewise under the direction of Professor Bacon. We met for practice every Sunday afternoon and gained considerable proficiency, especially in religious selections. For several years the Napa Male Choir furnished special music for the State Convention of the Y.M.C.A. Out of the choir came the development of a male quartet, consisting of Dr. W. H. Evans, E. S. Gridley, F. O. Mower, and myself. We were asked to sing on many occasions. But I could never be induced to attempt a solo!

During recent years I have not been associated with any musical organization; but I have never lost my appreciation for good music — though I may as well confess that some of the more recent and contemporaneous forms of so-called popular music — often employed for night entertainment — have no appeal for me.

In this connection I must put in a good word for "Peggy" our extraordinary buggy horse for a good many years. No common mare was Peggy. Of Hambletonian stock, she was well bred, plump, of comely form, a dark bay — slightly flea-bitten — in color. When idle she appeared indifferent, maybe a trifle lazy; but on the road she loved to "light out" and go "lickety-split" — other drivers learned better than to try to pass her. She was very gentle and safe — a real family pet. She could travel in several gaits: besides walking — she was not a very graceful walker — she could single-foot, trot, pace, and (as a saddle-horse) get into a keen gallop.

Peggy rendered high-grade service to four Hunt brothers in their times of courtship. While Frank was working in San Francisco and came home to Napa only at week-ends and holidays, he would write us a post-card reservation, as, "P. and B. mine for the Th." which meant he wanted to reserve Peggy and the buggy for his use on Thanksgiving Day. Mark took long drives to Tomales and Bodega Bay — for his Susie's home was over near the ocean. I drove to places too numerous to mention; but Peggy always knew the way home. George had an accident and smash-up one day: late in the afternoon he came into the yard slowly, with dejection written on his countenance, riding Peggy, but with no buggy. Father coolly took in the situation: all he said, very quietly, was: "Is it worth going back after, George?"

Peggy was a wonder, really a kind of institution, belonging to the Hunt family. We all hated to see her grow old.

The supreme gift of Napa College to me I have up to this point not even mentioned — it brought within my horizon the young woman who was to become my life companion and mother of our four children. That was a contribution overshadowing every course in history, every debate in the Orophilean Lyceum. It was something that stood alone, in a class by itself, not to be brought into comparison with anything else in my educational career.

How I first heard of Nancy Stuart I have always thought rather beguiling. In the late summer of 1887, with my close friend and fellow-student Artie E. Harris, I spent a week at the ranch home of our mutual friend and fellow-student, Homer G. Brown, a classmate in Commercial, '87, near the town of Dixon in Solano County. One day during that visit we three, with three neighborhood young ladies as our company, had a long ride in Mr. Jack Brown's light three-seater spring wagon: in late afternoon we had dinner together in the town of Suisun.

It was on that day, at an opportune moment, that Homer turned to me and remarked: "I understand the Stuart girls are going to College next session. You had better look out for that younger one, R. D." I had never heard of the Stuart girls — though long afterward I found out they were younger sisters of Emma

Stuart, who had graduated from Napa Collegiate Institute in 1879, and of Joe Stuart, who later took the commercial course there. The Stuart family then lived on a farm a few miles from the Brown Ranch.

Well, I remembered Homer's remark. When the fall semester opened, there were Nancy and Annie Stuart among the new students. I was still a bashful youth; but the student body was quite small, and gradually each member became acquainted with every other member. In the course of time I became acquainted with Nancy. But we were there for study — anything else was slow in developing. As a younger student she was in the Academy, or preparatory department; so we were never classmates together.

Nancy Stuart came from a deeply religious family and she was a devoted young Christian. Quite early at Napa she became active in religious affairs on the campus. The Student Volunteer Movement so impressed her that she joined a group, pledging herself to a life of Christian endeavor. Early in 1889 she was elected a vice-president of the Intercollegiate Student Young Women's Christian Association. On several occasions she was the active leader in the College devotional meetings. She was an earnest Bible student. Her religion was of the buoyant type.

I viewed the situation from afar — but not so very far! During my early college years I was interested — of course I was! — in the girls; but at the time I don't think any of them noticed it. I became specially interested in Nancy a good many months before she even suspected it. But by the spring of 1890, when I was a graduating senior and she a senior in the Academy, something had dawned on us both.

One evening, in the Ladies' Hall, at the conclusion of some social event, I made it a special point to say goodnight to Nancy. As we shook hands that night — nothing more! — I felt instinctively — or at least imagined — there was an unusual warmth in her hand as I clasped it, with just a tiny bit of added pressure as she withdrew it from my own. That pressure, ever so slight — or my imagination — was like a glorified electric current; it went through my being and sent me home with a new song in my heart.

Even so, it was months after that before I made bold to give the first kiss. I remember it well. We were enjoying a climb up the canyon in the mountains back of the Napa Asylum, alongside the gentle brook. While she was sitting quietly on a rock watching the water come down under the trees, I slipped up from behind, planted a kiss on her forehead, and said, "That's what I think" — or some such silly words.

At a later date, again in the mountains we both loved so much, we spoke the words that meant our engagement, never once saying the word marry, or wedding; however we had come to feel that we belonged to each other: "If in truth we love each other better than all others, we ought always to belong to each other." When I confessed it to her and she admitted it to me, the understanding was complete. Spring was at the point of dawning, the trees were already budding overhead, and at our feet the tiny fern was shyly peering upward.

It was still several years before our wedding day; but from that hour up there on the mountainside overlooking lovely Napa Valley, there was no wavering. We belonged to each other. Much happened to both of us since then: but that part of the story must be reserved for later telling. Napa College had made its supreme gift to me.

Some of the happiest occasions of my entire college experience, extending far beyond the separate existence of the college itself, were the alumni reunions. The first such occasion for me was the reunion and banquet of 1887, in connection with the graduating class of the Commercial Department, of which I was a member. The alumni reunion and banquet had become an established feature of commencement week.

No one has expressed the bonds of friendship and the warmth of sentiment generated, with greater fidelity than Lillian Hinman Shuey of the N.C.I. class of 1875, in her poem "The Yesterdays and Tomorrows." The first stanza runs —

> The sweet old days, the yesterdays,
>   I sing their songs once more;
> We clasp old hands, we dream old dreams,
>   We tread the paths of yore.

Part III of the poem opens with these lines:

> I sing the song of Tomorrow,
>   And Hope will strike the key;
> Robe her in light. How fair, how bright!
>   She rings life's harmony.

But of all the stanzas my favorite is this:

> Not all the gold from Tarshish brought
>   And from the new world riven,
> Could buy from me the heavenly wealth
>   The yesterdays have given.

If I were to pick out a single reunion of the many I have attended, as the acme of them all, it would have to be the one held in 1940, in celebration of the fiftieth anniversary of the graduation of the Napa College Class of 1890. It was at the beautiful campus of the College of the Pacific in Stockton, forty-four years after Napa College itself had ceased to function. Since there were only three members of the class, one of whom (Lorenzo Scranton) had died in the interim, it fell to Henry Tillman and myself to make all arrangements for the reunion.

The occasion was truly memorable. The excellent attendance included two of our former professors (D. W. Chilson and C. B.

Ridgaway) at least one Napa trustee (Lewis J. Norton), and two members of the class of 1879 (Judge Charles A. Shurtleff and Emma Stuart Coleman). The high point of the entire informal occasion was reached when Gertrude Thomas — "Gertie Carly" in her student days, was prevailed upon to sing; for Gertrude was the sweetest, most beautiful singer ever to come from Napa College. There was no piano, no accompaniment of any kind: she had retired from singing many years before. She stood in her place and lovingly sang a single stanza of "Long, Long Ago." The tenderness and sweetness and warm-hearted sympathy of her singing transformed the room into a hallowed place: many were moved to tears, all were deeply affected. No other reunion has ever been, for me, quite like the Golden Jubilee of the Class of N.C. '90.

CHAPTER FOUR

AN EARLY CRISIS

I had graduated from college. I was twenty-two years old. My record as a student was good — I was rather unusually "bookish," I think you would say. What next?

That the question "what next?" was not new at graduation is strikingly illustrated by a personal statement I wrote on the day I reached the age of twenty-one (February 3, 1889), while yet in my junior college year. This statement has only recently come to light. From it I may be permitted to quote:

> On this day, as I complete my twenty-first year, I feel strangely old, and cannot account for the time that has flown so rapidly by.... Twenty-one years old! Feel somewhat out of patience with myself because I have not done better in the past and because I have not yet settled upon a definite life work; and yet I have studied the matter dozens of times and it seems impossible to decide. It is always a serious question in my mind whether it is best that a person of my disposition and character should decide on a definite line of work, or whether he should first gain a firm foundation for any field and while doing this be on the constant lookout. This is what I'm doing and am sure I shall hail with delight any light on the momentous problem.... Tonight I gave myself anew to the service of God—determined that whatever I do I will "seek first the Kingdom of God," and that I shall ever aim to do nothing upon which I may not ask His blessing.

The curriculum at Napa had not called for a strong major study; I had liked all my subjects almost equally well; such an official as student counselor had not been heard of — my chief intellectual guide had been Doctor James N. Beard, President of the College; and fortunately for me his personal interest continued long after my graduation.

None of my college work could be called directly vocational — which is a matter of no personal regret now, as things turned out. I had a kind of philosophic bent that inclined me more toward the ideal of living a life than the more prosaic problems of earning a living. College education was viewed as a preparation for making a rounded man. For many the pendulum seems to me to have swung almost to the opposite extreme during a later generation.

I had my baccalaureate degree, but no decision had been made as to a life calling. I was living at home with my parents, helping as opportunity offered, working part of the summer on the ranch near Sacramento. I did not immediately seek any kind of permanent employment, although the importance of deciding what I should do was actively in my mind and gradually becoming more insistent.

But in the meantime I kept up my reading quite assiduously — I liked books better than almost anything else. I recall that I kept a record of the books I read that year after graduation, mostly in history — the list is rather impressive. With the encouragement of President Beard, I prepared a series of half a dozen lectures on the Protestant Reformation Period, which at his invitation I delivered before a small college class in modern history. That experience was a straw in the wind.

I pondered the question: What is to be my aim — what shall I do in life?

My father was a farmer, and there was the 500-acre farm: also, there was my next older brother, who had recently married and was about to follow in father's footsteps. I had due respect for the farming occupation; but neither my early experience nor my later observations yielded any particular appeal to me to settle down to the life of a farmer. And no member of the family advised me to look in that direction.

About that time I paid a visit to relatives in Tulare County. My Uncle Daniel Zumwalt of Visalia, a man of influence, was land agent for the Southern Pacific Railroad. I spent several days in his office, helping him with the chores and making my first acquaintance with a letter-press and a typewriter. Uncle Daniel took kindly to me: he informally offered me employment with him at what was then a very good beginning salary. His interest was sincerely appreciated; but almost instinctively I recoiled from the prospect of entering upon a business profession; though I still think the opening itself was attractive.

While my father never tried to dictate in any degree the life course of any of his five sons, I became aware that it would have been pleasing to him if I should take up the study of the law. Knowing this, and not yet having reached a definite decision, I went so far as to make preliminary inquiry by correspondence regarding requirements at one or two eastern law schools of good reputation. But candidly, my heart was not in it. I had observed a few young lawyers of my acquaintance, we had discussed the legal profession in the Orophilean Lyceum at college; my temperament failed to respond to its challenge — it might be all right for some of my friends, but I did not feel that it was for me.

I had become active in church work, especially in the Young Peoples' Society of Christian Endeavor and later the Epworth League. Some of my good friends in the church — I mention Dr. W. W. Case, Pastor of Central Methodist Church of San Francisco, in particular — were kind enough to suggest that I should study for the Christian ministry. But while I then had, as I have had all through life, a sincere sense of mission, I did not feel the inner call to become a minister: in fact, I confess that not much serious thought was given to the subject. I was to be a layman.

Before the end of my first year after graduation, having kept in touch with Dr. Beard, I was offered a teaching position in my *alma mater* at the munificent salary of $500 a year! Being un-attached and available, still living at home, without hesitation I accepted. Thus began my first regular year of teaching, at Napa College, in the autumn of 1891. I had a full schedule, part of my work being in the preparatory department, part on the college level.

The experience of that year, with $100 increase in salary for a second year, brought me across the Rubicon — the die was cast. I would be a college teacher! I had found my place. It was as if it were the voice of God: it required no argued defense, no wordy supplementation — this was *it*. To it my inner spirit responded.

If I could in time become a professor like Professor Damon or Professor Ridgaway, and earn $1,000 to $1,200 a year, what more could I expect or desire? Why should I look further? In the long retrospect of the years, that decision, made freely and without misgiving, with the enthusiasm of youth and with the sobering discernment that an educational career would never make me rich in this world's goods, has never been regretted — it is deeply gratifying to me after more than three score years to be able to state, that was the wisest decision I could then have made.

May I at this point be indulged, by way of a slight digression, a single reflection bearing on one's life work, or the legitimate demands upon one's profession — a subject to which I had devoted so little systematic thought?

Just what, in general terms, should one's profession be expected to yield to a young man who purposes entering it and is willing to prepare himself sincerely? In the light of some experience and considerable observation, I formed the opinion that his wisely chosen profession should be expected to yield him, first of all, a living — not necessarily any great wealth, but sufficient income to afford the comforts of life and the ability to maintain for himself and his family a reasonable standard of living. Secondly, he should be able to find satisfaction and enjoyment in his profession: genuine enthusiasm is one of the surest prerequisites for success. In the third place, the profession should furnish him with continuing opportunities for advancement in knowledge and progress in proficiency. Fourth, his profession should permit him to engage in some congenial avocation and thus find enjoyment in chosen cultural fields, such as music, the drama, or literature. Finally, what one does for a life-work should bring him friends, with a happy social environment.

But the profession, in turn, makes its legitimate demands upon the person. It demands a thorough and conscientious preparation, then a competent discharge of one's obligations. Furthermore, it calls for unflagging zeal, even in the midst of difficult conditions; but, not least by any means, there is the inescapable demand for a truly social viewpoint — one should constantly strive in practicing the chosen profession to contribute to the general weal no less than to advance one's own personal interests.

But at once there came to me the consciousness that I was not then prepared for the career I had envisaged: I must have more and higher education, ascend to the upper currents of true scholarship in fields congenial to myself and serviceable to my students. Then there was posed another personal problem of major concern: where should I go for the needed graduate study and experience that should most nearly fit me for the calling I had decided to enter?

That was indeed a difficult question for an inexperienced young teacher, who had never been out of California, neither of whose parents had enjoyed the blessing of academic training, therefore could not be expected to help now. Almost my sole counselor was Dr. Beard; but my mind was made up to look for the best university to suit my purposes and I was in the right frame of mind for the adventure.

A well-stocked bookstore has always had a strong attraction for me — even today it's not easy for me to pass one by when I'm in a strange city. One day, early in the spring of 1893, I think it was, I was in San Francisco and naturally gravitated into a big book store on Market Street. While casually looking at some of the newer items displayed on a table my eye caught sight of a publication of the Johns Hopkins University Press by John Martin Vincent. I looked within, and there I found such a bibliographical array relating to some specialized topic in history as I had never seen before. Now if any teacher of that day was more meticulous in preparing a bibliography and setting it up with Swiss-watch precision than Professor Vincent, I have never learned his name.

The discovery of that study in that Hopkins publication, in that San Francisco store, was like striking a match that lighted a torch that never went out. I was not long in reaching the decision that the Johns Hopkins University in Baltimore, not yet twenty years old, was the place for me for graduate study. And there must not be any delay in making ready.

I had correspondence with Herbert Baxter Adams, head of the History-Economics-Politics department: there was no obstacle placed in my way — I would be welcomed as a graduate student.

If I were called upon to name the one person to whom I owe more than to any other for my educational development, I would without hesitation declare, President James N. Beard of Napa College was that person. From the time he came to Napa in 1887 until he relinquished the presidency of the University of the Pacific in 1896, he was a constant inspiration to me and a never-failing source of encouragement in all the stages of my educational career. For this I shall never cease to be grateful. I have elsewhere referred to him in these words:

> Of President James N. Beard it may truthfully be said he was a man of commanding personality. His physical appearance — tall, dignified, with keen blue eyes and blond hair, clearly chiseled features —was such as to attract instant notice in any company. As a teacher he was always prepared, alert, exacting, and discriminating—but he was more than a teacher: he was himself always an intense student, an intellectual guide, ever abreast of the latest and best in his broad fields of interest. In matters of discipline he was adamantine for justice, treating serious infractions of college rules with a gravity and firmness that seemed at times almost relentless.

Among the many things for which I have long felt indebtedness to Dr. Beard was his advice to me to take up the study of elocution — a word that a little later fell into general disuse, yielding to the term "speech." This was in my junior college year. Evidently he had observed that such study would be of distinct benefit to me. While I had scarcely given the subject a thought previously, I knew in my heart that individual instruction in elocution would be good for me — it would help me to overcome my inherent shyness and self-consciousness when addressing others — it would add strength and poise where I felt myself perhaps weakest of all.

I followed Dr. Beard's advice, and took my first lessons from Corabel Tarr, preceptress and accomplished teacher of elocution, early in 1889. My principal teacher, however, was Emily Curtis, whose instruction proved invaluable to me. Some parts of it were taken a good deal as a child takes doses of bitter medicine, not because it tastes good but because mother says it is good for you. I believed my trouble had been correctly diagnosed; so I took the medicine on faith and endeavored to cooperate fully with the doctor!

For example, I remember yet the drilling I received in articulation and modulation. Over and over again, without end, I repeated the triangular formula, "Ip, it, ik," and the other formula, "Ee, oh, ah." But the particular exercise that galled me most — medicine I confess I needed — was that involving different types of laughter: I was compelled to laugh all kinds of laughs, before only my teacher, when there was really nothing funny to laugh at! Laughs in high pitch, or nervous tittering; then all the way dawn the gamut to the deep "belly-laugh" of the ruffian (though teacher did not use that word!); laughs based on the short *e*, the long *ee*, the *oh* and the *ah*, and clear down to *aw* and the *haw-haw!* Maybe it all sounded amusing to the instructor — she was cooperative — but it was tough going for her pupil! I took my medicine!

My study of elocution did not end with my college graduation. More than a year later I entered the California School of Elocution and Oratory in San Francisco, a private institution of which William T. Ross was principal, with Miss Curtis and Miss F. M. Estabrook associate teachers.

My residence in San Francisco during a number of months was a period of serious work on my part, but not very thrilling. I lived most frugally, my lodgment being a small, upstairs room, with virtually no opportunity to practice there. However, I obtained permission to practice in Central Methodist Church, on Mission Street, where I had become a member. Many a day I had there as my sole audience, the janitor of that big church.

For Professor Ross, author of the text-book used, I formed a real friendship. He taught Shakespeare and Articulation. Miss Estabrook instructed us in Physical Culture and Gesture — it almost gives me a "start" now as I think of myself going through the Del Sarte exercises, practicing the "feather movement," and all the rest. But I persevered.

In my graduating class, January, 1892, I was the only male member of the group of a dozen. My part on the program, however, was the only original oration, my topic being "Statesmanship versus Party Politics." In the *Proceedings* of the Second Annual Meeting of the National Association of Elocutionists (1893) I was honored in having my paper on "The Province of Elocution in Oratory" printed in full. For a year or two my early teaching included the subject of elocution in Napa College — my title was given as "Professor of History and Elocution." During one spring semester I coached thirty-four student "orators" individually at the approach of commencement time. This afforded me excellent opportunity to render secure and permanent the benefits derived from my own studies.

Many times I have wished that the subject of "Speech," a term that has largely supplanted "Elocution," might be required of all college students — on all sides I have observed the need of it. Relatively few who have attained eminence in science, or management, or technology, or even in the so-called "learned professions," can express themselves with real poise, dignity, and effectiveness. One will glue his eyes on his manuscript, another will uneasily shift from one foot to the other with painful rhythm, an after-dinner speaker, desiring to appear at his best, will reach down with his uneasy hand and move his napkin, or watch, or water tumbler a distance of six inches, only to move it back again two minutes later. Such distracting and embarrassing exhibitions and mannerisms have been witnessed by all of us: they might readily have been avoided by a modicum of training in youth.

Having been called upon times without number to address groups small and large, often with no previous warning, I have no apology for having studied what was called "Elocution" at the beginning of my educational career. Besides the benefits in articulation, modulation, and gesture, it has given invaluable self-reliance and poise. Even now my sense of gratitude to President Beard is renewed.

The power of influence is a very old theme. In the perspective of the years I cannot fail to observe that each of us has, in greater or lesser degree, a positive influence on the lives of others. I have found — sometimes in totally unexpected ways — that there are persons who have been influenced to do something, or to enter upon a manner of life where I have tried to point the way, often years before.

During recent years especially, numerous concrete examples have come to my notice. A few instances will serve to illustrate. The Superintendent of the Los Angeles City Schools (Claude L. Reeves), before winning his present position, wrote: "Occasionally I run onto friends in and around your district who tell me of your work, and it gives me an inspiration to know that you are still at it." A former superintendent of public instruction for the State of California (Vierling Kersey, also one of my students) wrote: "My own debt of gratitude and appreciation to you is constantly acknowledged." The president of Wabash College (Frank H. Sparks), who won his doctorate as my student, said in a letter: "You are a continuing inspiration." Rabbi Edgar F. Magnin, of Wilshire Boulevard Temple, Los Angeles (one of my students at Berkeley, summer of 1910), wrote in 1945: "You have been a very pillar of strength in everything that is fine.... The influence that you have had on thousands of students is beyond measure." Tiburcio C. Baja, a student at Southern California, years later, when Filipino Consul at Hong Kong, wrote: "Your kindness, sympathy, and understanding will ever be remembered as characteristic of American scholars. I like and love America, . . . I am telling my fifteen-year-old Ernest and ten-year-old Ruth to love America."

And just as truly, on the other hand, one's omissions and limitations are reflected in a negative way in the lives of others. There is no known way of accurately measuring the power of influence. But it is a general recognition of the fact itself that helps one to keep life in proper focus. Dr. J. R. Miller was unquestionably right when he declared: "The career and destiny of other lives will depend on what we do with our own life."

CHAPTER FIVE

Johns Hopkins University *and* BALTIMORE

Forthwith I began preparations for the trip to Baltimore in time for the fall semester beginning in late September, 1893. My college classmate and steadfast friend Henry Tillman had likewise decided to go — he to study science and mathematics. We were roommates during my entire stay in Baltimore, following which we have been lifelong friends.

Neither of us had ever been in the east before — the trip itself on the railroad was for us memorable. We spent a week in Chicago, availing ourselves of the unusual opportunity of seeing the Columbian International Exposition, the first of its character and scope in the United States. Shortly after reaching Baltimore we boarded a street-car for the University, and were dumbfounded to discover the conductor could not tell us where it was, had apparently never heard of it! In fact, we went half a mile or more beyond it without knowing it!

But eventually we found the University; and when we did we agreed that the street-car conductor's ignorance was at least more understandable — from the outside those buildings didn't look like a university, even to us!

From the beginning there had been the dream of a beautiful campus, at the Clifton Estate, but in the meantime a group of substantial three and four story brick buildings, located not far from the business center of Baltimore, constituted the home of the University. They were chosen on rather strictly utilitarian basis, but were virtually devoid of spacious grounds, lawns, trees and shrubbery; and of course no arrangement as an architectural unit was possible. There were the Administration Building on Howard Street, Hopkins Hall, Ira Remsen Chemical Laboratory, and the Biological and Physical Laboratories. McCoy Hall was not ready until the following year. The Library was departmentalized and thus made more directly accessible to students. The periodical list included many publications in other languages than English. Levering Hall was the Y.M.C.A. building.

Tillman and I located humble living quarters at 1111 Bolton Street, a plain room on the third floor of one of that row of deadly-somber three-story brick houses, with no semblance of a lawn. Mrs. James, our kindly landlady, we found to be a descendant of the FFV, in which she took unconcealed pride. Her husband, an ex-Confederate Army officer, seemed to have no visible means of support — except his hard-working wife: he spent many a winter evening before the open fireplace on the ground floor, smoking his strong pipe, from which issued fumes through the vent even into our third-floor room. Mrs. James was gracious and thoughtful in caring for us, leaving with us pleasant memories of our humble sojourn in Baltimore.

When the semester got under way the first week in October, the University presented a scene of intense life — the spirit of study pervaded the entire institution. At the time I entered, the Hopkins was only seventeen years old; but from its very beginning in 1876 it had enjoyed a reputation for advanced scholastic work that was second to none in America. I am reminded of a remark attributed to Professor Herman Von Holst, that "in America there is no real university — only the torso of one."

During its first year the total number of students was eighty-nine, fifty-four of whom were college graduates. Of the total of 522 students during 1893-94, 344 were graduates.

In President Gilman's thinking the college is a place "for the orderly training of youth in those elements of learning which should underline liberal and professional culture"; in the university "more advanced and special instruction is given to those who have already received a college training, or its equivalent, and who now desire to concentrate their attention upon special departments of learning and research." He made it clear that the Hopkins had no code of rules regarding conduct — everyone was simply expected to be a gentleman.

Johns Hopkins University was the first in the United States to operate on the theory that "students are best taught in the atmosphere of research." "Great universities," said Gilman, "are built not of bricks and mortar — but of men." To the inspired and inspiring leadership of its first president the prodigious advancement of the Johns Hopkins during the final quarter of the nineteenth century is due in a degree almost impossible to overstate. I would place him among the first three American university administrators of his time, an educator of personal grace and charm, of pleasant urbanity and surpassing social refinement, his work always showing maturity, never that of a novice.

Gilman exercised extraordinary care in selecting the original group of professors. First of all was Basil L. Gildersleeve, as professor of Greek, eminent classical scholar and trusted adviser. Next was James J. Sylvester, distinguished British mathematician, professor of mathematics. Then Ira Remsen of Williams College, professor of chemistry and later president of the University. Henry N. Martin, who had assisted Thomas Huxley, was to head the department of biology. One of the youngest of the group was Henry A. Rowland, called to head the department of physics — one of his students remarked, "It was a greater educational opportunity for a man to be neglected by Rowland than to be the favored pupil of any other living professor!"

My own master while I was a student in Baltimore was Herbert Baxter Adams, who as a student of Bluntschli at Heidelberg had received his doctorate and who held the only fellowship in history at the Hopkins during its first year. It may be appropriate to make further reference to him and to other of my teachers on another page.

My schedule of lectures having been satisfactorily arranged, I was at length ready to begin the serious work of a graduate student in Baltimore. But I had a boyish eagerness also to orient myself to my new university environment.

At the opening reception the youthful-faced person among the faculty men proved to be none other, I was told, than Maurice Bloomfield, eminent philologist; and that handsome, urbane gentleman, with affluent appearance, was Paul Haupt, leading oriental scholar and biblical critic. I had a curiosity to identify distinguished professors in any field of study, however remote from my own. There was another reception, intended more particularly for new students, given by the Young Men's Christian Association. This was more informal, with greater warmth of congeniality, reminding me pleasantly of things in California.

One of the first class lectures I attended was by John Bates Clark, who later gained recognition as the chief theoretician in economics in America. His subject was the theory of distribution; but his discussion was so rapid and so advanced that he wisely repeated much of it the second day for the benefit of bewildered students.

Another teacher was Professor John Martin Vincent, who came as near dwelling in the Middle Ages by virtue of familiarity with them as any modern man I ever knew. His bibliographies of *Geschichten und Handbücher der Mittel Alterthum* were astonishing — no one of us questioned his accuracy — (he had his own way about them). Perhaps even more astounding was the fact that Doctor Vincent, a medievalist, was able finally to leave a million dollar bequest to the Hopkins for the strengthening of the History department — a convincing evidence of his complete devotion to the work he so loved.

George H. Emmott, a typical British professor with high-pitched voice, expected great things of us in English Constitutional History and Roman Law, but seemed not much disturbed when we failed, one after another, to answer his searching questions. He fondled his old books as if they were his dearest treasures — and perhaps they were!

Then briskly stepped forth the master himself, Herbert Baxter Adams, both arms full of books and manuscripts, followed by his chore boy with a load of charts and maps. "Gentlemen," begins the bachelor professor, "my old master Bluntschli — there he hangs above the door — used to say again and again to his disciples, 'Bücher, Bücher!' Jones, what have you read during the past vacation?"

Adams always was in full command at the weekly seminar — "seminary" at the Hopkins. Each of us in turn presented an original paper, or report, thereby submitting himself to the sharpest kind of criticism. But also there were words of commendation when merited. Membership in Adams' seminary was a memorable experience — he kept the men on the *qui vive*. Perhaps it would be inaccurate to call Adams a finished scholar of widest erudition, nor was he a particularly brilliant lecturer; but as an inspirer of young college teachers and research students in American history, I doubt if we have ever had quite his equal.

The first week you have enough thrown at you from various angles to engage you for a lifetime! You feel tired and homesick; then you wonder just what you are getting into. But after all, you reflect over the week-end, no professor will expect the impossible of you; and why did you come to Baltimore if not to get the most out of your university experience? You enter upon the second week with refreshed spirit, better poise, and something like a true perspective begins to unfold. If others can do it, you can!

Among my other teachers at the Hopkins I must mention a few. James Schouler was an eminent authority in American constitutional history. His lectures were solid, though lacking in vivacity, and with no sense of humor. I would say his renown rested more on his scholarly writings than his ability as a teacher. Henry Carter Adams, then professor at the University of Michigan, was my teacher in the subject of Railway Transportation, also a splendid course in the relation of the state to industry. Dr. E. R. L. Gould conducted an exploratory course in theoretical sociology, and Dr. David I. Green an applied course, including numerous excursions to a variety of institutions. (Sociology had not yet won for itself a definite place among university disciplines.) Sydney Sherwood was my teacher in economics: while not a brilliant lecturer, he was a constructive thinker who, unfortunately, did not live to reach his zenith. My own chief inspiration for the study of economics came from John B. Clark, then professor at Amherst, who later was recognized leader for many years at Columbia University.

Dean Edward H. Griffin was respected instructor in the history of philosophy, in which came one of the longest examinations I ever wrote. The dean was becomingly modest, but thorough in his presentation; and he could be firm on occasion.

Unquestionably the most finished lecturer among all my teachers at the Hopkins was Woodrow Wilson, then of Princeton University, who gave nonresident courses at the University in Baltimore. When he appeared before his class in comparative politics or administrative law, his subject matter was well organized, ready at hand, and his delivery left nothing to be desired. Wilson was not only a finished lecturer: he had already proven himself a brilliant essayist, earning the title, "the Walter Bagehot of America," and was later to show himself a political orator of high rank and a master in the writing of state papers.

The University Library was then not large but was well stocked with selected references for graduate requirements. It was admirably supplemented by the Peabody Institute Library in Baltimore, and secondarily by the more popular Enoch Pratt Library.

But as I had come to Baltimore all the way from California, the University was to me far greater than any one of its departments. I was eager to make the most of my exceptional opportunities. I desired to see some of the eminent scholars in other fields in action — men like Gildersleeve, Remsen, Rowland, Haupt, and Bloomfield. And entirely outside of the regular Hopkins faculty, distinguished leaders were brought there for special lectures. So I got to hear Howard Furniss, Shakespearean scholar; Edward Eggleston, widely known American historian; Sir Archibald Geikie, great biblical scholar; Charles Eliot Norton, brilliant Harvard literary critic; Simon Newcomb, noted astronomer; Caleb T. Winchester, professor of English at Wesleyan; Levasseur, distinguished French economist; Helmholz, one of the greatest of German physicists; and still others.

Here I pause to make mention of a little personal incident. As an undergraduate I had engaged in many debates, written essays, and delivered orations on appropriate occasions: but it had not occurred to me that I might sometime be the author of a book. It was while listening to the lecture of Edward Eggleston on "Modes of Travel in the Colonies," that December evening in 1893, that the notion of writing a book myself, with implications in California history, came to me. I then queried, "shall I ever act on the idea?" The answer is seen in the dozen volumes in California history I have had published.

Among the other lecturers I make special mention of two. One was Felix Klein, preëminent mathematician. I went into the amphitheater-shaped room to hear him, more because of his eminence than because I knew anything about higher mathematics. I paid dearly for my curiosity! What with his not-too-good English and his running barrage of symbols and formulae flashed upon the blackboard, I understood absolutely nothing he talked about from beginning to end. I could not follow my impulse to leave without creating a disturbance; so remained to the end—a rather bitter end it was! But I derived some comfort the following day when I was told that only two persons of that audience did understand what Klein was talking about, and they were Professor Craig, head of mathematics department, and Simon Newcomb, the noted astronomer!

The other lecturer was William T. Harris, Hegelian philosopher and distinguished U. S. Commissioner of Education. It was a privilege during my studenthood to attend his series of lectures on the philosophy of history and the philosophy of art. It was President Gilman's policy to bring before the students notable scholars and educators, both national and international: he was usually present to introduce the visitor, and never have I seen a more gracious introducer than Daniel C. Gilman. Such experiences were most enriching to us.

A feature that I must not overlook was the brief morning prayers, or devotions, conducted by Dean Griffin, as chaplain. The attendance, which was purely voluntary, was never large: but it was my practice to be there for the quiet, reverent service, believing it to be a good way to start the day's activities.

While in Baltimore I identified myself with the Methodist Church, located at the campus of Women's (Goucher) College, of which Dr. Frost was pastor. On several occasions, however, I went to Mount Vernon Place Methodist Church to hear Luther T. Townsend, most eminent Methodist preacher of the area. Perhaps still more influential as a Christian leader, however, was

Maltbie Babcock, a Baptist minister, whom I heard at the University.

One of the greatest thrills I received during my entire stay in Baltimore came not from any lecture or sermon — not from the University at all. It was a revelation to me in an entirely different field. It is vivid in my memory today. It was Grand Opera!

Despite the fact that I was more than busy with my studies and the preparation of my dissertation, despite the further fact that I was compelled to live most frugally, when the New York Metropolitan Opera Company announced a season in Baltimore in February, 1895, I surprised myself and resolved to go! I went to "Faust" and "Othello." What if I did feel compelled to buy the cheapest tickets — to the top balcony? That was nothing. I had always loved music, but never had I heard or seen anything even faintly resembling those performances in Harris' Academy of Music. There were Melba, Tamagno, Eames, Maurel, De Reszke, Nordica; there was the superb orchestra, conducted by Mancinelli, and the wonderful stage setting. I had discovered a new world, and I have never forgotten the thrill it gave me.

During those student days I applied myself diligently: but I was systematic in my work, maintained regular habits, and I tried to conserve my energies. My health was excellent, partly because I did much walking for exercise and pleasure. In one of my letters to my mother I wrote, "No, you needn't expect that I'm going to spend my time in being sick; haven't time for such nonsense." My regular retiring time for the first year was eleven o'clock; but because of special pressure it was advanced to eleven-thirty for the second. In a letter I said, "My principal natural safety-valve against over-work is sleepiness, and of sleep I am bound to have a liberal share."

My original intention had been to spend one academic year in graduate study at the Hopkins, then to California, marry the young woman to whom I had become engaged before going to

Baltimore, and resume my teaching. Naturally, I earnestly desired to make the most of that year's experience.

However, before the end of that year I discovered what looked
like a possibility, by hard work and severe application, of winning
my doctorate in one additional year. It was a day in March, 1894,
when I made bold to confer with Dr. Adams on the subject.
After listening attentively he stated the matter wou'd be greatly
simplified if I could produce from President Beard of Napa
College a certificate of a year's work after graduation. Such a
certificate, if honored at the University, might enable me to
enter the following autumn as a candidate for the degree.

That was my chance! You may be sure I decided to make the
most of it. If I could by any possibility earn my Ph.D. in one
more year, I could never afford not to try my earnest best to
reach the goal. Dr. Beard was co-operative: he knew I had devoted myself to study during 1890-91 and had not engaged in
teaching. The certificate was forthcoming; and after another
conference Dr. Adams endorsed it and referred it to the proper
committee. I was on the high road.

I had made another important discovery during that first
Hopkins year — it was that my own native California had a
history and in that lay my own best prospect for research. I had
not failed to note the eagerness and concern with which my
fellow students searched for acceptable thesis topics, how they
looked into every nook and cranny of New England history, or
Virginia history, which had been plowed and harrowed over and
over again, trying to find some spot, or place, or time, or person
that had not been fully exploited by other sprouting candidates.
The search for a topic was sometimes painful.

This put a thought into my mind: I asked myself, hasn't
California got a history, too? Why should I try to compete with
students living in the east by delving further into the founding
of Massachusetts Bay Colony, or Jamestown, or the exploits of

William Penn? When I approached Dr. Adams with the thought, he said at once, "You're quite right! History like charity begins at home — California is your field." From that time till now, more than sixty years, I have never lost my interest in California's history.

My decision to study the beginnings of California statehood during the exciting days of the Gold Rush added justification to my natural desire to spend the summer vacation period of 1894 at my home. Even before making the trip, however, I made the acquaintance by correspondence of General John Bidwell, pioneer of 1841, who at once took an interest in my study, and whose personal acquaintance, from that time till the time of his death, is still dearly prized by me. While in San Francisco I availed myself of an opportunity to call on Hubert Howe Bancroft, whose stupendous History of the Pacific States in thirty-nine volumes had been completed a few years earlier. Also I made a personal call on Theodore H. Hittell, author of the history of California in four large volumes. A third person whom I interviewed was Horace Davis, prominent business man, author of valuable special studies, and president of the University of California from 1888 to 1890. With these and other practical experiences on the ground, I felt better qualified to proceed with my researches in Baltimore.

Great was the surprise of some of my fellow students when I appeared at the opening of the fall semester as a *third-year man* — they knew I had been at the Hopkins but a single year; they did not know that I had received credit for a year's work done before coming to Baltimore. I had set my hand to the plow and my face to the future. I must succeed if at all possible.

I shall never forget how Adams greeted us that day, preceding his first lecture — it was ominous! Looking down from his rostrum at the group of hopefuls before him — there were eighteen third-year men in the department, and his word was law — he announced a pontifical decree, as follows: "Men, there are too many candidates this year! It is not right to turn out so many young doctors — the market cannot absorb them all. It's not right."

We were dumbfounded! We shook in our boots — all of us, for even Tom Moran, the department fellow, knew not what might happen, for the words of Adams sounded like the voice of doom.

About a week later it was noised about that one of our number had been called into the office and quietly advised that the state of his health would not permit him "to come up this year." Then we learned of another, who had been working nine months on his thesis, but had been forced to abandon it because there appeared one day on the library table, in a fresh batch of publications from Europe, a printed thesis in German on his identical topic. He dropped out of the race. None of us felt entirely secure. I recall that Charles Estes, then the Y.M.C.A. secretary, and I, came to an agreement that in the event that the master called us in to advise us that our health was not good, we would have the hardihood to reply that we would be willing to assume that risk — then see what happened! We were both in a good rugged state of health. Fortunately, for us, nothing happened — we were not called in! It remains only to be said that of the eighteen candidates at the beginning of the year a full dozen finally did win the doctorate in June, 1895. In all, forty-six Ph.D.s were granted by the Hopkins that year, the largest number conferred by any American university up to that time.

My total experience while a student at the Hopkins was most rewarding. It was not all bookish. I remember a tramp over the wooded hills of Maryland in late autumn time; the trees, the running brook, the gently-sloping hills were beautiful. I recall the lake in Druid Hill Park on New Year's Day, 1895 — skating was good, and several thousand people, of all ages and conditions, singly and in groups, were enjoying themselves on the ice. There was a baby carriage, college boys were playing hockey, and one neatly-dressed gentleman was cutting graceful figures when — lo, and behold! — in a backward sweep he went plunk into a hole near the edge of the lake where someone had been harvesting ice! Even I ventured to put on skates, for the first time; but I kept well out at the fringe! On the third trial I found I could keep upright and make at least as much speed as in walking.

One of my classmates was a Japanese, named Takaki. In a most friendly spirit and wishing to do me a particular favor, he said to me one day: "Hunt, the graduate men in the Hopkins stand well socially with the city folk in Baltimore. I think it would be an excellent idea while you are here if you would look around and find yourself a good wife. For example, there's Miss White, on the faculty of the Latin School — I think she would make you a very fine companion." I thanked Takaki profusely, but did not reveal to him that I had been engaged to a girl in California for two years, that I was regularly receiving from her two letters every week, and that she was eagerly awaiting my return to California, when we were to be married.

My first visit to New York was at Easter time, 1895. My roommate, Henry Tillman, and I went together, our special object being to see our third classmate from Napa College, Lorenzo Scranton, who was then studying law at Columbia University. Within a few days we saw a good deal of the metropolis, including the Easter Fashion Parade on Fifth Avenue. There were other trips, to Washington, Mt. Vernon, and Annapolis. All these enriching experiences were treasured up in my memory.

Not having expected to be at the University for a second year, I was rather hard pressed to meet all financial obligations. Fortunately, I was able to obtain a position as evening teacher of commercial subjects at the Baltimore Y.M.C.A My modest earnings proved to be a godsend. But, on the other hand, this added work made serious inroads on my time, increasing the intensity of my efforts to achieve my major objective. At the graduating exercises of the Association night school, after some kind words regarding my services, my students presented me with a silver-mounted silk umbrella.

At this point allusion may be made to an incident that put to the test my decision and plans regarding my life work. A very earnest letter, dated February 28, 1895, came from my revered teacher, Professor W. C. Damon, at Napa College, who had been attracted to the Willard Cooperative Colony at Harriman, Tennessee, with its projected American Temperance University. Named after the illustrious Frances Willard, the Colony was to be a militant exponent of prohibition, of national scope "in the matter of training men and women for the great reform work now pressing upon the country."

Professor Damon made a strong appeal to me to join forces with him in that noble effort. "My heart turns to you. I believe you can make a success of it," he wrote. "People have money for this work. If you feel the call to be from God let me know and we will see that you are provided for. *It is a life work*. What greater task can you undertake?" And Professor Damon himself became President of the enterprise.

There I was at the Hopkins in my final student year, looking for a position; and here came this earnest entreaty from my beloved teacher — of all men! I had much sympathy with the chief objective; but as I thought it over I greatly feared the plans as outlined lacked the elements of practicality that would afford a reasonable hope of success — and I was expecting to be married in a few months. My honest judgment was against it. Regretfully I was constrained to decline the gracious invitation. Later developments proved my judgment to be correct.

Late in the spring semester, there appeared on the official bulletin board the schedule of final oral examinations for the doctorate, mine among the others. The doctoral examination is the culminating test, an event in the young scholar's career seldom forgotten in subsequent years. It is attended not only by the candidate's committee but by any professor from any department who desires to sit in and participate, if he wishes, in the questioning.

I remember my doctoral examination well, with President Gilman presiding, half a dozen professors from other departments present, and Herbert Baxter Adams, chief inquisitor. I thought Adams was very considerate. Regarding my dissertation, dealing with early California history, I enjoyed a rather unusual advantage. When the questions turned to other fields, however, I was not so well fortified, except perhaps in the period of Protestant Reformation. At the mention of Martin Luther, up spoke Professor Wood of the German department, inquiring more closely about Melanchthon. At the conclusion I felt that my performance was by no means brilliant; but the committee was charitable.

My doctoral dissertation had to do with the fascinating formative period of California history, from the American conquest of 1846 to the actual admission of the Minerva-state into the American Union in 1850. It dealt almost exclusively with the political and governmental aspects, although some reference was inevitably made to military operations and to the sensational effects of the gold discovery.

The major part of my product was accepted for publication by the University, under the title *The Genesis of California's First Constitution, 1846-49*. It appears in Volume VIII, Thirteenth Series (August, 1895) of the Johns Hopkins University Studies in Historical and Political Science, of which Professor Adams was editor. I was gratified to have it published by the Hopkins Press.

While I had previously prepared one or two short papers as newspaper articles, which might be called "historical recreations," I would refer to *The Genesis* as my first serious publication in

California history. My long chapter, "Legal Status of California, 1846-49," was published by the American Academy of Political and Social Science in *The Annals* (November, 1898).

Finally came Commencement Day, on the afternoon of June 14, 1895, the exercises being held in the Academy of Music, in Baltimore. After the orchestral rendition of Bach's "Festival March" and the opening invocation, President Gilman, after reminding the audience that it was the one hundreth anniversary of the birth of Johns Hopkins, the philanthropist, and of George Peabody, who did so much for Baltimore, introduced Professor Marion Learned, who delivered an address on "The Rewards of Literature." After another orchestral number, Professor Fabian Franklin presented an address on the treatment of political and economic questions. Admitting, after many years, that both these addresses were learned and packed with wisdom, I may now make full confession that I remember nothing of the substance of either of them! I had other reason for being there than to listen to erudite addresses!

But the great moment came at length, when Professor Minton Warren presented to the President the candidates for the Ph.D. degree — myself included! To state that I was elated when Daniel Coit Gilman, with his ever-gracious smile, handed me that small diploma, would be a gross understatement! Weary as I was, my finances gravely depleted, 3,000 miles away from home, there was a song of triumph in my heart, not without a deep sense of humble gratitude — I had reached a life goal!

The time came for me to take my leave of the University, and Baltimore; and return to my own California, which had become far dearer to me during the interval. When I bade farewell to Dr. Adams, he was kind enough to say, "Well, Hunt, I think you will get along just about as well as if you had stayed here another year." This was indeed gratifying to me. I went in to shake hands with President Gilman, who knew California well, and loved it; he gave me his best wishes. I have always had a sense of pride in knowing that his signature is on my diploma.

As to my record as a student at the Hopkins, I have never to this day received any report, or grade mark for any class — nor has that ever given me a moment's concern! I was aware of the fact, however, that my schedule was too crowded to permit me to achieve the rank of which I felt myself capable, under normal conditions. It was the mental climate of the University which Woodrow Wilson described as the "quality of intellectual daring, a youthful enthusiasm," that gave me what I needed. It was at the Hopkins that I made the discovery that education is never ended, the lessons are never completely learned — truth forever beckons us onward. Looking back after the decades, I am grateful that my footsteps were directed to Baltimore for graduate study. Today I pay grateful homage to the Johns Hopkins University, happy to renew my pledge of loyalty.

Again I was headed for the West — and a Westerner I have always been. I had my doctorate and have never ceased to be grateful for the courage it required to remain that second year and by hard work to reach my goal.

I have always held the motto of the Johns Hopkins in the very highest esteem, even reverence: *Veritas Vos Liberabit.* And I have expressed the wish that when I die the simple headstone at my grave should bear the inscription —

THE TRUTH SHALL MAKE YOU FREE

With sincere appreciation the first and third stanzas of the Johns Hopkins Ode (words by William Levering Devries, music by Elizabeth Ellen Starr) are quoted here:

> Truth guide our University
> And from all error keep her free!
> Let wisdom yield her choicest treasure,
> And freedom reach her fullest measure;
> O let her watchword ever be,
> The truth of God will make you free.

The truth will crown her sons with fame,
Their lives inspire with noble aim,
Their names make known throughout our borders
As learning's guides and wisdom's warders;
Then let their watchword ever be,
The truth for aye shall keep us free.

As an alumnus of Napa College undoubtedly the most memorable of the many reunions I attended was the Golden Jubilee of the class of 1890 — not at Napa, for the College had closed its doors in 1896, but at Stockton, the seat of the College of the Pacific, in 1940. Two members of the graduating class of three, Henry Tillman and myself, had planned the celebration and we were there to enjoy it.

Now, in the summer of 1955, I wish to record one other celebration, memorable in my life — the sixtieth anniversary of my Ph.D. degree at Johns Hopkins University, at the lovely Homewood Campus in Baltimore.

Of the dozen men of the History-Economics-Politics major, under Herbert Baxter Adams, receiving the Ph.D. in 1895, I was saddened to learn that only one besides myself is still living, and that he, Arthur F. Bentley, was unable to be in Baltimore on this anniversary because of failing health. Heavy, indeed, is the toll Time has taken during six decades.

For two years or longer it had been in my mind, quite vaguely at first, that I would like to return to Baltimore in 1955 to celebrate the sixtieth anniversary. Hearing me casually mention the idea one day, my son Lloyd took it seriously and encouraged me to carry through. Later, plans were laid, my oldest son, Paul, having expressed willingness to accompany me.

On June 12 we flew to Baltimore, were treated to a tour of the campus and special lunch the following day, through the courtesy of Osmar Steinwald, director of alumni relations. President Lowell J. Reed presented me with the beautiful medallion designed for the "Fifty Year Alumnus." On Commencement Day — June 14, exactly sixty years after I received my doctorate — I put on my academic costume, marched in the academic procession, and was assigned a seat in the front row on the platform, from which I could readily observe the body of candidates and their friends assembled in front of stately Gilman Hall. The speaker of the occasion was Dag Hammarskjold, Secretary-General of the United Nations, on whom was conferred the honorary degree of LL.D.

Following the conferring of degrees came the President's Reception and Lunch, attended by a small but select group of men and women. Seated at my right at the lunch table was Dr. George H. Evans, professor of political economy, and at my left the wife of Dr. Carl Swisher, professor of political science. It was a very happy occasion.

To me it was indeed a privilege to visit the University sixty years after my graduation. I was graciously treated on all sides. I gained the impression that the Hopkins has maintained its reputation for high standards and sound scholarship; and my own choice of university for advanced study, made more than six decades before, was reconfirmed. I returned to California with a deep sense of gratitude and sincere gratification at having returned to Baltimore sixty years after graduation. I regard the visit as one of the significant events of my life.

CHAPTER SIX

Uɴɪᴠᴇʀsɪᴛʏ
of the PACIFIC

In the early spring of 1895, as the time approached when I expected to receive my degree at the Johns Hopkins, a very practical matter, of vital concern to me, was the question of finding a teaching position, presumably in a college. It was the more urgent because I was definitely anticipating matrimony soon after commencement that summer, and my fiancée in California was eagerly waiting for me.

I soon discovered that the demand for young Ph.D.'s at that time was far from brisk. I had become fairly reconciled to the thought of accepting a satisfactory position in almost any location, within reason; though I was sure it would not be easy to leave California, to which I was bound by so many and such strong ties. There were my parents and my friends, there was the home of my future wife and her family, there was the college where I had received my early education.

But at the very time, Napa College was in process of uniting with the University of the Pacific, at San José; Dr. Beard had been elected president of the consolidated institution: the trustees had voted that as a result of the merger, Napa College must finally close its doors in 1896, when all activities would be centered in San José. Need for the strictest economy was stressed.

In personal letters, President Beard, who had continued to be very friendly and helpful to me, clearly indicated that he would like to have me on his faculty, but he feared the trustees could not offer me a satisfactory salary. I received letters also from Lewis J. Norton of Napa, one of the more active trustees and a highly esteemed personal friend: a deeply devoted worker in the Methodist Church himself, he expressed real eagerness to have me return to California and join forces with the Christian institution.

As I look back upon that spring and upon my search for a position, I think I was perhaps not as aggressive in the search as I might have been if my own longing to return to California, with a strong possibility of the position there, had been missing. At least it seems not unreasonable to think I might have found a better paying position elsewhere if I had been more diligent in my search.

At any rate, conditions being as they were, I finally accepted the position of professor of history and economics at the University of the Pacific at a salary of $1,000 a year — which was considerably lower than most Hopkins Ph.D.'s had been receiving. But I was to return to California — and I never was very commercially-minded. My face was westward.

At mid-June, 1895, with my Johns Hopkins "sheepskin," with my position assured in my native state, with my intended bride, family, friends and future also out there, it is quite unnecessary to say that I lost no time in taking my leave of Baltimore and was on my way back to California.

One phase of the merging Napa College into the University of the Pacific resulted in the plan that I was to teach the first semester of 1895-96 at San José (College Park campus) and the second in Napa, which was to be the final semester of Napa College, the place that meant so much to me. But before I tell about my first semester at College Park there came a diversion in my life, even more important than my teaching — it was my marriage. Some of the details are found on other pages.

In the late summer of 1895 my bride and I took up residence in College Park, a suburb midway between San José and Santa Clara, preparatory to the opening of the autumn semester at the University of the Pacific. Our first home was in the upper story of Captain Fieldsted's residence on Myrtle Street, located near the campus.

At that time the enrollment in the college department was distressingly small, largely as a result — I soon discovered — of the "exodus" of students following the "Hirst trouble" of 1890-91. This serious defection had brought one of the gravest crises in the entire history of the University, all the more acute because at that very time (1891) Stanford University, less than twenty miles away and widely heralded as richly endowed, opened its doors: its superior attractions proved irresistible to many of Pacific's students. As if this were not enough, I found that very few of the Napa students, who felt a keen sense of resentment because of the closing of Napa College, transferred to San José.

To be sure, there were more students in the Conservatory of Music, the Commercial Department, and the Academy: at the time the Conservatory was probably the strongest division of the University: but *bona fide* college students were numerically at a very low ebb. When the student reporter, Percy Milnes — nicknamed "Pud"— reported to the San José *Mercury* an increase of "almost forty percent" in college students, he did not wish to be merely humorous; he was telling almost the literal truth, for the returning students in that department numbered barely more than a score — his percentage was not far wrong!

But "Pud" did posssess a good sense of humor. As a student he seemed friendly to me from the beginning. I usually carried a small hand-bag — not then owning a briefcase — to class, containing a few reference books for use during the lecture hour. This student was not accustomed to see a professor bring extra books to the classroom. One day — I had been there only a fortnight or so — "Pud" met me on the campus as I was carrying my little satchel of books, and, mistaking it for a traveling bag, he tauntingly remarked; "Well, Professor, I know the faculty turnover here has been pretty rapid of late: but you're not leaving us yet, I hope." He and I remained on the best of good terms.

As I looked over the faculty list I discovered that I was the only active member holding the Ph.D. degree at that time, and one of the youngest men of the group. During that year President Beard divided his time between Napa, College Park, and San Francisco. His larger plans for the University, with San Francisco as official headquarters and the locale for graduate and professional work, failed to materialize, for lack of adequate support. That year proved to be the final year of Dr. Beard's administration. Most of the detail was handled by Professor Moses S. Cross, professor of Greek and Latin, who a few years later was acting-president *ad interim*.

The preceptress was Bessie J. Mayne; her sister Lulu M. Mayne, was leading teacher of English literature. Among the men my own closest associates were A. C. Bothe, professor of natural sciences, Heber D. Curtis, professor of Latin, and J. W. Riedeman, professor of German and French: for several years a strong bond of friendly comradeship continued between us.

The literary societies had an important part in the college life. In the college department there were the Archanian Literary Society and the Rhizomian Society for the young men, and the Emendian Literary Society and Sopholechtia for the young women. Archania, founded in 1854, has the distinction of being the oldest organization of its kind west of the Mississippi River: only four years later Emendia became the pioneer society for young women.

Archania had been looked upon as a society to assist in the preparation of prospective ministers, though membership was open to all "who are honestly seeking literary training." Rhizomia, founded in 1858, from the beginning professed an "active and progressive spirit," standing always for "the love of liberty and freedom." The keen rivalry between them has continued through the years. Emendia's early programs consisted chiefly of essays, recitations, and music. Sopholechtia, organized in 1881, placed greater emphasis on the social amenities, as in the study of etiquette, though literary and musical features were by no means neglected.

More recently, about the time when the College moved from San José to Stockton (1924), in harmony with a more or less general trend, all four organizations which I had known as literary and debating societies, adopted Greek letter names and became fraternities and sororities. Archania became Alpha Kappa Phi; Rhizomia, Rho Lambda Phi; Emendia, Epsilon Lambda Sigma; Sopholechtia, Alpha Theta Tau. However, the old names of the men's societies — Archania and Rhizomia — are still respected.

The University was founded by the Methodist Episcopal Church, and was the first institution of collegiate grade in California to receive a state charter (July 10, 1851). It is still under the control of the California-Nevada Conference of the Methodist Church. In 1911 its name was changed, on the recommendation of President William W. Guth, to College of the Pacific: it continues as one of the church-related colleges of American Methodism.

Attendance at daily chapel services was compulsory, as was attendance at church on the Sabbath. Denominational preference, however, was not tolerated. College Y.M.C.A. and Y.W.C.A. were actively maintained. Very little emphasis was placed on athletics at the time; there was no adequately equipped gymnasium: Pacific's traditional rival in sports was Santa Clara College, a Catholic institution only three miles distant.

The smallness of the student body was largely compensated for by the mutual acquaintance among students and the individual attention and closeness of contact between students and teachers. It was a center of earnest work.

Following the resignation of President Beard, after a brief interim during which Doctor Cross was acting-president, Dr. Eli

McClish was elected president, serving for a decade (1896-1906). He was warm-hearted and sympathetic. If he could not be rated a great scholar, he was a devoted leader, full of noble endeavors, for whom both students and teachers were drawn by a sentiment that amounted to real affection. Following his resignation in 1906 the Conference Committee on Education stated:

> Leaving the field of technical education to re-enter the pastorate, he does it bearing the love and esteem of the faculty, the board of trustees, and the Conference....

During the period of my teaching, beginning in 1895—as during most of my mature life—I was reasonably active in religious work. Each man on the liberal arts faculty was expected to take his turn in leading the devotional exercises at chapel, which regularly included a scripture reading, announcement of a hymn, and the morning prayer. To certain members this was by no means a light or spontaneous function. I recall, for example, that Professor Heber Curtis, with considerable labor, wrote out his prayer each time he officiated, and to avoid any confusion read it word for word — but always with fair success. Student Don Williams, who never failed to see the humorous side, after some droll remark about the different professors, one day said to me, "But you pray for everybody — not one of us but is covered in your prayers."

The Y.M.C.A. was rather feeble, I thought, at the time. I was glad to be identified with it and offer such help and encouragement as I could.

But my chief religious activity was centered at the College Park Methodist Church. Pastors whom I remember were Rev. T. B. Hopkins, T. A. Towner, W. P. Grant, and C. E. Irons. The Sunday School, like most of them I have known, was always in need of teachers. In that capacity I have served many years. At College Park I had a class of boys about twelve years old. But later I was made superintendent. We had two little boys of our own then,

ROCKWELL D. HUNT, ABOUT 1896

Paul and Lloyd, aged about five and four. They were of course in the primary, or infant department.

It was customary, once a month, to have the little ones of the primary department march in to the main school for the closing exercise. On one of these occasions, perhaps the first for Paul and Lloyd, when they came marching in they suddenly spied their father standing at the pulpit conducting the exercise. Without warning, or asking leave of anybody, they immediately broke ranks and dashed down the aisle, calling out: "Papa, Papa!" They came right up to the pulpit stand, and there I took their hands, one at my right, the other at my left, while I conducted the closing exercises. So far from chiding them I felt a sense of pride in my little ones: even today to recall the incident gives me a pleasurable sensation.

It was while I was at the University of the Pacific that the Seventeenth International Convention of the Young Peoples' Society of Christian Endeavor was held in San Francisco, in July of 1897. This great organization of young Christians, with membership open to all Protestant denominations, had been founded by Rev. Francis E. Clark, who was its first president, the original idea being "to spread the word of God and build up the Christian church." Having been an active member of the society in the Napa Methodist Church, I had opportunity to attend the San Francisco Convention. I had no place on the extensive program, but did enjoy singing in the combined chorus choir.

In most Methodist churches the Christian Endeavor was followed by the Epworth League, which became an official part of Methodism. Quite naturally I became an active member of the League. Indeed, my activity took on a considerably wider scope when I was elected president of the San Francisco District Epworth League.

In the course of time I was asked to serve as a member of the official board of the church; then, later, in another church as a member of the board of trustees. Thus I have been active in different phases of church work, but in it all have remained consistently a layman. The total experience has constituted an important aspect of my life through the years: while it has been personally satisfying, and has brought rich spiritual blessing, a sense of mission has always been a chief incentive — I have believed religion essential to my life and to what we know as Christian civilization.

During my incumbency as president of the San Francisco District Epworth (1897-98) I was called upon to address anniversary meetings and conventions in a number of churches. As a constructive measure I devised a simple system of comparative statistics of membership, attendance at meetings, and spiritual interest manifested. The District Secretary was to compile statements, to be sent monthly to each League to be read or posted.

The Seventh Annual Convention of the District Epworth League was held at San José, April 27-29, 1897. I presented an address on the final day of the Convention, in which I stressed the importance of intellectual preparation for the work of the church, concluding with the thought that there is no danger of over-education. On a similar topic I addressed the Annual Convention of the Oakland District, May 13, 1899.

In the meantime, first announcement was made of the California Conference Epworth League Convention, in San Francisco, April 21-24, 1898, with Rev. E. P. Dennett, as Conference President. It was my privilege to have a part in the program of the Convention as president of the San Francisco District.

In addition to my activity in the Epworth League I served as a lay delegate to the Annual Conference of the church for several different years. In this capacity, however, I was never very aggressive: many of the discussions did not appeal to me as possessing very vital significance. I never aspired to official position in the Conference.

During one semester (1898-99) I had the experience of conducting a class of about twenty-five students in Pacific Slope History at Stanford University, commuting for each lecture hour from my home. In this I was, in a way, a successor to Mary Sheldon Barnes, who was a pioneer in California in teaching local history. In the Stanford register for 1898-99 I was listed as Lecturer on Pacific Slope History.

Dr. George Elliott Howard was the dynamic head of the history department at Stanford: it was through contact with him that my course was arranged, virtually voluntary on my part from the financial side. I found the experience pleasant and valuable.

It brought me into touch with the members of the history department, including Dr. Howard, Dr. A. B. Show, and Dr. Clyde A. Duniway, also with a few other professors, notably E. A. Ross, of the economics department.

I formed a very favorable impression of Dr. Howard as scholar, lecturer, writer, and friend. He stood high in the esteem of President Jordan — which made his summary dismissal a few years later, occasioned by his outspoken attitude in relation to the "Ross trouble," all the more lamentable. Howard's tirade against the firing of Ross, before his class in the French Revolution, placed him in what Jordan, perhaps under pressure from Mrs. Jane Stanford, deemed an impossible position: I have never doubted that the decision to drop Howard was one of the most painful that Jordan ever made in his long career as administrator. As is well known, numerous other faculty members presented their resignations in protest against the dismissal of Ross, and in sympathy with Howard.

Another phase of my association at Stanford was as a courtesy member of the History Seminar. When I was preparing a report to be presented at a certain date, I made some mention to Dr. Duniway about the shortness of time, and received the very dubiously comforting remark, "You have the satisfaction of knowing that the nearer the scheduled date comes, the nearer ready you will be with the report."

My experience at Stanford as a young teacher also offered me an opportunity to become somewhat personally acquainted with Dr. Jordan, who certainly stands as one of the foremost of California's educators. Naturally, I was gratified to receive his kind letter of appreciation at the conclusion of my course.

Of all the California educators I have known I shall rank none above David Starr Jordan, organizer and first president of Leland Stanford, Jr., University. In my opinion he was masterful, imperturbable, and — above all — human. He never seemed hurried, but always had momentum. His multifarious duties as administrator, teacher, creative scholar, never disfigured his poise. Without impetuosity he applied himself diligently to his task: in the end, he accomplished the work of a man.

Since my first year at Johns Hopkins University my interest in the history of my native state has never been lost. I have taught courses in the subject at several institutions; most of the books I have written have been in the field of California history.

One of my most popular teaching subjects in the University of the Pacific was Pacific Slope History. I had not been at College Park long before I discovered that William Lewis Manly, a well-known California pioneer, was living quietly within two or three blocks of my own home. I had acquired a copy of his book, *Death Valley in '49* and had become interested in the exploits that had earned for him the title "Hero of Death Valley." His story fascinated me.

I thought to myself, wouldn't it be a treat for my students if I could prevail upon this dear pioneer to come over to my classroom some day and tell his story, simply and directly, to my young students? Mr. Manly was at the time bowed over, his gait somewhat unsteady, with hands shaking, because of the infirmities of age. But, much to my delight, he agreed to come over to West Hall and talk to my class.

At the appointed time he was there. He and I sat together behind the desk on the little rostrum while the students came in and took their places. I was happy to have at my side the pioneer who, about a half-century before, had by his heroism and devotion been instrumental in saving the lives of the famishing party, back yonder in the desolate camp in the midst of Death Valley, with no other chance of ever finding their way out.

With brief introductory remarks I presented my honored guest to the class, saying, "Mr. Manly will now tell you his own story." But, as I turned to him I observed that his hands were shaking violently — I don't suppose he had ever addressed a group like that before: the dear old pioneer became more agitated as I was introducing him. He was stage-struck and tongue-tied — could not utter a single word!

Fortunately, I was somewhat familiar with his story, for I had been reading his book. I leaned over to him and very quietly asked him some simple question, which he answered with a nod; then another and another, to which he replied, "Yes, that's so," or, "That is correct." Within a few minutes his power of speech came back to him; he turned to the class and modestly narrated how he and young John Rogers had answered the call to venture forth on the relief expedition, which proved successful, and which resulted in rescuing the famishing Death Valley party of the winter of 1849-50. I count myself highly favored to have had the personal acquaintance of William Lewis Manly.

One phase of my experience while on the faculty of the old University of the Pacific is recalled with mixed feeling — it was the financial side. We were painfully aware of the constant struggle of the institution to keep its financial head above water. At times it seemed faced with disaster.

Our salaries were admittedly too low, and the chief justification seemed to be that we, like the trustees, must be willing to make sacrifices in behalf of the cause of Christian education. Certain it was that the duties of the trustee who served as treasurer — there was then no comptroller — were not only onerous but personally distressing, particularly when the meager monthly stipend of professors was several months in arrears.

I can remember even now the call of T. C. MacChesney, the treasurer, at my home, where I was trying to support my wife and growing family, when, with sad countenance he propounded this agonizing question: "Doctor Hunt, what is the very least amount you can get along with till the first of the month?" With my grocer's and doctor's bills staring me in the face, what a question that was to be confronted with! When I answered with what self-respect and humility I could summon, Mr. MacChesney reached into his pocket, produced two or three twenty dollar gold pieces, which he handed me, then left, still bearing a sad countenance. As I reflect in retrospect on those conditions, I think my devoted wife was really the chief sufferer; yet she bore the burden with Christian fortitude.

Mr. MacChesney presented his resignation as treasurer in September, 1896 and was succeeded by Jere Leiter, who inherited a thankless task indeed. But Mr. Leiter did possess the capacity for smiling on occasion! In a speech to the faculty he smilingly warned the professors to get ready for a fare of spare-ribs and bacon.

The demand for retrenchment and rigid economy was so sweeping that no one's position seemed quite secure. I found out afterward how near I came to being a victim, in late May, 1897. When it was reported that, purely on grounds of economy I might not be retained for the following year, a group of my colleagues, whose confidence in me was most rewarding, quickly let it be known that if Hunt were dropped they would resign in a body. Hunt's election by the trustees followed immediately. It was a novel — and I may add, unique — experience for me. No criticism whatever of my work was presented: from the trustees' standpoint it was simply one of a number of attempts to discover a point at which an economy might possibly be effected, a pointed — and poignant — illustration of the desperate straits "Old U.P." found herself in at times. While I deeply sympathized with the objectives of the college and appreciated the self-sacrificing spirit everywhere in evidence, there was an inner feeling that the financial pressure on the faculty members was too heavy, that the treatment they and their families were subjected to was not quite fair. Almost unconsciously I was gradually preparing myself for a definite change, not with a spirit of rebellion, or resentment, but in justice to my family and my future.

While connected with the University of the Pacific, at San José, I enjoyed pleasant experiences as lecturer and teacher at the Chautauqua Assembly in Pacific Grove during a series of summers. The Assembly Program, under direction of Rev. Thomas Filben, extended over periods of approximately a fortnight in July - August, and proved quite attractive to individuals and families wishing a wholesome vacation period at the quiet, attractive seaside, a short distance from Monterey.

My function was two-fold: first, to teach a small class in California history; second, to present special lectures at some of the general sessions, held in the Methodist Church. For example, I gave one lecture on the French Revolution, and once or twice used a stereopticon with slides for a travelogue talk; also conducted a Forum Hour, with Historical Question Box. Other instructors included Josiah Keep, on Conchology; C. H. Meeker, on Nature Study; C. L. Anderson, on Marine Biology; and John Ivy, on Art. Star feature lecturers included such notables as James M. Buckley, editor of the *Christian Advocate*, Bishop William Quaile, of the Methodist Church, and Eli McClish, President of the University and of the Pacific Grove Chautauqua.

Perhaps the main attraction, from my personal standpoint, lay in the fact that the Chautauqua afforded my young family a fine outing at the seaside, under very favorable conditions, while my part on the program proved to be sufficient to pay the bills. Mrs. Hunt and the two boys we then had, Paul and Lloyd, spent many hours happily along the beaches, clambering over the rocks, and watching the waves of the Pacific. My recollection of this experience is most pleasant. I still have in my possession the little album of snap-shot photographs taken by J. D. Sweeney, one of my students in California history, and presented to me as a keepsake.

In the light of the longer perspective, one of the most interesting experiences during my seven-year incumbency at the University of the Pacific (1895-1902) came to me in connection with the Golden Jubilee Celebration, in 1901. It was deemed most fitting that the fiftieth anniversary of the chartering of the institution (July 10, 1851) should be commemorated with appropriate ceremony.

The Jubilee Exercises were held in the Conservatory auditorium, in connection with the Annual Commencement, May 22 and 23, 1901. As professor of history, it was my task to prepare a résumé of the history of the University, which was published in *Overland Monthly* for May, 1901, under the title "Golden Jubilee of the University of the Pacific." Reprints of the article were made to insure wider distribution.

Also, at the Semi-Centennial Exercises held Wednesday afternoon, May 22, I presented the address, "The Harvest of the Past," which was largely historical in character. This was published in the *California Christian Advocate* of May 30, 1901. In the course of my address, which I had prepared with care, I said:

I am aware that there has recently been—and perchance the echo yet resounds—no slight clamor for the abandonment of university and even college ideals and advanced instruction; nor need I be reminded that other colleges in California of limited resources have succumbed before the swelling tide of consolidation and centralization: but I desire to register the humble conviction that if we are to enter upon our rightful heritage and build a fitting superstructure upon the foundations that have been laid both deep and strong; if we are to grasp matchless opportunities for enlarging the kingdom of light and righteousness in a point of world-focus; then the University of the Pacific must be preserved and strengthened into actuality.

One further reflection: to me it is passing strange — perhaps it is quite unique — that it fell to my lot, a half-century later, again to be connected with dear old Pacific, and to participate actively in in her Centennial Celebration, in the city of Stockton. Moreover, yielding to urgent requests, I prepared the history of the institution from the beginning, which was published as a 240-page volume; and this was a feature of the notable Centenary.

Continuing my active service through the summer of 1954, I thus have completed two seven-year cycles in the College that was chartered in 1851, the first cycle beginning in 1895, the second ending fifty-nine years later. If there is any virtue in the ancient tradition that seven is a perfect number, then I may not be over-bold when I lay claim to being a perfect exemplification of the hallowed tradition!

CHAPTER SEVEN

SAN JOSE
HIGH SCHOOL

With my growing family, while I was faculty member at the University of the Pacific at San José, I found it far from easy to "make ends meet" financially, with my salary of $1,000 a year, and with the supposedly regular payments often several months in arrears. After some thought on the matter I decided to go down to the County Superintendent's office and inquire just what I should require to obtain a certificate to teach in a public high school — not that I had any definite expectation of ever using it, but on general principles and as a possible insurance for the future.

One day, I think it was in 1901, about the time our third child was born, I called on Superintendent Chipman to make my inquiry. "What is that you have in your hand?" he asked, seeing the small roll I had with me. "That's just a diploma," I quietly replied, handing him my Johns Hopkins Ph.D. "Oh, that's all you need!" he immediately declared, on opening up the roll. "We don't see many of those around here."

And that was literally all I did need. The certificate was issued without further question — no examination, no education course: the little diploma was the talisman.

I cannot help thinking how different the Superintendent's reply to my inquiry would have been a generation later, after pedagogical requirements for the general secondary credential had been fixed by statutory provisions and regulations set up by schools of education! As it was, my certificate was valid even without credits for a single course in education; and, as will appear, I had the good fortune to continue as a high school principal long enough to earn a teacher's life diploma.

At this point I am constrained to add that my personal experience in this matter is not to be taken as a general indictment of schools of education, nor am I wishing to give unqualified endorsement to all the more recent requirements of amassing multiplied credits in different departments of education for various and sundry teaching credentials. There has been too little attention to the art of teaching by many highly trained specialists; possession of a higher academic degree is not always sufficient evidence of "pedagogical" dexterity. To be a most fruitful and inspiring teacher of advanced students I hold that a man should be actively engaged in some definite research work, and at the same time he should possess the power and skill of imparting while he himself is learning.

It could not have been very long after obtaining my high school credential that something quite unusual happened — that is, something unusual in my experience.

Late one afternoon, clad in overalls and grimy jumper, I was engaged in the unlovely but necessary task of clearing out the drainage at the rear of our modest home on Asbury Street. I must have looked more like a confirmed hobo than a college professor — in just about the most unpresentable condition to receive polite company that one could imagine. It was precisely at that time, with me engaged at that dirty task, that the unusual happened.

President Eli McClish of the University of the Pacific — my President — without a moment's warning walked briskly down the side walk, immaculately dressed, with his broadcloth Prince Albert coat, and found me there! Paying no attention to my appearance, he announced, "Judge Lewis is out front in his carriage; he'd like to see you." I looked myself over for a hasty moment; but seeing no alternative, I said, "All right, I'll go out with you."

I was aware that J. R. Lewis, a retired judge from a Rocky Mountain state, had recently been made president of the reform board of education for the San José School District, but at the time I had no personal acquaintance with him. What he wished to see me about I, of course, had no way of knowing. He invited me to a seat beside him in the carriage. Then, coming directly to the point, he addressed me substantially as follows:

"Doctor Hunt, as you no doubt know, Mr. Shumate, principal of San José High School, has just recently been elected City Superintendent of Schools, which leaves a vacancy in the principalship. The two leading candidates for the position are two of the faculty men — Mr. Gleason and Mr. Brownell. We do not propose to elect either one of them: there is a good deal of jealousy, and to make either of them principal would bring trouble and disharmony. After talking it over, we have decided that the position is yours if you will accept it — let me know tomorrow!"

That was the unusual thing! I had not taught a single day in any grade in any public school! And in this totally unexpected manner had come, almost in my own back yard, this unequivocal invitation to accept the principalship of a comparatively large city high school. The salary was exactly double that I was currently receiving.

I was then thirty-four years old, in good health, with a growing young family consisting of wife and three children. Almost at once I felt "in my bones" that I could not afford to reject Judge Lewis' invitation; but there must be no hasty action. My good wife offered no objection, leaving the decision entirely to me. Since I had my doctorate from Johns Hopkins, and my necessary certificate, with good health and faith in the future, the decision was not a very difficult one — I would accept the principalship. Judge Lewis was duly informed, as he had requested.

That decision brought a major change in my early career as an educator. For six years I continued as principal of San José High School. A few of the many and varied experiences of that period are briefly told on succeeding pages.

At no time during the period of my principalship did I expect to remain permanently in the field of secondary education: my own temperament and inclination, as well as my special qualifications pointed, I sincerely believed, to the field of higher education — I expected sometime to return to college or university work. Nevertheless, while I was engaged in high school administration I threw myself heart and soul into it, for I deemed it a worthy and important undertaking.

I could not fail to recognize my inexperience and my limitations; but I enjoyed certain initial advantages that helped to compensate for deficiencies of which I was keenly aware — though I was careful not to parade these deficiencies! In the first place, I was taller than any man on my faculty — even the new superintendent good-naturedly said to me, "At least, we shall have to look up to you!" More important, I was the only member of my first faculty who had the Ph.D. degree — many of them seemed pleased to refer to me as "Doctor Hunt."

Then, I had enjoyed some years of experience as a college teacher, an experience few if any of the faculty could boast — I had seen something of the results of secondary training as revealed in the entering college classes. Two letters of endorsement that were published were more than generous. President McClish said: "I have no member of my faculty whose services I would surrender with greater reluctance than I would those

D. R. HUNT AND FIVE SONS: GEORGE G., MAJOR C., FRANK L., ROCKWELL D., MARK T. (ABOUT 1904)

of Dr. Hunt. But ... I cannot do less than give this expression of my high appreciation of him as a Christian gentleman, a broad scholar, and an enthusiastic and inspiring teacher." My Johns Hopkins Professor Herbert B. Adams wrote: "Dr. Hunt is an excellent scholar, a man of religious character and sterling integrity.... His influence upon his pupils is uniformly good and hopeful. I predict for him growing usefulness and wider recognition as a lecturer and writer upon historico-political subjects."

It is gratifying to record that, speaking generally, the faculty of men and women over whom I was called to preside treated me with a higher degree of respect than might have been anticipated, especially knowing, as they did, my own total lack of experience in public school work.

It is not possible here to refer to each individual faculty member; but I cannot refrain from making reference to the vice-principal, Charles M. Gleason. His loyalty and devotion were beyond praise, and as a master of detail in arranging classes and counseling students he was a prodigy. He had served as vice-principal under my predecessor as principal, and continued in the same capacity under several succeeding principals. Multiplied thousands who passed through the halls of San José High School are grateful today for the kindly manner and benign influence of Vice-Principal Gleason.

Many of my experiences while principal were interesting, a few were grotesque, only a very small number really disagreeable. Several that seem in retrospect rather humorous, perhaps ludicrous, come vividly to mind even now.

For a year or two I was called upon to supervise two eighth-grade rooms that were taught in the High School basement. During the noon hour one day the father of one of the boys who had hopelessly failed in his studies, came to my office to pressure the principal to pass his boy contrary to the teacher's judgment and recommendation. When I informed him I could not do that, for I respected his teacher's excellent judgment, he became insistent and undertook to cajole me into yielding. Perceiving that his method was unavailing, he changed his tactics, came very close to me, and said appealingly, "Promote the boy — money talks!", as he patted the pocket of his trousers. But by that time I was fully convinced he had been drinking; so I managed to engage him in conversation with a faculty man, while I quickly stepped into my inner office, called the police department on the telephone, asking them to come and remove the man from the school grounds. In a little while, two officers made their appearance and very quietly led the man away — and that was the last I ever heard of him.

Mr. Bryant was an excellent teacher of algebra and geometry, but unfortunately quite devoid of humor in the classroom. In his class in algebra one day — a class of about twenty-five boys and fifteen girls — while he was writing a formula on the blackboard, with his back to the class, some-one let fly a piece of crayon that happened to hit the professor on the back of the head. Mr. Bryant was horrified! He had been basely insulted!

At once he proceeded to try to find out which boy had committed the terrible act in order that he might be properly disciplined. But no boy volunteered to confess guilt, and the teacher's temperature was rising rapidly. At length he resorted to a systematic screening process, coming face to face with every boy in the class and with long forefinger pointing directly at him, asking in sepulchral tone, "Did *you* do it?" Every boy denied guilt! By that time the teacher's temperature had reached a danger point — he was frustrated. Suddenly he scribbled a hasty note on a piece of paper, handed it to a frightened little girl on the front row, saying, "Here, take this to the Principal at once." I glanced at the note, which read: "Please come to my room immediately," his name signed at the bottom.

When I opened the door to enter that room, the atmosphere

was so heavy that one could almost cut it with a knife! "Dr. Hunt," Mr. Bryant proclaimed, "some boy in this class is a liar! I turn the matter over to you!" Just handed it to me, like that!

All eyes were turned on me—what should I do? I had never read in any pedagogical book how to treat that kind of situation! My first impulse was to laugh; but that would never do—the teacher was in deadly earnest—he was a good teacher—that would insult him. I turned quietly to the expectant class, with a faint suspicion of a smile, told them that much worse things had happened, but of course they all knew such an act was improper. Then I said, "I'll tell you what I think we'd better do: let's forget about this now; proceed with the lesson of the hour; and let the boy who threw the chalk come quietly alone to my office sometime during the day and tell me about it."

It worked! Shortly after the noon recess, in the quiet of early afternoon, a contrite little chap appeared before me and confided, "I'm the boy that threw the chalk." A friendly talk with the boy convinced me he would never repeat the offense in a thousand years. Of course no further discipline was needed.

But the story has a sequel. Next morning when Professor Bryant came to his room he found pinned to his door a caricature of himself, bending over an erring boy, his aquiline nose exaggerated, his bony forefinger pointing menacingly, while underneath was printed, *"Did you do it?"*

As was only natural and to be expected—something every high school principal knows—there were many incidents along the way, new situations to be met, individuals to be dealt with. One question of immediate concern was that of fraternities and sororities, since recent legislation had pronounced them illegal in California secondary schools. At San José the problem was briefly somewhat more sensitive, since one or more of the popular teachers were believed to be sympathetic with the continuance of the Greek letter societies. As principal I was in complete harmony with the act outlawing fraternities and sororities in high schools, largely because of the immaturity of the pupils; but I gave every encouragement to literary and debating societies as a splendid agency for the promoting of extra-curricular education.

I discovered, soon after assuming the principalship, the custom of having a class rush between the graduating senior boys and those of the next lower class, near the end of the semester, and that these rushes sometimes were precipitated in the halls, inside the school building, involving an element of serious physical danger. I decided that rushing inside the building must stop: being on the alert, I acted vigorously and was able to nip the first such rush in the bud. In anticipation of the event, I had quietly stationed myself in the main hall, where I saw a leader of the rushing class suddenly grapple a leader of the graduating class. Instantly appearing on the scene, my authority was respected — there was no general rush. Thereafter there were none in the building, although there was an occasional good-natured rush outside, usually on the public street.

Partly as a means of becoming better acquainted with the members of the senior classes, I insisted on teaching the Civics course myself — sometimes also American History — in addition to carrying the principalship. This teaching proved to be an interesting experience.

I recall that one day County Superintendent Bateman quietly dropped into my Civics class, took a seat in the rear and sat through the period. At the conclusion he explained to me that he heard that I employed some specially interesting method in my teaching; so he wished personally to observe. I felt complimented, though I have to confess that up to that time I was not aware that I had any "method" at all. Naturally I did aim to be systematic in my teaching, and to maintain a lively interest in the subject in hand, always seeking to keep it from becoming remote or purely abstract.

In those days high schools were accredited by subjects, for admission of their graduates to the freshman class of the University of California. Every year the school was visited by the official inspector. The teachers were eager to learn when they were to be inspected; for they wished to appear in "best bib and tucker," and were anxious to have their pupils put on their best performance. The program of inspection may not have been an ideal system in all respects, but it certainly acted as a spur to keep teachers on the *qui vive*. There was widespread criticism directed against the dominant influence of the University over the state's secondary education; on the other hand, it did much in standardizing requirements for high school graduation and admission to freshman standing. Incidentally, it afforded me, as principal, excellent opportunity to become acquainted with Dr. Alexis Lange, head of the School of Education of the University of California at Berkeley.

San José High had a full quota of literary and debating societies, which played a significant part in the life of the school. For the boys there were: Logeion, the Senate, and Ecclesia; for the girls, Philalethea, Delphic, and Ephemerian. Some very good young "orators" were developed. The student body had its regular staff of officers. The school magazine, published by the senior class, was *The High School Bell*: the souvenir editions, published each June, were ambitious efforts involving much labor and skill—they represented the pride and loyalty of the youthful editors.

Other features included athletics, orchestra, glee club, and still other activities common to high schools. There was no lack of animation at San José High—a wholesome atmosphere pervaded the scene.

As principal of the High School I was always conscious of my responsibility to the families of my pupils and to the community. A single expression of my feeling may be found in a circular letter addressed to parents under date of April 22, 1907, which, in part, I reproduce here:

Dear Parent:

I am taking the liberty of addressing to you a letter on a subject that must be of vital interest to you, as it is to myself and my associates as principal and instructors. The subject is the highest welfare of your children, who are now pupils in the San José High School. These have been entrusted to our care and instruction; and our earnest desire and constant solicitude are not only for their success in their studies, but none the less for their establishing habits of study and habits of living during these plastic years that will insure to them sterling characters in the days to come. I believe that a closer cooperation of parent and teacher in the endeavor to attain these ends will prove helpful and yield salutary results to the pupil.

The public school is the great nursery for citizenship; but the school is never at its highest efficiency unless sustained by the home, the 'chief prop of the state.' If the school is to be of most use to the community, parents must first have an appreciation of its ends and aims, then actively cooperate with the school authorities. This should involve an alert interest in the school work of the pupil and a reasonable enforcement of the instructor's directions for hours of study, and concentration of attention during a given time.

I therefore earnestly request that you as parents take an active and sympathetic interest in the work of your children in the High School. Reinforce the teachers' directions for the timely preparation of lessons and school tasks. ...

We are now in the very midst of the school term and the conditions are most favorable for the best work. The perplexities and conflicts of the term opening are of the past; the warm weather and numerous distractions attendant upon the closing weeks are yet before us. The most effective work of the entire year should be done *now*. Each day is important. Absences from school should be very rare and only for imperative reasons.

In closing, I wish to pledge to parents and friends the best endeavors of principal and teachers in behalf of the hundreds of pupils entrusted to our tuition; also to invite fathers and mothers to visit the High

School and its teachers with a view to becoming more intimately acquainted with its work and to establishing mutual relationships that may result beneficially to our sons and daughters coming up through the transition stage.

Faithfully yours,

ROCKWELL D. HUNT

During my six years of incumbency it was found necessary to inflict the penalty of temporary suspension on fewer than half a dozen boys. In the three cases I can now recall, the punishment had a definitely salutary effect upon the boys, as indicated by what followed — which was particularly gratifying to me.

Viewing the lively scenes of those years in retrospect, after decades of mellowing experience, I can readily understand that a good many of the pupils, and some others, thought me pretty severe in the matter of discipline, perhaps austere to the point of puritanism. It may be there was ground for such a feeling. But I can frankly say that I would rather have erred in holding up too high a standard of individual and group ethics than in the direction of condoning loose morals or winking at wrongdoing that merited appropriate discipline.

Perhaps it may serve to illustrate my personal adherence to ethical principles to reproduce here a statement I prepared for the Women's Christian Temperance Union when some of its members approached me for my opinion on what appeared to be a trend toward the wider use of the cigarette among boys. That was years before smoking among girls was even thought of — my statement might require certain modification to fit conditions obtaining a half-century later than it was written. Here is the statement I gave the women:

> In my opinion the cigaret habit is one of the most vicious and pernicious that afflict American boys of today. I can at present conceive of no high or worthy interest to which it is not hostile. It is

hostile to the perfect growth of the boy's physical organism, and to keep this sacred edifice pure and clean is a God-given law; it is hostile to the normal development of the expanding intellect, warring against mental alertness, precision of thought, and breadth of comprehension; it is hostile to the moral nature, inducing habits of stealth and stultifying the higher self; it is hostile to the religious principle, for nothing can be truly Christian which is alien to bodily growth, mental development, and moral culture, and which tends to quench that inner light, instinct with the spirit of devotion and making for universal integrity and righteousness.

The most serious case of discipline with which I had to deal came in the sixth and final year of my principalship. It may serve to illustrate the statement in preceding paragraphs. The boy in question was called to account for having a leading part in the outlaw baseball game, in connection with which the name San José High School was misused. The faculty agreed that he had acted without authorization, tending to bring the school into disrepute in the field of sports. It was therefore voted, after full consideration, with the concurrence of the principal, that the offender be deprived of participating in certain school sports for the remainder of the year.

This episode in itself, would not merit mention here if it were not for the fact that the boy's father took violent exception to the faculty action, apparently making the incident an occasion for bringing complaint against the principal. Pressure was brought to bear to have me remit the penalty. But the heavier the pressure, the more firmly I resolved to stand for the right as I saw the right. The boy's father, without coming to me for the plain facts in the case, talked to the superintendent of schools, and to the president of the board of education who had succeeded Judge Lewis. Now it so happened that all three of these men were members in the same fraternal society — and I was not a member! Thus I found myself in the unhappy situation of being opposed temporarily by both the superintendent and the president of the board. I could readily clear the whole matter up simply by admitting I was wrong and remitting the boy's penalty!

But I was not in the wrong — my own sensitive conscience was guiding me and my backbone was in the right place — I could not, would not yield.

Now the president of the board was a good lawyer — later a superior court judge in the county — and when this incident reached its climax in a real showdown, the facts were brought into the open; and when the lawyer weighed the clear evidence, he concluded that as principal I had pursued the right course, and was therefore vindicated. Moreover, he was constrained to write a note to the *Western Journal of Education* in which he stated that the action that had been taken was in the best interest of amateur athletics as applied to high schools.

Looking back to that particular incident of half a century ago, I am inclined to wonder how I was able to withstand the pressure brought to bear, and to remain calm and unperturbed through it all, never losing my poise at any time. There I was, with devoted wife and four young children; but willing to stake everything upon my position and simply stand firm. I am certain that the experience proved fruitful in fortifying my own moral character.

At graduation exercises each year, I aimed to have a good speaker for the main address, but representative students were also given places on the program. At the time the diplomas were presented, as principal, I delivered a brief message to the graduates intended to stimulate their minds to further preparation for life and to the higher ideals of living. For example, in greeting the class of 1906, I said:

> You came to us four years ago as boys and girls; today you go from us as young gentlemen and young ladies. You came as pupils; you go as students. You came as unformed but impressionable beings; you go with distinct characters that will abide. Marvelous has been the

ROCKWELL HUNT NEW HOME, AFTER THE EARTHQUAKE OF 1906

transformation wrought by the quadrennium. . . . Having passed your preliminary training, you are to enter progressively into your rightful heritage. My wish for you is that largeness of vision and that steadfastness of purpose which will give assurance that you each shall come to your full stature of manhood and womanhood. . . .

At 5:13 o'clock in the morning of April 18, 1906, a fortunate hour from the school standpoint, the great San Francisco earthquake dealt a death-blow to the large three-story brick building that housed the San José High School. That morning I was busily engaged in trying to salvage the situation at my own home, where our two-story house, occupied at the time by nine persons, was ruined beyond repair, when Everett P. Carey, one of my faithful faculty members, appeared and reported, "The High School is destroyed."

No need even to try to describe the activities that followed. My family must be cared for; our home must be wrecked and a new house built; the school building must be abandoned, except for a few basement rooms; temporary quarters must be obtained elsewhere for half-day sessions. A multitude of details must be left to the reader's imagination. At Stanford University, which suffered heavily the caprice of the temblor is illustrated by the toppling of the heroic statue of Louis Agassiz, which fell head-downward, piercing the concrete pavement below, "fitting symbol of 'the world turned upside down.'"

With excellent coöperation adjustments were made quickly, in good order. At the June Commencement of that spring, I said to the graduating seniors:

> Have you been mourning the destruction of your school by the quaking earth? The school is not destroyed, but only the poor shell of it. The school is really spiritual, and is immune from such rude material shocks. Yet we shall hope that in the fullness of time there will stand, staunch and beautiful, a dwelling place, symmetrical in all its dimensions, perfect in all its appointments, fit for the spirit that is to inhabit it.

The period of my principalship extended over six years. On the basis of this tenure I received a state life diploma. During my sixth year I was honored in being elected president of the California State High School Teachers' Association, which brought me into touch with many leading authorities in secondary education.

My active association with San José High School was concluded with a farewell reception tendered Mrs. Hunt and myself by the School's literary societies, attended also by many alumni and friends. Mark Grimes presided. As a central feature of the evening program, Walter Case, with complimentary remarks on behalf of the literary societies, presented me with a beautiful loving cup. Following my brief response, W. Cortez Shelton, for the alumni, spoke generous words of appreciation: he was a member of my first regular graduating class at the School and a foremost debater, later a prominent attorney of Los Angeles. All in all, with a varied musical program and opportunity for social mingling, it was a heart-warming occasion for Mrs. Hunt and myself, on the eve of our departure for Southern California.

President Benjamin Ide Wheeler of the University of California wrote me as follows:

> I am very sorry to hear you are leaving the San José High School. You have made a great success there, and if you are to be decidedly better off in the University of Southern California, I want to congratulate you heartily. We feel, however, as if the foundation were being taken out from under us whenever they take away a good principal of one of our large high schools. It seems to me that the material is singularly deficient for that kind of public service.

The time had come for a change. What that change was to be and how it came about, must be told on subsequent pages. But in the meantime I must make a leap over half a century to refer to a recent experience that was deeply gratifying to me.

In the autumn of 1952 I received a courteous invitation to

present an address on the occasion of the dedication of the new
San José High School on the 2nd day of the next November.
Rereading the invitation, with real emotion I noted that it was
exactly fifty years since the time when I had assumed the principalship of that School. What a thrilling experience was this, to
be asked to come back, after half a century from my 'debut' at
Old San José High to dedicate the beautiful New San José High
on its spacious fifty-acre campus, with buildings all spotless and
gleaming with newness! For my address I chose the topic "Half
a Century Onward." In the large audience I was delighted to see
a few of the fine teachers who had served on my faculty: at the
close a group of the "old boys and girls" who had been my pupils
gathered about me in happy reunion. How could I help ex-
periencing one of the biggest and most heart-warming thrills of
the entire year! It was great to be there! The formal dedication
ceremony was conducted by the Grand Parlor of the Native Sons
of the Golden West.

One thing more. After the preceding pages had been written
something has happened that must be recorded here. It was the
receipt of a beautiful hand-written letter from one of the many
pupils of San José High School half a century ago, a letter that
went straight to my heart, like a bright flash of early springtime
after a long winter. So more-than-generous is this letter that I
share a portion of it with the reader. It is dated at Altadena,
March 2, 1955, signed by Libbie Wheeler Templeton:

> Recently I attended a luncheon where a small group of San José
> High School graduates were present. We all attended High School
> when you were Principal and your "ears should have burned" as we
> reminisced about our school days....
>
> We had all admired and loved you in our school days. As the years
> have passed you have continued building into your life those intrinsic
> values for which we have all striven. You have accumulated recogni-
> tion and honors of many kinds. So we have grown more and more

proud of you, realizing that our youthful confidence in you was well placed. . . .

I know I am speaking for this luncheon group when I congratulate you for all that you have contributed to life and for the inspiration you gave your students.

Today we greet you as "Mr. California." We are deeply impressed with this signal citation for you, proclaimed by Governor Knight. We know it means that our entire state has found in you those fine qualities which commanded our affection and respect when you were our San José High School Principal. . . .

Affectionately,
LIBBIE WHEELER TEMPLETON.

Many kind expressions have come to me over the years from students and friends, augmenting the flood tide of my psychic income: none has moved me more deeply than Libbie's surprise letter, which completely convinced me that my six years as principal of San José High School were fruitful years.

CHAPTER EIGHT

MARRIAGE
and FAMILY

The time came for me to leave my California to enroll as a graduate student at Johns Hopkins University, in Baltimore. The parting from my fiancée was not easy — but we both believed it best. Neither of us entertained the slightest doubt as to our single-hearted devotion to each other. To Nancy the tongue of ever-busy gossip said, "You will never hear from him again, after he reaches the City of Baltimore." To me the plausible tongue whispered of opportunities that would come to a Hopkins man three thousand miles away from home. Neither of us had the least misgiving as to our mutual fidelity. And so the event proved.

My student days in Baltimore were busy days — but not too busy regularly to write two letters each week to my loved one in California. The two that came from her as regularly as the weeks rolled by were an added incentive to do my best in preparing myself for the great day to which we were looking forward. While I refused to live the life of an ascetic, nothing that I did was permitted to bring into question my relationship to my fiancée out in the Golden State. The parting in the summer of 1894, that is, for my second year at the Hopkins — how well I remember it! — was particularly difficult: it had been wholly unanticipated by either of us the year before. But, again, we believed it best.

The consuming topic with me, as I returned to California with my doctorate in the late June of 1895, was the wedding set for the next month. In the meantime Nancy had been active. With true forethought she had made nineteen substantial rugs from rags, and had acquired two or three fine redwood chests for storage purposes. Simple arrangements for the day of days were readily completed.

On the 24th day of July, 1895, we were united in matrimony at Nancy's home, near the town of Oakdale, in the presence of a family group, including her parents and some other relatives, and my parents and three brothers. The ceremony was performed by Rev. Frank H. Horton. As the bride and groom passed down the walk and through the gate to enter the carriage that was to take them to Modesto for the train trip to San Francisco, my brothers sang "God Be With You Till We Meet Again."

After a brief honeymoon we proceeded to the old Napa home, where my parents were still living, for a short stay before my teaching duties began at the University of the Pacific, at San José. That year, 1895-96, witnessed the consolidation of Napa College with the University, at the conclusion of which, in the spring of 1896, the institution at Napa was to close its doors finally. As one part of the arrangement, I was to teach at San José during the first semester, at Napa the second semester. And so it was.

Years after my marriage I essayed the delicate task of trying to state and analyze the specific reasons why I wanted Nancy to be my wife — an outcrop, I suppose, of my social science meditation. While admitting to myself that the thing could not be done with complete finality, I nevertheless ventured to present categorically the particular reasons. I found seven, and here they are, leaving all elaboration to the reader's imagination: 1) Satisfactory acquaintance before the wedding day. We had been engaged for about two and a half years, following a personal

NANCY STUART HUNT

acquaintance of several years, including visits in both our homes.
2) Well-rounded physique, with wholesome, pleasing personality.
By this I do not mean a prize-winning beauty, with scintillating
"charm," but I imply an attractiveness based upon good looks,
unaffected grace, and the absence of artful guile. 3) Good
marriageable age. At the time of the wedding I was twenty-seven,
she was twenty-four. Preparation for professional life often brings
matrimonial delay, posing a serious social question. I regretted
that my educational program and financial status prevented our
marriage at an earlier date. 4) Clearly observed and expressed
love for little children. Nancy and I were both from prolific
families: we believed that the normal and sacred function of
the marriage relationship is the rearing of offspring — we were
desirous of having children. 5) Marriage for love rather than
for money. On this point we were both very pronounced. We
never did have much money: but no amount of money could
have taken the place of our love for each other and for our family.
6) Worth of character above accomplishments — not to imply
that we did not value real accomplishment, but rather to assert
that mere accomplishment, however graceful or brilliant, is not
to be compared with nobility of character. Fortunately, high
accomplishment may itself result from sterling character. 7) Secure
anchorage afforded by the religious spirit. In our religious life
Nancy and I were sincere and humble — religion was the chief
foundation stone. We looked to it as the sustainer of righteous
conduct and as the guide of daily life.

In stating these specific reasons I am conscious that not all has
been said. Life is more than meat; so the cord of love is something
more than its seven strands. At the risk of being deemed presumptuous or perhaps even bordering on the mystical, I venture
to advance the thought that the scarlet thread running through
and through and binding into a single cord of love the seven
golden strands was that "kind of eugenic prevision that is deeper

than consciousness." Identifying this intuitive prevision with a divinity that shapes our end, I could gratefully affirm: "What God hath joined together let not man put asunder."

A year before our marriage we had agreed in a wish for four children; but there was no discussion as to time or sex! We had our four children — all boys; but each child was by the mother dedicated to the Father of All, long before birth.

Our first real housekeeping, during the fall semester of 1895-96, was at the home of Captain Fieldsted on Myrtle Avenue, two blocks from the University campus. It was in College Park, a suburb of San José, equally distant from the town of Santa Clara. We rented the second story rooms of the house. Strangely enough, after moving several times, we finally purchased the place, and there it was, though in a new house, that we were living at the time I accepted a position at the University of Southern California, in 1908.

During my seven-year term at the University of the Pacific three of our children were born — the fourth while I was principal of San José High School. I must tell of the naming of our boys. Paul Adams, the first born, derived his first name from Nancy's favorite sister-in-law, Pauline (always called "Pline") and the Apostle Paul; his middle name is from my head professor at Johns Hopkins, Herbert Baxter Adams — a bachelor. The second child was born on Bunker Hill Day (June 17); so a good neighbor suggested the super-patriotic name "Bunker Hill Hunt," which was a little too strong for us: we finally agreed on Lloyd Freeman, thinking of William Lloyd Garrison and Edward A. Freeman, whose names savored of both patriotism and liberty — with Bunker Hill in the background. In the case of the third, I yielded to the wish of his mother and agreed he should be named after his father — Rockwell Dennis Hunt, Jr. — with the definite understanding, however, that he must not be called "Rockie," or "Rocky," for as a child I had come to dislike that name intensely and was unwilling to have my child suffer as I had suffered when they called me by what I regarded the effeminate name "Rockie." Hence, at home, in school, everywhere, our third boy was known as "R. D." (or "Ardee"). The first name of the youngest of the four, Clarence Stuart Hunt, is from a young cousin who had died as the result of a tragic accident; the "Stuart" preserves the family name of his mother.

All that remains to be said at this point is that as parents we aimed to give our children good foundations in character and education, rather than life security in a financial sense. Just as our own parents were anxious to give us better opportunities than they had enjoyed, so we earnestly desired to afford our sons opportunities and facilities superior to our own.

There is little that need be recorded here concerning our home life. The furnishing of our home was always very modest — we did not have the means or the current income that would justify display; but fortunately, I think, neither Nancy nor I permitted that limitation to impair our inner happiness or peace of mind. With the necessities of the situation, there was a willingness to practice strict frugality and personal thrift. There was no buying of expensive articles on long credit, nor on the installment plan with small down payment. I had my books and periodicals; but as I view it in retrospect, Nancy did not have all the quota of things making for intellectual and esthetic enjoyment that she richly deserved. For the sake of the family she was willing to go without.

She was essentially a "home body"; her interests were centered in the family, first of all. Closely linked to this was her devotion to religion and the church. We were as one in seeking to give our children the fullest benefits of education and in inculcating the principles of integrity and personal rectitude. We believed sincerely that the best wealth is the wealth of character.

THE ROCKWELL HUNT FAMILY
TOP ROW: PAUL, LLOYD; LOWER ROW: "R. D.", CLARENCE

While she deeply appreciated her comparatively small circle
of intimate friends, most of them associated with her in church
activity, she cared little for what is commonly called society life —
much of it seemed to her to lack the ring of complete genuineness.

Both Nancy and I had spent much of our earlier life on the
farm, with a kind of freedom to which the city boy and girl
are strangers. We desired for our own boys something of the
freedom we had enjoyed. Accordingly, our two older sons having
reached high school age, we disposed of our humble home in
Los Angeles and purchased a little two-acre "farm" at Lennox,
then commonly known as "Rancho," an unincorporated community some two miles beyond the town of Inglewood, a dozen
miles from the University where I was teaching. Our modest
home was located on Fir Avenue. The move was intended purely
for the benefit of our children. Paul and Lloyd entered Inglewood
High School, and R. D. attended the nearby Jefferson grade
school. I traveled by street-car to and from my regular work.

On that little two-acre place we had a good number of chickens,
a few Muscovy ducks, and for a while, a pig and a cow. On the
vacant acre we raised a crop of hay. There was ample space for
our vegetable garden and berry patch. We were really out in
the country.

The local Methodist Church was not strong enough financially
to support a regular pastor; but Carl S. Knopf was at first the
very acceptable student pastor. He was the young man who later
became dean of the School of Religion at the University of
Southern California, from which post he was called to be president
of Willamette University. It was in that small church that G.
Bromley Oxnam (now Bishop) preached his first sermon. The
Hunt family became active in the Lennox Church. Among the
women, Nancy came soon to be regarded as a natural leader.
She was held in affectionate regard, was frequently called upon
to lead in the missionary and other meetings, and her counsel was

sought by her associates. She linked closely together her interest in the work of the church with her devotion to home and her family.

In short, we became an integral part of the community in which we lived. In due time our sons Paul and Lloyd were graduated from the Inglewood High School and were ready to enter college. It was but natural that our sons should attend the University which I was serving as professor. There were clear indications that the time was at hand when we should move back to Los Angeles.

Professionally, I had been aware of the certain handicaps I experienced by living so far away from the University and the city, a quarter of a mile from the street car, and an equal distance to walk from the nearest stop to the campus — an automobile was not to be thought of when we moved to Lennox.

Under such conditions, after about three years, we leased our two acres and returned to Los Angeles, where we lived in a rented house on Thirty-fifth Street, adjoining the University campus. But the tenant at Lennox did not prove to be wholly satisfactory: hence it seemed imperative that we return. This we did.

The next change came in 1920, when we applied our little "farm" as part payment on the purchase of a residence property located on Brynhurst Avenue, Los Angeles. In the meantime I had purchased a used Buick automobile, which eased the transportation problem somewhat.

The Swiss chalet type house, pleasantly situated on the gently sloping Baldwin Hills, two blocks above wide Mesa Drive (now Crenshaw Boulevard), proved to be our last family home. For Nancy and me it continued to be home for years after our three remaining sons — R. D.'s death is told elsewhere — had married and established homes of their own. Indeed, it was there, in that dear home, that I, with sad heart, said my last farewell to my companion of forty-three years.

Nancy and I always loved having our children come back to the home nest, whether for an hour's hasty call or as long as they found it convenient to stay. The pantry and the back door were always open — no permission was ever required to help themselves to mother's pies in the cupboard. She was specially fond of gathering the family together on Thanksgiving Day, or Mother's Day, or some member's birthday. And the family dinners she prepared were superb and more than ample.

But there came a time when her health showed unmistakable evidence of weakness. The lack of her former resilience became more marked. In our solicitude we took her off to hot springs in the desert, to the baths at Elsinore; she spent portions of several summers at son Paul's timber claim in Oregon. Besides engaging the best medical service available, I repeatedly consulted the specially recommended member of the University's medical faculty in behalf of the one I loved above all others. But she never regained her normal, satisfactory health, despite all our efforts.

One morning in May, 1938, in our Brynhurst home, in the quiet of the breakfast hour, she suffered a heart attack, and within a few hours, her spirit had taken its departure. The cord that had bound us together in love for more than four decades was broken. The doctor pronounced the final stroke coronary occlusion.

I was again alone — yet not wholly alone, for I had a wealth of beautiful memories, and my sons and their families, they were with me. Profound was my bereavement: but I would not give myself up to overwhelming grief.

Following simple services in the University Methodist Church in Los Angeles, with which we had been actively associated so long, she was laid to rest in beautiful Inglewood Memorial Park: on the simple marble marker above the grave are carved the words: "I am the way, the truth, and the life." Alongside, above the grave of the dear boy who had gone before his mother, is another marker bearing words she herself had lovingly selected; "In Thy presence is fulness of joy."

For a good many years now, I have walked alone, without the companion who had become so much a part of myself. During the months and the years, however, I have not given myself to useless brooding, neither have I allowed myself time for loneliness. My son's homes are always open to me, and it is a pleasure to pay visits to them all. But, being in good health and engaged in my own activities, I have preferred not to make my home with any of them. I have wished to live my own life, surrounded by friends and books, while permitting those of the younger generation to maintain their own patterns of living. This plan, I believe, has been conducive to the happiness of all concerned.

The call to duty and further service has not been unheeded. Had I relaxed my activity my days would have been more lonely, and my sense of mission in life would have been violated. I am blessed to have enjoyed the love and companionship of my precious wife, the mother of my children — there is no bitterness, no remorse; but there is humble gratitude and an abiding peace.

When in 1944 my first great-grandchild was born I felt a bit "puffed up" with great-grandfatherly pride: so I sent to the little new-comer, Paula Mardel Gann, in care of her mother, my lovely granddaughter Dorothy-May, a gift of a $100 government savings bond. In acknowledging the gift the happy mother wrote: "Grandpa, I hope you live long enough to have a great-great grandchild." Well, that was a dozen years ago — and who knows? At any rate, to the date of this writing, four other hundred dollar bonds have been disposed since the first one — I must be an impartial great-grandfather — and happy at that!

My good wife and I always tried to avoid even the slightest semblance of favoritism in dealing with our children, by which I

do not mean that they were treated precisely alike. They were far from being alike; accordingly identical treatment was not always appropriate or applicable. Our third boy was Rockwell Dennis Hunt, Jr., whom we always called "R. D." Because of his affectionate nature, and because he was my namesake, it may be possible that I had been emotionally affected in a higher degree toward him than toward any other child. I do not know. I do not admit that he, above his brothers, was "the idol of my heart"; neither will I deny that he was extremely precious to me.

The accidental drowning of this child, a fine lad, full of promise, when twelve years old, was a stunning blow to his father and mother. Our family had gone from our Los Angeles home to the Oakdale fruit farm, which had been inherited by Nancy, the parents to have charge of harvesting the crop, the children to enjoy a vacation.

"R. D.," with his brother Paul and several other boys, had gone to the Stanislaus River for a swim. But my precious namesake never returned. After hours of distressing work, the body was recovered just before sunset. The speaker at the services was Fay Donaldson, a graduate of Napa College, at that time pastor of the Oakdale Methodist Church. The remains now lie at the side of his mother's in Inglewood Memorial Park. There is scarcely need to add that for three-quarters of a century the vacant place has never been filled in my heart, my dear namesake is still missed — but the memory is sweet and hallowed.

We received an unusually large number of letters from friends expressing their loving sympathy in our hour of bereavement. I quote briefly from the words of my senior colleagues at the University of Southern California. Doctor Thomas B. Stowell said:

> I am too shocked to write.... One can understand why a man of advanced years, whose work is done, should be taken from the world; but why a bright, promising youth, whose life is all before him,

ROCKWELL DENNIS HUNT, JR., ABOUT EIGHT

should be lost to the world, passes explanation.... Please tell the boys [his brothers] how I sorrow for them in their loss, and that now each one must increase his burden one-third more, to give to the world Rockwell's contribution; one-third more of love to father and mother, one-third more of earnest work for the world; for a great and good life has gone.

Dr. James H. Hoose wrote;

Although your other sons sit at your table, yet his chair is vacant— and only memory will fill it for you—till you all shall gather at the home "Over there." Your comfort lies around the fact that your son was a noble boy, born and bred by your own lives—an honor to parenthood and a glory to immortal life.

Each of our three living sons is a native of California and a graduate of the University of Southern California — each has taken studies beyond the baccalaureate degree. Paul Adams, the oldest, qualified for the high school teacher's certificate and became a teacher of physical education in Thomas Starr King Junior High School of Los Angeles. After serving in that capacity for a considerable number of years, he acquired a fruit farm near Oakdale, in Stanislaus County, the acreage that had been a part of the original Stuart Colony. He is distinctly the out-doors type, having long had special fondness for hunting wild game, from the dove to the bull elk, and for fishing, whether for brook trout, river bass and salmon, or deep water species found in the ocean. As a director of the Oakdale Irrigation District, member of Stanislaus County Recreation Commission, and past president of the local Kiwanis Club, as well as fruit farmer, he is a widely known and respected member of the community.

Lloyd Freeman, the second son, followed his early bent and majored in electrical engineering. After graduation he spent three years in the employ of the Westinghouse Company, in Pittsburgh: then he took a position with the Southern California Edison Company, of Los Angeles. By steps he rose rapidly to the rank of Chief Electrical Engineer, which position he held until 1954, when he was made Consulting Engineer for the corporation. He has attended numerous national and international conventions, in whose programs he has frequently participated. From earliest childhood his practical interest in machinery and mechanical things and electrical devices was so marked as virtually to eliminate the problem of vocation—nature provided the answer.

The youngest son, Clarence Stuart, chose the law, graduating in 1923 with the J. D. degree. As a mere child he had become a very rapid reader, and his retentive memory seemed to be a natural gift. His vocabulary expanded rapidly: in his numerous examinations, both before and after graduation, he ranked among the highest. His first regular appointment was as Deputy District Attorney for Los Angeles County, stationed at Long Beach. He rose rapidly in status by virtue of successful promotional examinations. Soon after the conclusion of World War II, however, he entered private practice in Long Beach, in association with Joseph Ball. At present (1955) he is second in the large firm of Ball, Hunt and Hart, which includes seven attorneys. His selection as president of the local bar association and his service on state and local committees illustrate his standing in his profession and his community.

Each of our sons has made his contribution to the nation's war effort. Paul enlisted in a Base Hospital Unit in the first World War, left college before graduation, and served actively in France for the better part of a year. Lloyd was summoned on several occasions to join in special research work for the government at Washington, Columbia University, and elsewhere. Clarence applied for and received a commission as lieutenant in the U. S. Navy in World War II and was given the choice assignment as Intelligence Officer on the presidential cruiser *Augusta*. In that capacity he served until the war was ended.

Each of the three has established a home of his own, all of them in California. Paul resides near Oakdale, Lloyd in Glendale, Clarence in Long Beach. They are still my "boys," though the youngest of them has now passed the half-century mark. My three daughters-in-law, Imogen, Dorothy, and Leota, are ladies of talent and accomplishment: in each of their homes there is always a welcome for "dad."

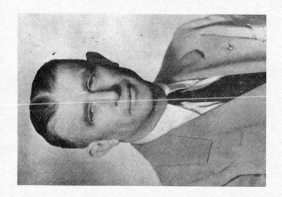

PAUL, LLOYD, CLARENCE

CHAPTER NINE

UNIVERSITY *of* SOUTHERN CALIFORNIA

Three men, each of them my senior, and each a trusted friend, took special and personal interest in the question of locating me at the University of Southern California. They were Dr. Freeman D. Bovard, Judge J. R. Lewis, and Attorney William M. Bowen. I could not fail to be grateful to each of them, though I realized that it was incumbent on me to make my own decisions.

Dr. Bovard was editor of the *California Christian Advocate*. I had made his acquaintance and at several different times had sent him contributions which were published in the *Advocate*. He had known me while I was teaching at the University of the Pacific, and had shown interest in my work as principal of San José High School. One year he accepted my invitation to be commencement speaker there. It was on that occasion, I distinctly recall, that he drew me aside and said to me, quite earnestly, "You ought to be at the University of Southern California — that's the place for you." His special interest in that University is the more readily understood when it is remembered that at its opening, in 1880, he was its vice-president and professor, his older brother, Marion M. Bovard, its president, and at the time he talked with me his younger brother, George Finley Bovard, was president of the University, at Los Angeles: thus I needed no introduction to him.

Judge Lewis it was who, as president of the San José Board of Education, had come to my home and treated me to a surprise by offering me the principalship of the High School, and had steadfastly supported me in that position as long as he remained in San José. When he moved to Los Angeles he became interested in the University there: then it was he thought of me and wished me to become a member of its faculty. He wrote me at length on the subject and, unknown to me, went so far as to interview one or two of the influential leaders at the University.

William Bowen at that time and for many years afterward was a trustee of the University of Southern California. I had known him well from the time of my student days at Napa College. He did not graduate at Napa, but for a few years was one of the most active members of the debating society, the Orophilean Lyceum. My brothers and I became intimately acquainted with him, and he was a frequent visitor at our home; a warm friendship sprang up between us. Following the early acquaintance he completed his law studies and later with his family moved to Los Angeles for the practice of law. Seeing a possibility of attracting me to the University of which he was a trustee, he actively set about trying to effectuate a realization. In the end, it was he who brought about a conference with President Bovard, the result of which was my acceptance of the invitation to a position as professor of economics and sociology at the University. But further details about my actual introduction to the Southern California position will follow in subsequent paragraphs.

Those were the three men who believed in me and were convinced that I could render useful service in the Los Angeles institution, who were most influential, next to myself, in bringing about my long term of active service in the University of Southern California, in all a period of thirty-seven years.

My actual introduction to the University of Southern California was due almost wholly to my steadfast friend Mr. Bowen. Knowing my desire to re-enter college work, he invited me to go to Los Angeles to be his guest at the "Greater University Banquet" on the occasion of Washington's Birthday, 1908, and while there to have a conference with President Bovard relative to a possible position.

The banquet was a noteworthy event, for it was there, in Levy's downtown restaurant, that the "Greater University" idea was definitely launched. The seven different schools and colleges of the University were well represented, the decorations were profuse and elaborate, the attendance was large — it was a spirited and gala event. I was the guest of Mr. and Mrs. Bowen, in my new tuxedo — the first I ever owned!

On the following morning by appointment I called on President Bovard, who met me with real cordiality. He assured me that because of what his brother Freeman had told him he had no need of further evidence as to my educational qualifications, and that therefore the only real question was whether I could agree to accept a position as professor for the very modest salary the University was then able to offer. It was a very real question.

My current salary as principal of the High School at San José was then $2,200 a year; but the time had arrived when I wished to enter college teaching if offered an acceptable position. I fully expected it would be necessary to make some financial sacrifice, especially if I went to a church-controlled institution; but when Dr. Bovard informed me that the best he could offer at that time was $1300 a year, I was a good deal surprised and disappointed — could I possibly afford, with my family obligations, to make that sacrifice? My question whether it was not possible to make it $1500 met with a reluctant negative response.

Being convinced of President Bovard's sincerity, also that there was a real future for the University and that I would be among the best of friends there, I finally decided, partly as an act of faith, to accept the position and cast my lot with the University of Southern California. I was told there would be opportunity for some additional earning in the small summer school being planned, previous to the opening of the fall semester. It was not an easy decision, but I was convinced that the time had come for the change and that there was a real opportunity in the making.

President Bovard was exceedingly gracious to me. He took me about to the various departments as if I were some distinguished visitor, and invited me to address the student body on the subject of world peace.

One thing in particular that impressed me and that I have never forgotten was his special request. "Dr. Hunt," he said, "you have now had valuable administrative experience; my own knowledge of university administration is quite limited. I shall deem it a favor to me if you will at any time call to my attention anything in any department that you observe and think is out of line or in need of correction." I have always appreciated that confidence and the spirit that inspired it; and I have wondered how many administrators would be willing to make such a confession to a newly employed professor and make a similar request of him.

My title at the University was to be Professor of Economics and Sociology — not simply a "chair", nor merely a "settee", but an entire cubicle of sittings, for I was called upon to teach also a course in Pacific Slope History and another in Political Science! But the University was then young and its resources severely limited. By way of contrast, the "Trojan" University arrived at such status, some years before these lines were written, as to require seven full-time teachers in Sociology alone, a similar number in Economics, to say nothing of the large departments of History and Political Science, or the College of Commerce, with its thousands of students. I was privileged to have a significant part in the development and expansion of the University with which I had cast my lot. That part will be outlined somewhat more fully on subsequent pages.

President Bovard gave me a favorable introduction to the liberal arts faculty, not a large group in 1908, for up to that time the total registration at the University had barely reached 1,000 for any one year. But it seems appropriate to make specific reference to some of my early colleagues.

The one man who stood out above the others as a great teacher — and a great soul he was — was James Harmon Hoose, professor of Philosophy and Education. Laird J. Stabler, professor of Chemistry, later Dean of the College of Pharmacy, who served the University effectively through many years; Tully C. Knoles, professor of History, later to become president of the College of the Pacific; Paul Arnold, professor of Mathematics; Albert Ulrey, professor of Zoology; Roy Schultz, professor of Spanish; Ruth Brown, professor of Latin; Edgar von Fingerlin, professor of German and French; James Main Dixon, professor of English and Comparative Literature — these were some of the members of the faculty with whom I became acquainted during my first year in Los Angeles. My association with them and others was happy from the beginning.

One of the first questions of more general interest that came to my attention was that of scholarship standards. It gave me an uncomfortable feeling to learn that the top-ranking high school graduates of the vicinity were not generally being advised to enter the University of Southern California. As a high school principal, I had become somewhat acquainted with William H. Housh of Los Angeles High School, also through his writings with Lewis R. Ashley, probably the most prominent teacher in the Pasadena High School. To learn that the cream of their

graduates were being advised to go to the State University at
Berkeley or to Stanford University — and not to Southern California — was disconcerting. In the minds of the leading principals,
there was at that time no real university in the south, and
scarcely a first-class college.

I felt called upon to do whatever I could to improve that
situation. My high school experience proved valuable, in affording
me an approach to local administrators and an understanding of
the rather unfavorable attitude toward the institution of which
I had become a part. I regarded Mr. Housh very highly, and for
all the remaining years we remained the best of good friends.
Equally friendly relations have been maintained with Mr. Ashley,
who has been for many years one of the most influential leaders
in secondary education by virtue of his widely-used textbooks
as well as his splendid teaching.

To bring about a mutually satisfactory relationship between the
University of Southern California and the best high schools and
administrative officials required much time and careful planning:
but the problem was not lost sight of, and the rapid development
and improvements at the University calculated to assist in bringing
about a solution, were well on the way.

While the Master of Arts Degree was conferred on a relatively
few individual candidates, there was no organized graduate
department until the autumn of 1910. In the meantime, largely
through the importunity of Doctor Hoose, Doctor Thomas B.
Stowell, former president of Potsdam Normal School in New
York, was brought to Southern California in 1909, and almost
immediately the demand for higher studies was greatly stimulated.
At this stage of development Dr. Stowell proved a tower of
strength, first as professor of education, then as founder and first
dean of the School of Education.

On the basis of a special report approved by the Committee
on Graduate Scholarship, October 26, 1910 and concurred in

by President George F. Bovard two days later, the Graduate Department of the University of Southern California was founded. To have charge of this department was to be the function of a group of senior faculty members appointed by the President, and known as the Graduate Council. The announced purpose of the Graduate Council was thus defined:

> (1) To give due prominence to the Graduate Courses of instruction offered by the University; (2) To insure systematic and efficient administration of this higher work; (3) To provide instruction for graduate and upper division students.

For the Master's degree, due emphasis was to be placed on the required thesis, and it was stipulated that "The work of the candidate must show marked excellence."

It is worthy of record that the charter members of the Graduate Council were as follows: President George Finley Bovard *(ex officio)*; James Harmon Hoose, Professor of Philosophy (chairman); Thomas Blanchard Stowell, Professor of Education; James Main Dixon, Professor of English Literature; Gilbert E. Bailey, Professor of Geology; Edgar M. von Fingerlin, Professor of Modern Languages; and Rockwell D. Hunt, Professor of Economics and Sociology (secretary).

As the secretary, I came to know my colleagues of the Council intimately and well — an acquaintance I have long cherished as among the happiest memories of my long service at Southern California. Youngest of all the members at the beginning, I have for many years been the sole survivor of the group. I deem it a privilege to devote a paragraph to each of my honored colleagues of the original Council.

George Finley Bovard, a younger brother of the first president, Marion M. Bovard, and a member of the University's first graduating class in 1884, was president from 1901 to 1921. He was privileged to guide the University's growth from a weak, struggling college to a place of leadership among institutions of higher learning of the great Southwest. Under his devoted administration it was well advanced on the way to the real metropolitan University it is today. Seldom is it given to one to receive in his lifetime such expressions of affectionate regard and sincere appreciation as were tendered to President-Emeritus Bovard by the trustees of the University on the occasion of his retirement as active trustee.

James Harmon Hoose was called the Nestor of the University during dark days of the 1890's, when it struggled against almost insuperable odds. To him, as Professor of Philosophy, students and faculty alike looked for counsel and guidance — he was prudent and wise, ever resourceful, completely consecrated to his noble task. At the celebration of his eightieth birthday he was pronounced "philosopher, dreamer, seer — a man who has proved that ideals and visions are the most real things of life." He was a great teacher, a teacher of men rather than of mere subjects. His rugged, kindly personality stamped itself indelibly upon his students.

Thomas Blanchard Stowell, founder of the University's School of Education was a life-sized man of wide learning, planetary experience, ripe judgment, and thoroughgoing loyalty. As Doctor Emory S. Bogardus said of him: "He inspired in his pupils, young and old, not only an abiding interest in facts, details, and principles but also a deep-seated love of nature, of little children, and of God." He endeared himself to all who knew him. His service to the teaching profession of Southern California during the decade of his activity was without equal.

James Main Dixon, a native of Scotland, educated in St. Andrews University, remained always a true Scot in speech and manner. With a personality unmatched for its uniqueness, he rendered conspicuous service to the University during a long incumbency. His mind was truly encyclopedic, his versatility remarkable, more than compensating for his lack of pedagogical methodology and techniques. He could hold his own in any theological discussion, was an authority in teaching English and comparative literature, and was an interpreter of Robert Burns without a peer.

Gilbert Ellis Bailey was an unusually interesting personality. Conspicuous in any company because of his great height, weight, and impressive presence, he never lacked a lively sense of humor and he was a most congenial friend. The popularity of his classes in geology was enhanced by his previous experiences in Mexico, Central America, and South America. In his writing he blazed new trails in *The Use of Explosives in Agriculture, Vertical Farming,* and *California, a Geologic Wonderland.* Dr. Bailey's loyalty to the University was absolute and complete, which won many influential friends.

Edgar M. von Fingerlin was a representative of the true type of old German nobility, combining in himself the best of European culture with the bearing of true aristocracy. He had become a loyal American, with the fine spirit of Western democracy. As a teacher of modern languages, he was always gentle and patient, the student's guide and friend rather than master and disciplinarian. His tastes were simple, his manner that of the true scholar — never aggressive, never place-seeking for himself, always content to play his part with fidelity and integrity. None other could have filled the place he held.

Such was the personnel of the first Graduate Council at the University of Southern California, charged with the responsibility of establishing and maintaining the requirements for all graduate degrees. Inevitably changes came from time to time. After twenty-five years the Council numbered twenty-five members, and I was the only member appearing in the second group, known under the von KleinSmid administration as the Council on Graduate Study and Research.

I shall now give an outline of the history of an achievement that gave great impetus to the newly organized Graduate Department, an event perhaps second to none in placing the University of Southern California on the high road to becoming a great metropolitan university.

For years the only institutions authorized to issue the recommendation for the state high school teacher's certificate were the State University (at Berkeley) and Stanford University, both of them hundreds of miles to the north. It is quite understandable that teachers trained in the north would naturally recommend their graduates to go north to college — at least a partial reason for the situation described on a previous page. Dr. Stowell, himself a teacher of teachers, became deeply interested in the matter of obtaining authorization from the State Board of Education for the University of Southern California to issue recommendations for the coveted secondary credential. To win this privilege was worth our best effort.

As secretary of the Graduate Council I was intimately associated with Dr. Stowell in the quiet campaign to obtain the needed authorization. We gave the matter our most earnest study. Interviews were sought with those who were in positions to aid us in shaping a satisfactory program of development and of procedure leading to the goal. More than any other member of the State Board its then president, Dean Alexis Lange of the University of California, was the key person. I had become acquainted with him a few years earlier, when he was examiner of high schools for accreditation, and while I was principal at San José. I can still remember vividly the time I called upon him at his home near the University and how we two walked together over the Berkeley hills, while I explained to him the plans for our Graduate Department, the requirements for the master's degree, and our earnest desire to make ourselves worthy of the privilege of issuing the High School Recommendation. Dr. Stowell as leader was likewise busy laying foundations.

Our formal application was made to the State Board at Riverside in April, 1910. The Board was not ready to grant the petition, but authorized a special committee "to continue its investigation with a view to determining whether or not the institution might be properly accredited at the end of another year."

In December, the Graduate Council received a communication from State Superintendent Edward Hyatt, setting forth definite conditions on the fulfillment of which the authorization might be issued. Each condition was carefully considered and President Bovard then pledged, on behalf of the University, that the conditions would be met.

The final meeting of the Board, at the Riverside Mission Inn, was not without its dramatic moments. The University was represented by President Bovard, Attorney William M. Bowen, Dr. Stowell, and myself. The scene had apparently been set for favorable action, when Frederic Burk, president of San Francisco Normal School, turned to our president and asked, "What guarantee, Mr. Bovard, can you give this Board that these conditions will be fully met?" President Bovard was ready. Looking squarely at Dr. Burk and pointing his long forefinger directly at him he replied, "When you require a special guarantee from the State University and Stanford University, the University of Southern California will meet them." There was nothing more to be said.

On the 10th of February, 1911, the University was duly accredited, which placed it on a level, in that respect, with the northern universities and gave assurance of at least one year of graduate study in a group of academic departments, in addition to the required courses in education. It was a signal achievement, giving U.S.C. a unique position among all the educational institutions of Southern California.

Among the conditions to be met, one had reference to the

augmentation of the library and laboratory facilities needed for graduate research, another pertained to the limitation of teaching hours on the part of professors whose work was to be primarily on the graduate level. Perhaps nothing was more important or of more far-reaching significance than the strengthening of the faculty by adding young specialists of thorough training and future promise. The four such men employed to begin service in September, 1911 were: Allison Gaw (English Literature), Lincoln Edwards (Zoology), Emory S. Bogardus (Sociology), and Leroy S. Weatherby (Chemistry). Each of these had his Ph.D. degree; together they constituted the important addition to the faculty to enable it to meet current needs and inspire confidence for the future. Of the four, Doctor Bogardus gave the record period of service to the Universty, as professor of sociology, dean of the School of Social Work, dean of the Graduate School, and editor of the bi-monthly *Sociology and Social Research*. Indeed he has devoted virtually his entire distinguished academic career to the University of Southern California.

At this point it is pleasant to record a striking reversal of sentiment, regarding academic standards, I found when I came to Los Angeles in 1908. Now many principals and teachers in intermediate and elementary schools were glad to enroll as candidates for the high school credential and for the master's degree. Among my own students were several who later became city superintendents of schools, including Frank Bouelle and Vierling Kersey, and more who later were high school principals. During 1917-18 more than 300 graduate students were registered. A decade later 450 students were enrolled in the Graduate School, in addition to 398 graduate students in the School of Education. The early disparagement of U.S.C. as an institution to which principals might recommend their brightest graduates had vanished. Instead of it, teachers in all grades of public schools were registering in greater and greater numbers. This was due, in

ROCKWELL D. HUNT AT ABOUT FORTY-EIGHT

part, to the personal interest taken in the registrants by their professors and the administrative officers concerned, as well as to the offering of courses specially adapted to the needs of the student candidates. The new scene was really marked by an unusual spirit of mutuality and cordiality between faculty and students.

In 1920 the Graduate Department was organized into the Graduate School. I was appointed its first Dean, my incumbency continuing to the time of my retirement twenty-five years later. The Graduate Council, over which the Dean presided, was regularly continued, the University Registrar serving as secretary. Methods of procedure were developed to meet the needs of the rapidly increasing graduate student body. The credentials of each applicant were carefully scrutinized before admission to the school.

The exercises "in dedication of George Finley Bovard Administration Auditorium, Hoose Hall of Philosophy, and Stowell Hall of Education" (June 19-23, 1921), including group conferences, musical features, and culminating in the Commencement Exercises, proved to be the most elaborate of all such exercises at the University of Southern California to that time. The volume of Proceedings, edited by Ralph Tyler Flewelling, contains this dedication:

Dedicated to
GEORGE FINLEY BOVARD
Who made the Greater
UNIVERSITY OF SOUTHERN CALIFORNIA
An Accomplished Fact

In the Preliminary Statement, presented by Wilbur H. Long, occur these words:

> The George Finley Bovard Administration Building is the first of a group of university buildings to be erected on the university campus.

It is designed to furnish the central unit of a group composing the Greater University, and contains the offices of administration, the offices of the departments of instruction, and the auditorium, together with 27 classrooms, lecture halls, and seminar rooms.... Plans call for a University Library Building, a home for the Maclay College of Theology, and buildings for other departments and colleges.

The Sermon of Dedication was delivered by Bishop Adna Wright Leonard, of the Methodist Episcopal Church, president of the board of trustees — his theme "I Am a Debtor." Special tributes were paid to James Harmon Hoose and Thomas Blanchard Stowell by Tully C. Knoles and Emory S. Bogardus, respectively. Two organ recitals in dedication of the splendid new organ were presented by Edwin H. Lemare of San Francisco; the Annual Commencement Exercises were held in Exposition Park.

My own part in the proceedings consisted in membership in the committee on arrangements, a brief dedicatory address on "Doctor Hoose as Colleague," and as presiding official at the Exercises in Recognition of Delegates. Responses were made by E. P. Clarke, Susan M. Dorsey, and James A. Blaisdell. The Annual Alumni Address was presented by William S. Bovard, a brother of President George F. Bovard. I quote the closing words of the fraternal greeting presented by Dr. Carl S. Patton, of First Congregational Church, Los Angeles:

I rejoice in the progress that this day signalizes; and upon all the labor which this day crowns with success, and all the promise that it speaks of a better commonwealth, wise in the things of the spirit. I, a representative of a sister church equally interested in education, bring you my heartiest felicitations. God bless the University of Southern California, and make her, in His Kingdom, a city upon an hill that cannot be hid.

The Commencement Address June 23, was delivered by Professor Robert W. Rogers of Drew Theological Seminary. In his stirring discourse Dr. Rogers sounded no minor note. Said he:

> Nay, far from it, this is a clarion call to this sovereign common-wealth, to this astoundingly beautiful, this lovely and puissant city here, to build gloriously a great university worthy of the past and its present achievement, but worthy also of the unmeasured and unmeasurable opportunity of tomorrow. Nothing is too great, no ideal too lofty, no hope too rich and deep for what may here be achieved. Upon these foundations already well and truly laid, let great and numerous buildings stand. Let their halls resound with the hurrying feet of tens of thousands of high-spirited youth, making haste to laboratories, libraries, lecture rooms and seminaries of the highest research. . . . Let those who teach remember the glorious succession in which they stand . . . let them do and dare mighty things undreamt before, nor yield to the enticement of any lesser ambition.

I had been happy to suggest the name for the Bovard Building, a name adopted by the trustees, which was universally deemed most fitting and deserved. The President had already expressed a desire to be relieved of his responsibilities. The Dedication Exercises marked the close of his illustrious term. Bovard Administration Auditorium set the pace for subsequent buildings. No less was the affection and respect for the man during his remaining years, as President-Emeritus. I am grateful to have enjoyed the privilege of serving under him during a dozen fruitful years.

When President Bovard retired from active duty in 1920, search was immediately begun for a man who would come to head the University, and, standing on the secure foundations already laid, plan wisely to build for the larger future by integrating the various schools and colleges, guide the development of the institution into a full-fledged university and thus meet the higher educational demands of the wider, rapidly growing community.

After months of diligent searching an invitation was extended to Dr. Rufus B. von KleinSmid, President of the University of Arizona, to accept the position. A telegram of acceptance was received October 10, 1921 — Dr. von KleinSmid had seen a vision of the great future for Southern California.

I remember well the eagerness with which we of the faculty looked forward to the actual arrival of the new president, to take the helm. We were hopeful that everything would work out to the general satisfaction of all — the man from Arizona, with the rather forbidding name, would be well received.

After anxious weeks, the president-elect appeared on the campus in early December, 1921 and became president-in-fact. He entered upon a term that ended only with his retirement in 1947.

Dr. von KleinSmid had already won many honors in Latin-American countries, including a number of honorary degrees conferred by their universities. Recognizing in the occasion of his formal inauguration an unusual opportunity, the joint committee of faculty and trustees, acting on a suggestion of the new president, decided to hold a great Pan-American Conference on Education. We of the faculty gave the project our full, loyal support.

The Conference, held April 27, 28 and 29, 1922, was believed to be the first conference of its kind ever held in any university. Fourteen Latin-American governments were represented, with a total of some 400 delegates present. Never had there been such a gathering of Latin-Americans in California.

The formal inauguration ceremonies took place on the forenoon of April 28. The academic procession included the faculties of the University, board of trustees, Latin-American delegates, other distinguished guests, and members of the senior class. President-Emeritus Bovard very appropriately presided. Bishop Adna W. Leonard, after delivering the formal address of the occasion, introduced Rufus B. von KleinSmid as the new President.

Immediately after his inaugural address on "A World View of Education" the president conferred honorary degrees upon a group of eminent persons recommended by the committee. Among those receiving honorary degrees was former U. S. Senator Cornelius Cole, distinguished California pioneer of 1849, then in his one-hundredth year. It was my rare privilege to present him to the president for his LL.D. When the venerable Senator stepped forward to receive his diploma and doctor's hood, the vast audience rose to its feet as one man and gave the modest centenarian a heart-warming ovation. Others who received honorary degrees included Dr. Norman Bridge; Orwyn W. E. Cook; José de Galvez, Director Universidad Nacional de Chili; José Vasconcelos, Minister of Education of Mexico; Gumero Villalobos; John Barrett, Chairman International Pan-American Committee; Frank M. Porter, Dean of U.S.C. School of Law; and President-Emeritus George Finley Bovard.

The presentation of the large number of delegates was a pleasing and dignified ceremony. Included among the delegates who honored the University by their presence were more than a score of university and college presidents, a group of distinguished Latin-Americans, and numerous representatives of learned societies.

The Inaugural Banquet took the form of a trustees' dinner to delegates and specially invited guests. At the personal invitation of President von KleinSmid I served as toastmaster for the occasion. In introducing the President-elect for his address I took occasion to use these words:

> Combining in himself unusual breadth of training, excellence of scholarship, successful administrative experience, the rare ability of meeting men of large affairs, wide and intimate acquaintance with our social and commercial problems, and the high qualities of a cultivated Christian gentleman, Dr. von KleinSmid faces a matchless

opportunity as he assumes the duties of the presidency of the leading institution of higher learning in the great Southwest.

The new president had gotten off to an excellent start — the Pan-American Conference had been an outstanding success. Interest in international affairs was greatly stimulated, and was actively followed up later by the founding of the Los Angeles University of International Relations in 1924 and the establishment of the Annual Institute of World Affairs at Riverside in 1926. In both of these Dr. von KleinSmid has continued as chancellor.

Announcement of a $10,000,000 campaign to strengthen the University was made within six months after inauguration, which proved to be over-ambitious for the time; but another movement, on the more purely academic side, was started, which was of more direct interest to me and in which I was to have a leading part. This must be described in some detail on subsequent pages.

As an administrator President von KleinSmid possessed such personal charm and suavity of manner, combined with patrician bearing and urbane affability as to mark him as a person of distinction in any company. He carried the University presidency with an air of effortless ease. His handsome, finely chiseled profile was further enhanced by his wealth of black hair, turned snowy white in more recent years. He exhibited remarkable versatility in public address, responding generously to invitations to speak before a wide variety of groups. A marked personal trait was in his fine sense of the dramatic and in perfect timing. It seemed quite the natural thing for the assemblage of students to greet him on appearance by standing and applause.

As an instrument of graduate instruction in any university, the department seminar long since came to be regarded as indispensable. Its one chief objective is "to give training for and practice in research," and research is the very genius and spirit of graduate work. It may be said that scarcely any university department maintaining instruction on the higher levels of creative scholarship, or stimulatng independent research, is without one or more seminars. To be most effective the group must never be a large one—usually not to exceed twelve to fifteen members.

The first seminars in the University of Southern California, introduced in the formative period of the Graduate School, were doubtless rather feeble and faltering for lack of qualified personnel and in some cases competent leadership. But they gained rapidly in strength and character—in due time becoming firmly established as an important instrument of advanced instruction.

As I conceived it, the member's major task for the semester or the year consists in the preparation of the seminar report, in thesis form, based on individual investigation. When presented before the group, the report is subject to criticism both as to subject matter and to methodology. Subsidiary exercises vary with the subjects of departments concerned. Reviews of recent books and attention to scholarly periodical literature are important. Anything in the nature of personal bias or unscientific spirit is definitely frowned upon. As some one has expressed it, an important goal of the seminar is a "genuinely critical spirit, a sense of evidence, and a sustained suspicion of false deductions." As professor of economics and dean of the Graduate School during the period of its early development, it was gratifying to have a hand in the progress of the seminar in the University as "the most important instrument of graduate instruction today."

A brief résumé will show that the Graduate School of Arts and Sciences was authorized by the University trustees on the 27th of January, 1920, and that on the 24th of February of that year I was appointed Dean of the new School and authorized to proceed with its further organization. The specified objectives of the School were:

1) To give due prominence to graduate courses of instruction offered by the University;

2) to insure systematic and efficient administration of this advanced work;

3) to provide separate instruction for graduate and upper division students.

In the year book for 1922-23 was published my statement on "The Graduate Attitude," in part as follows:

> ... The undergraduate student is chiefly acquisitive and receptive: the graduate steps out, first toward becoming a master of arts, and finally discoverer, creator, leader among students and masters.... The attitude of the graduate ... is one of increasingly independent effort, whereby the candidate reinforces his claim, by worth and by labor, to the fuller recognition of the University and in the goodly company of scholars.

As Dean, beginning with 1922-23 I prepared each year a report to the president and board of trustees. Reference to this series of reports is now a convenient way of refreshing my memory as to changes and developments that took place during the period of my administration. The Council on Graduate Study and Research had been considerably enlarged and its functions more clearly defined. A mass of detail was handled by the administrative committee, appointed by the dean.

With the rapid growth of graduate work, and the establishment of new schools — including those in Education and Commerce, a reorganization was effected whereby the Graduate School of Arts and Sciences became "The Graduate School of the University," which symbolized the movement of integrating the various divisions and units of the University into a unified whole.

As the number of candidates for the master's degree increased, with more and more departments of study offering major work, another important question forced itself upon the minds of those of us directly concerned: should the University of Southern California prepare itself to offer the highest academic degree, the doctor of philosophy? It became more and more obvious that serious attention must be given to this question, in view of the growing demand in the large area represented by the University.

Another and very pragmatic situation, which some of us in responsible positions could not fail to perceive, unquestionably had an influence in bringing the Ph.D. question to the fore without undue delay. In 1917, Dr. Ernest C. Moore of Harvard University, and one-time city superintendent of schools in Los Angeles, was called to be president of the State Normal School there, with the understanding that it should be metamorphosed into a branch of the University of California. If, as at first appeared, it was to be of junior college level, the logic of time clearly indicated that full collegiate stature would be demanded within a few years; and a four year college being well established — the population of Southern California increasing rapidly all the while — could it not be foreseen that this "Southern Branch" would be forced to offer also graduate work? The wisdom of a prophet was not required to see what was actually happening. And the thing that was happening gave added reason for the University of Southern California, with its years of experience and as an established institution, to proceed as rapidly as consistent with actual facilities to assume the stature of a full-fledged university and plan to confer the highest university degree.

In my report as Dean of the Graduate School to the President and Board of Trustees, for the academic year 1922-23, and dated June 22, 1923, the following paragraph appears:

> Thus far the Graduate School ... has contented itself with meeting the requirements of the master's degree and the California High School Credential. There has developed, however, during the last few years a very considerable demand for work leading to the degree of doctor of philosophy. This year the demand has become more insistent —in fact, several holders of the master's degree have been pursuing further graduate work with the hope that it may later be accredited to them towards the doctorate.

Early during that year I had addressed letters to more than a score of representative educators, requesting their opinions on three questions:

1) Should the University of Southern California definitely plan to offer work in a group of departments leading to the Ph.D. degree?
2) Is the time ripe for beginning work in accordance with such plan?
3) What departments, in your opinion, should be the first to invite candidates for the doctorate?

Replies to my letters were favorable to the University's undertaking the advanced work at the earliest date compatible with financial ability. One well-known administrator expressed the view of many when he wrote:

> One of the greatest needs educationally in southern California has been the completion of a higher portion of its educational system.

Because of my official position and my academic experience, I felt that the introduction of work justifying the conferring of the Ph.D. degree would be one of the most important steps in the University's history, and that any initiative must come from the dean's office. Despite the favorable response to my letters and urgent expressions from some of my colleagues, however, I was painfully aware of our limitations, and firm in the resolution to proceed without unseemly haste — if the University of Southern California was to offer the Doctor of Philosophy degree it must be on a high and defensible level. I was keenly sensitive to the responsibility resting directly upon me. In my report to the President I stated:

> The requirements for the Doctor of Philosophy degree at this University should be uniformly and unequivocally high, the more because of our very youth in the field of graduate work and our tendency to phenomenal growth.

I had already laid before the Council a series of eight basic propositions for consideration. Then I set forth some specific needs, including more ample endowment, the addition of faculty men of broad scholarship and specialized learning, more adequate laboratory facilities, and, as a "compelling necessity" "a suitable library building, fire-proof and modern in construction, and thoroughly equipped in all appointments."

The Dean's 1923 Annual Report on the Graduate School was concluded in these words:

> Our opportunity as an institution in southern California, happily situated in the metropolis of the great Southwest, is unique; and we must not be unmindful of the fact that opportunity brings corresponding obligations. I believe the work of the Graduate School . . . is now only in its infancy, but that it is destined to grow rapidly in magnitude and excellence to meet the very real demands upon us and the challenge of a future indefinitely great.

In the Graduate Bulletin of April, 1924 appeared the first public official announcement regarding the degree of Doctor of Philosophy. No student was to be admitted to candidacy for the doctorate previous to May, 1925, no doctorate conferred before May, 1926; and for a time candidates would be received in a strictly limited number of departments only. The time schedule was intended to afford selected departments an opportunity to augment their facilities, and also forestall the attempt of any prospective candidate to win his doctorate at Southern California with a bare minimum of work there. The precaution proved to be wise.

In actual fact, no doctorate was conferred in 1926: in 1927 a single candidate (D. Welty Lefever) was successful in winning the degree. Dr. Lefever continues a highly respected professor in our School of Education at the time this is written. Each year since 1927 has seen a group of successful candidates leave the University with the coveted doctorate.

The first group of departments authorized to invite candidates for the Ph.D. included Education, English, French, Philosophy, and Sociology. Other departments were added as they were adjudged to be adequately equipped for the purpose.

As Dean I suspected that some of my colleagues thought of me as a kind of watch-dog at the gate and were sometimes inclined to wish me to move a little faster or open the gate a little wider. But I insisted on proceeding conservatively, for I believed deeply that the crowning work of a university is in the quality of the young doctors it turns out and that standards must be maintained on a high and dignified level. At the time of which I write I prepared, with my best care, an article setting forth my ideas on "The Doctor of Philosophy Degree," which was published in the magazine *School and Society.*[1] Here is a concluding paragraph:

> In a word, I am pleading for the scrupulous insistence upon such qualifications for the Ph.D. degree as will insure the infusion from the universities into contemporaneous life of a succession of worthy and promising scholars—well rounded, sharply focused—who shall be able while passing along the torch of learning to assist in advancing to ever-widening bounds the frontiers of human knowledge.

From the early years of the present century, as the population of Los Angeles maintained its almost dizzying rate of increase, the University administration was under pressure to venture into some new field, establish some new college division, or add to the curriculum new or more specialized courses in keeping with some group demand. I at once became aware of this progressive, venturesome spirit, and, while always inclined to urge caution and avoid undue haste, I sympathized with a number of plans brought forward for expansion along comparatively untried lines. In more than one field I was even cast in the rôle of leader.

---

[1] Vol. XXIII, No. 576, (January 9, 1926)

I introduced what may be called a slight innovation during my very first year at the University, in the form of a course in Municipal Problems, a special feature in which was a weekly lecture — talk to the class by a practical on-the-job official or authority in Los Angeles. I was greatly assisted in arranging this weekly series by my friend William M. Bowen, who had personally introduced me to a number of key persons about town as potential speakers. On the 5th of September, 1908, I addressed the Los Angeles City Club on "Problems of the Modern City," presenting as my main thesis "that municipal problems is a subject worthy of a place in the curriculum of every American university." I announced the series of addresses, about a score in number, to be presented in my class by practical experts on significant topics in their respective fields.

The plan worked well and gave a practical touch to the course that no amount of reading in books could have accomplished. No book or printed report could present so graphically the picture of bringing water to Los Angeles from Owen's Valley, 250 miles away, as could Engineer William Mulholland, standing before the class; the treatment of juvenile offenders by Judge Curtis D. Wilbur; and so with the work of the City Playground Department, as told by the commissioner, Mrs. Willoughby Rodman, and the social activities of the Bethlehem Institution as described by its director, Dr. Dana W. Bartlett.

The institution of that series of practical talks on specific local problems, beginning in 1908, was many years later said to be the modest forerunner of a major division of the University, the School of Government, acknowledged to be one of the best of its kind in the country. In 1940, in connection with the Institute of Government conducted by Dean Emery E. Olson, the *Daily Trojan* reported:

> Dean Hunt thirty-two years ago resorted to a technique which is recognized today as being most efficient and effective; this program

was that of arranging for a series of lectures by public officials from the city and county and the state, as well as by leaders and captains of private industry.

What might be called a by-product was seen in the introduction of a regular course in City Planning, with Gordon Whitnall as instructor. His first class numbered two students! Since that time the development of the study of city planning, with the problems of zoning, street-layouts, parks, playgrounds, industrial districts, etc., has been a sensation in American municipal life.

A university in a city has a responsibility to the community to furnish leadership and guidance to the people of the locale it serves.

As the University developed *pari passu* with the rapidly growing Southern California area, there seemed to be emerging more and more clearly a need for better preparation for bigger business. I was senior member of the teaching staff in the department of economics, but theoretical studies in economics did not fully meet the demand coming stronger and stronger from the banks, the incoming factories, and large business firms. Still less were elementary business colleges of an older type able to fill the bill. There was need for something more adequate, involving training on higher levels.

As thought on the subject rapidly crystallized there emerged the vision of a new college, such as had been founded in a few universities in the land, a college of commerce and business administration, separate from the academic department of economics, to be regarded as a major division of the University. Should the University of Southern California, despite its inadequate endowment and limited income, undertake to establish such a college or school?

With the help of Professor O. J. Marston I set to work to draw up the framework for a curriculum of such a college, for more serious consideration. The general idea won the approval of President Bovard, who stated, however, that the University was not in a position to guarantee its financial underwriting.

Nevertheless, as had been done in several other historic instances, the decision was reached to venture forth and announce the advent of the College of Commerce and Business Administration, which was formally authorized by the trustees January 27, 1920. It was a bold step. It must be admitted that the first planned curriculum, on paper, consisted almost wholly of courses drawn from the economics department — obviously not adequate for a completely equipped college of commerce. But a start was made, the formal opening took place in September, 1920, and there was faith that the future would provide.

The interest shown in the new venture was such that there was no thought of retreat. That was in 1920-21. When I was approached to serve as dean of the fledgling I replied that I had already been given the post as Dean of the Graduate School and had no desire to hold two deanships. As a compromise I consented to act as Director for the time being, until a regular Dean should be found.

Such, in brief, was the status of affairs during the precarious first year of the history of the College of Commerce. If it was to continue into the second year, it was clearly obvious that there must be substantial reinforcements in the teaching staff — but for these the University had no provision in its budget. What next?

I had become convinced that leading financiers and business men of Los Angeles would be willing to give support to such an institution as we had projected if it could be properly presented to them. While in San Francisco on one occasion, to attend a meeting held in the interest of world peace, I found an opportunity to talk briefly with Henry S. McKee, vice-president of Citizen's National Bank of Los Angeles. I sketched to him our plans for a college of commerce, and tried to impress upon him something of the significance of the movement to the city and community. I found him interested and responsive.

Not long after that there was a simple, informal lunch meeting in the Angeles Hotel in Los Angeles that proved to be historic in the annals of the College of Commerce. Only three persons were present — Henry McKee, Emery E. Olson (my lieutenant), and myself. I quite frankly stated the situation as I saw it. There was need in Los Angeles for an institution of high grade and collegiate level that could prepare young men and young women for responsible positions in finance and business — junior executives, auditors and accountants, transportation and foreign trade experts, and the like. There was no such institution then functioning to meet the demand. The University of Southern California had undertaken to fill the gap, but was presently confronted with the difficulty that because of budgetary limitations it was not in a position to supply the funds imperatively needed to guarantee the offering of courses that would meet the community needs. Three or four new specially prepared instructors should be employed at once — and it was not sufficient to express the hope or expectation that the tuition fees of students attracted by the opportunities would be adequate to pay the salaries of new professors.

It was then that Mr. McKee, who had listened attentively, offered a suggestion that led to the establishment of the College of Commerce on a firm basis. Said he, in effect, "Why don't you get twenty of us bankers and business men to underwrite your proposition? It would be easy for me to 'phone over and get Henry Robinson at First National, J. A. Graves, and a number of others to join me for $1,000 apiece, and that would start you going." He couldn't have made a speech that would have pleased us more!

And he was as good as his word. He did call several of his friends who agreed to underwrite the College to the extent of

$1,000 each for the ensuing year, provided we secured a list of twenty signers in all. It did not take me long to draft the appropriate statement to be signed by the guarantors; and with the very effective assistance of Olson and Harold J. Stonier it was but a matter of days when there they were — twenty valid signatures on the dotted lines, each agreeing to put up one-twentieth of any legitimate deficit, not exceeding a maximum of $1,000, for the year 1920-21.[1] Is it any wonder that I thought that list of signatures a beautiful document, or that I treasured it with fond and vigilant eye? So valuable was this list of sponsors deemed to be that for years afterward their names were printed in the regular catalogs of the College, and they were given special invitations to the Annual Commerce Banquet.

At once we began the search for additional members of the Commerce staff. Four young men of special training were employed. Of these, one — Clayton D. Carus has remained at the University as Professor of Trade and Transportation down to the time of retirement, in 1953, rendering conspicuous service not only to the College of Commerce and the University but the entire metropolitan community. It has been to me a personal pleasure to be associated with him throughout the years.

But the story of the twenty guarantors is not ended yet. At that time the College of Commerce kept its own accounts, had control of its own budget. It was my function as Director to sign checks issued in all payments. So successful was the reinforced College in attracting students to its offerings that by early spring it was found that because of the large income from tuitions there would be no deficit whatever. It can scarcely be imagined with what pleasure I wrote each of the guarantors, thanking him for

---

1 Here is the full list: Henry S. McKee, Henry M. Robinson, H. D. Lyman, J. E. Fishburn, Marco H. Hellman, W. H. Brophy, A. M. Chaffey, R. D. Judkins, J. A. Graves, D. T. Babcock, R. H. Moulton, R. B. Hardacre, Jay Spence, F. W. Braun, R. J. Schweppe, A. C. Balch, Donald O'Melveny, W. B. Kline, R. H. Ballard, and W. Ross Campbell.

his moral support but treating him to the surprise announcement that the College would not call upon him for a dollar of his generous guarantee! That unique experience made each of the score a friend of the College forever. We had won the confidence and the good will of the business community. The College of Commerce and Business Administration of the University of Southern California was well on its way.

Since I was then Dean of the Graduate School, it seemed natural, I suppose, for Commerce students and faculty members also to address me as Dean. After holding the title of Director for a year I finally yielded and accepted the title of Dean for two more years.

President Bovard was fully aware of the fact that I did not wish to hold two deanships indefinitely. The reason for my continuance was twofold. First, Dr. Bovard feared that any qualified person who would be brought to the deanship in Commerce might underemphasize the liberal arts foundations to the commerce course, and therefore wished me to continue as Dean during the formative period; secondly, both he and I were cognizant of the fact that Emery E. Olson, then Assistant to the Dean, strongly desired to succeed to the deanship if or when I relinquished the position, and we agreed he was not yet sufficiently mature to assume the responsbility of the position. I am sure that Olson himself would concur in these statements. So it happened that both the president and Olson wished me to continue longer as Dean.

One day in casual conversation with Dean Ezra A. Healy, of the School of Religion, and at the time President of the Board of Trustees, our talk ran along something like the following:

"I understand," said the good Dr. Healy, "that you expect sometime to give up one of your deanships. When that time comes, which will you choose to retain?" Without hesitation I replied, "I prefer to continue as Dean of the Graduate School.

I'm having a fine time as Dean of Commerce, and my relations with the Commerce faculty are most happy; but by natural bent I prefer the graduate work."

"But," queried the good Doctor, "is it not likely that in years to come, the Commerce dean, in the nature of the case, will receive a larger salary than the Graduate dean?" "It is not only likely," I replied, "but it is inevitable; but that will not alter my decision."

Just how right I was in my prognostication is illustrated by the fact that within a few years thereafter, the Dean of Commerce was receiving 40% more salary than I had received while holding both deanships, and the salary of the Graduate dean remained unchanged.

Dean Ezra A. Healy, who had earlier served as pastor of University Methodist Church, is well remembered for his wholesome good humor, his mellifluous orotund voice, his chaste diction and urbanity of expression, his deep and abiding conviction of right and duty, his affable personality, and his symmetrical life and character. To know him was to love him.

When I relinquished the Commerce deanship in 1924, I was succeeded not by Emery Olson but by a newcomer, D. Walter Morton, a man of special qualifications coupled with practical experience fitting him well for the position. At the same time, however, Olson was made director of the new evening division of the University called Metropolitan College (now known as University College), thus introducing him to an important administrative position. He it was who later brought the School of Government to national eminence as its dean.

An important adjunct to the College was the publication of a monthly magazine, *Commerce Journal*, under the dean's editorship. The staff included Emery E. Olson, managing editor; Grace D. Walker, assistant editor; Harold J. Stonier, business manager. I have always enjoyed editorial work.

Within a few years we had developed a unique feature, an Advisory Editorial Board, representing the Southern California Commercial Teachers' Association. This proved to be a splendid cooperative arrangement, for it enlisted the active interest of commercial teachers from Los Angeles to San Diego. In addition, there was formed a significant list of cooperating business organizations — publicity directors, purchasing agents, and the like — thus tying in with the College the secondary institutions and also the metropolitan business community.

Some issues of *Commerce Journal* reached to upwards of forty pages. Carefully prepared articles appeared on such topics as "Can Business Depressions Be Prevented?"; "The Human Value in Business Compared with the Property Value"; "Unfair Methods of Competition"; and numerous others. The editor's contribution was usually fairly brief. Three editorials during my final year as dean dealt, respectively, with Business as a Profession; Perspective; and "Conservation." This last subject has long been one of my favorite themes. "Finally," I said in the *Journal* for December, 1924, "the very culmination of the larger thrift is *human conservation*, without which every other form of conservation would be without significance."

Commerce Journal unquestionably served a useful purpose during the formative years of the College of Commerce and Business Administration. Five volumes had been published. But it was not long after I surrendered the deanship that the magazine was discontinued, to my own personal regret.

The formal dedication of the Edward L. Doheny, Jr., Memorial Library on the 12th of September, 1932, was an event of extraordinary interest to me as Dean of the Graduate School. In the Dean's Annual Report for a number of years I had emphasized the commanding importance of having on the Southern California campus an adequate, fire-proof library building as an imperatively needed feature to support the rapidly developing graduate program of the University. The total inadequacy of library facilities up to this time was fully recognized: accessions to research materials of the library itself could not be expected to keep pace with the demand in the absence of a new, well-equipped building. "From the standpoint of the Graduate School," I stated in the Dean's Report for the year ending June 30, 1930, "the one supreme need, that eclipses all others, is that of the great new University Library."

Through the munificence of the Edward L. Doheny family the need for the Library Building was handsomely met. The 12th day of September, 1932, is therefore a highly important date in the annals of the University of Southern California as a whole, and of its Graduate School in particular; for on that day, with elaborate public ceremony the Edward L. Doheny, Jr., Library, which now dominates Alumni Park and faces George Finley Bovard Administration Building, was solemnly dedicated.

Obviously it would be impracticable for me to describe all of the various steps in the development of graduate studies at the University during the first quarter-century of the Graduate School's history, although they came within my purview as Dean. In such an expanding institution, under such a dynamic leader as President von KleinSmid, changes were normally to be expected, the wisdom of some of which could be determined only in the light of history. I am certain that on more than one occasion the theoretically wise course was not pursued because of what is called the "personal equation"; but this is far from saying that my University stood alone in that regard. There are doubtless times and circumstances when tact is the better part of wisdom and when prudence looks beyond tomorrow.

In 1928 the School of Education was authorized to submit recommendations for the graduate professional degree of Doctor of Education. Since that date the School of Education, and later certain other professional schools, have operated autonomously as separate divisions in the matter of advanced degrees. Thus for several transitional years the Graduate School was neither strictly a school of liberal arts nor a school operating uniformly throughout the graduate level of all divisions of the University, in accordance with the act of 1923. I was well aware of the illogical situation, which proved somewhat embarrassing at times, but which, after all, proved to be but temporary.

As Dean of the Graduate School I felt keenly the need of encouraging members of the faculty to lay emphasis on original, creative work in their respective fields. It was my earnest desire that a spirit of research should pervade the atmosphere, to the end that a zeal for true scholarship should characterize the University and make it worthy of its proud name.

With such thoughts in mind, a further step was taken in 1933 when, within the Graduate School, which had become numerically quite large, there was created the School of Research, whose membership was to constitute a more selective group, collectively an instrument in the realization of and emphasis upon the highest university ideals. Dr. Allison Gaw, in his volume on the development of graduate work in the University, referred to this new school as "The capstone of the entire structure that has thus been erected by the University Administration after fifty-five years of development."

Membership in the School of Research included, in addition to the regular specialized staff: 1) every graduate student who has been formally admitted to candidacy for the degree of doctor of philosophy; 2) other graduates holding the master's degree who are specially recommended by their respective department heads as possessing undoubted capacity for independent research; 3) visiting scholars and scientists may be admitted by vote of the Council; 4) junior faculty members who are actively engaged in research may, on recommendation of their respective heads, be admitted by vote of the Council. As a mark of distinction any member of the School devoting himself primarily to research may be elected to a special group known as Associates in Research.

A bi-monthly publication bearing the title *Research News*, for limited circulation, was launched, under the editorship of the dean. This four-page journal appeared regularly during my incumbency, and during the four years administration of my successor Emory S. Bogardus. Subsequently it was discontinued, and the School of Research, under reorganization, lost its individual identity.

One other feature, introduced for the purpose of giving further encouragement and added impetus to the personnel of the Graduate School, was the Annual Faculty Research Lecture, instituted by the dean in 1933. The selection of a faculty member to present the Research Lecture in the field of his own specialty was deemed a recognition of his past achievement and a well-deserved honor. The lecturer is chosen by a special committee of the Council, with the approval of the President. Announcement is made a year in advance, thus affording ample time for the completion of his investigations.

Beginning in 1933 the Research Lecture has been a regular feature each spring — now a well established tradition. Most of the lectures have been published in pamphlet form. In more recent years the Anniversary has been made the occasion for a day devoted to research reports from numerous major departments of graduate study at section meetings on the campus, the entire program culminating in the Research Lecture in the evening.

The general plan has been carried out with conspicuous success. It is to me highly gratifying to have had a part in establishing the Annual Faculty Research Lecture. A mere listing of lectures and topics to the time of my retirement as Dean reveals something of the variety, scope, and scholarly effort involved:

1933 George P. Hammond, "Resources of the Mexican Archives"
1934 Harry J. Deuel, Jr., "Studies in Acidosis"
1935 Herbert D. Austin, "Roma, Maria, Lucia: A Dante Study"
1936 Ralph T. Flewelling, "Chinese Influences in the European Enlightenment"
1937 Emory S. Bogardus, "Social Distance and Its Practical Implications"
1938–39 Edgar L. Hewett, "Native American Race in the Drama of History"
1939–40 Milton Metfessel, "Relationships of Heredity and Environment Behavior"
1940–41 Garland Greever, "America's Third Man of the Renaissance"
1941–42 Richard E. Vollrath, "Photography, with Particular Reference to Astronomy"
1942–43 John M. Pfiffner, "Function *vs.* Hierarchy"
1943–44 John F. Kessel, "Journeys into the Field of Microbiology"
1944–45 J. Eugene Harley, "Sovereignty, Equality, and Force as Factors in a World Security Organization"
1945–46 Thomas Clements, "The Geologic History of the Channel Island Region"

Following my retirement as Dean, I was one day surprised and — I must in honesty admit — pleased and honored, when notified that I had been selected to be the Fourteenth Annual Research Lecturer. I chose for my topic, "1850: A Year of Destiny."

Sometimes an institution that is functioning under rapidly expanding, constantly shifting changes and conditions is inclined to seize upon any good opportunity to stage a public celebration, partly as a means of taking current stock of its course and progress, partly to afford a new impetus or stimulus toward further advances.

As we approached the year 1935 at the University of Southern California, I thought I saw such an opportunity; for that year would mark the twenty-fifth anniversary of the formal inauguration of graduate studies at the University. When the matter was brought to the attention of President von KleinSmid he readily consented to the general plan for the quarter-century celebration: he forthwith appointed the Dean of the Graduate School chairman of the general committee on arrangements, and named as other members Emory S. Bogardus (vice-chairman), Hugh C. Willett (secretary), Ruth W. Brown, Allison Gaw, Wilbur Long, Irene McCulloch, and Laird J. Stabler.

The celebration, intended to mark the accomplishment of the twenty-five year period, was held at the University, November 21-24, 1935. Two eminent visitors, United States Senator Elbert D. Thomas and George W. Zook, presented leading addresses dealing with current trends in scholarship. Senator Thomas made an eloquent plea for clearer understanding of nations through common aims in education; Doctor Zook, President of the American Council on Education, extolled higher education for its contribution of breadth of understanding and professional training.

At the first general session Vice-President Frank C. Touton spoke words of welcome, and introduced visiting scholars, including Senator Thomas, Dean Carl E. Seashore, President Tully C. Knoles, Bishop William Bertrand Stevens, President Remsen D. Bird, and others. More than 500 persons attended the Quarter-Century Dinner, where President von KleinSmid presented a number of delegates for brief remarks.

A feature of the celebration was the Third Annual Research Lecture, by Herbert D. Austin, on the topic "Roma, Maria, Lucia — A Dante Study." The lecture was published in full in the proceedings. My own particular contribution was an address on "Foundation Years," in which the keynote may be found in these lines:

> Firm foundations are not for display but to support a worthy super-structure. Perhaps the world at large was not even aware of the foundations that were being laid—they were not to be seen of men, but they were for a purpose. So it was with the foundation years of our beloved University: they were years of humility, passed perchance unremarked but building on the rock.

A major portion of the celebration consisted of an extensive series of Group Conferences. I may mention here only the group names and their respective leaders: Social Sciences, Clarence M. Case; History and International Relations, J. Eugene Harley; Psychology, Milton Metfessel; Languages and Literature, Garland Greever; Physical Sciences and Mathematics, Arthur W. Nye; Philosophy, Ralph Tyler Flewelling; Education, Lester B. Rogers; Biological and Medical Sciences, Clinton Thienes; Religion, John G. Hill. Each group had its own special program of papers and discussions. Never before at the University had such a series been undertaken. The volume of proceedings was edited by Herbert W. Hill, who stated in the Foreword:

> ...The celebration, however, was more than a mere record of achievement or prophecy of things to come. It brought forth real contributions to scholarship.... The universities invited to participate responded cordially and generously. To them is accorded in large measure the success of the occasion.

For my part as dean I was honored by the presentation of an illuminated parchment, reading,

Presented by the Faculty to
ROCKWELL DENNIS HUNT, A.M., PH.D., LL.D.
As a symbol of their esteem, upon the
Occasion of the Twenty-fifth Anniversary of the
Inauguration of Graduate Studies in the
University of Southern California
November 22, 1935

In my own student days at Johns Hopkins University I had felt the need of a closer bond with other graduate students, especially those outside of my own particular department. Students coming from institutions in widely separated localities often find themselves severely limited as to personal acquaintances and social contacts among fellow students, thus missing an element in the enrichment of their lives which should bind them more closely to the institution.

It is recognized that the usual "student activities" of under-graduates cannot be duplicated among the graduates: but for that very reason I felt that specific attention should be given to what I regarded as a real social problem pertaining to the graduates.

After considerable observation and some serious thought, as dean I decided to encourage the students of the Graduate School to effect some simple organization and plan a limited program of events that should at once be stimulating in character and socially pleasurable.

During the year 1927-28 such an organization came into being under the title "Associated Students of the Graduate School," a name later changed to "Associated Graduate Students." Weekly luncheons and an Annual Banquet were featured. Experience brought variations in student activities; but through succeeding years the organization served a useful purpose in developing the "sense of belonging" among the members. It was not always easy to find among the busy graduates those individuals who felt they could afford to take the time demanded by the duties of the officers; and there was need of encouragement and frequent assistance from the dean's office. In all this my capable secretary, Ruth Bohnett, proved to be most helpful. Among the most inspiring events may be mentioned special addresses given by eminent scholars, such as President James A. Blaisdell of Pomona College, Professor Frank Fetter of Princeton University, and

President Herman Liu of Shanghai University. While I cannot state that the social problem we had in mind was completely solved, it was clear to me that those who participated actively in the affairs of the Associated Graduate Students found real enjoyment and in many cases cultural benefit in the relationship.

One of the main purposes in celebrating the Twenty-fifth Anniversary of the Founding of the Graduate School was to stop and discover what point had been reached in graduate studies at Southern California. "By self-appraisal," I then declared, "we may foresee some of the possibilities and get a glimpse at the needs of tomorrow on the graduate level." The celebration took place January 25 to 28, 1945.

The theme adopted was "The Future of Graduate Studies in a World Reborn." The three day program was a notable one arranged by a General Committee consisting of John D. Cooke, Chairman, Emory E. Bogardus, Ruth W. Brown, Thomas Clements, Mary Sinclair Crawford, and Ernest W. Tiegs. President Rufus B. von KleinSmid and Dean Rockwell D. Hunt were each given the title "Honorary Chairman." Eleven professors were appointed chairmen of respective group conferences; five were named chairmen of special committees, such as Reception, Invitations, and Publications.

Among those participating in the elaborate program may be mentioned J. Eugene Harley, Albert S. Raubenheimer, and President von KleinSmid of the Southern California staff, President Franklyn Bliss Snyder of Northwestern University, Chancellor Oliver Cromwell Carmichael of Vanderbilt University, Claude A. Buss of Stanford University, and Bishop James C. Baker of the Methodist Church.

The Proceedings of the Anniversary, edited by Emory S. Bogardus, were published in a volume of 216 pages, including names of representatives from 120 institutions and societies. The *Southern*

California Alumni Review, in reporting the occasion, made this comment:

> It was a bold step to undertake now with the whole world intent on the panorama of global war, but the emphasis laid on future planning gave the conference important significance at this time; a veritable "shot in the arm" for the whole graduate school scene in America.

At ten group conferences a total of fifty research papers were presented, summaries of which appear in the printed proceedings. The respective chairmen of groups were as follows: Economics and Commerce, Joy L. Leonard; Education and Philosophy, Ernest W. Tiegs; Engineering, Robert M. Fox; Fine Arts and Music, Max T. Krone; Languages and Literature, Louis Wann; Philosophy and Religion, Wilbur H. Long; Sciences, Thomas Clements; Social Sciences, Wilbert L. Hindman; Sociology, Bessie A. McClenahan.

A part of my function was to present an address on "Development of Graduate Studies at the University of Southern California." I referred to the graduate school as "the keystone in the impressive arch of higher education. It deserves well of the city and of the Republic, but it must not fail in its high duties and heavy responsibilities to the public." In closing I quoted chaste words from Benjamin Ide Wheeler:

> Here in these stately halls, for centuries to come, each generation will transmit to its successors the lessons of the past; here, by the contagion of sympathy, each generation will inspire its sons and daughters to noble living; here by the mystery of inspiration, vision shall awaken vision and personality shall give of its spiritual lifeblood to the handing on of life, like a fire by the handing on of the racer's torch.

On Saturday morning I had the rare pleasure of presiding at the Dean's Breakfast, to which all the doctorate alumni to that date had been bidden, and which proved to be an exceptionately happy occasion.

Delegates and representatives from more than 125 universities and learned societies were in attendance.

At the Anniversary Dinner in Los Angeles University Club, Dean Albert S. Raubenheimer of the College of Letters, Arts, and Sciences presided. Addresses were presented by President Snyder of Northwestern, Chancellor Carmichael of Vanderbilt, and President von KleinSmid of Southern California.

This celebration of the Twenty-fifth Anniversary of the founding of the Graduate School in a way represented the culmination of my active service at the University of Southern California. It was at the conclusion of that academic year that by virtue of my retirement my title was changed to Dean-Emeritus. As editor of the proceedings Dr. Bogardus generously added:

> Dean Hunt has ever been quick to appreciate the special problems that arise in the varied fields of graduate study, to keep in mind the personal problems of graduate students, and to direct the attention of faculty and students alike to the program of graduate research in tangible relation to the need of the larger community, that is, of the city, of the nation, and of mankind. In short, Dean Hunt's major contribution to the growth of the Graduate School and of the School of Research of the University may be found in his ability to stimulate all the interests involved in the complicated tasks of graduate scholarship; and at the same time to keep all these factors moving forward together in an effectively balanced way.

In a complimentary editorial on the eve of the Celebration (January 24, 1945), the Los Angeles *Herald-Express*, after referring to the value of the University to the city of Los Angeles, paid generous tribute to the Graduate School as "not the least of its contributions to the educational field," "so wisely directed and governed by Dean Hunt," then continued:

Not only did he found this institution, but through more than a score of years he has lived its life, has dreamed its dreams, and has worked to make that life worthwhile and those dreams come true....

The University of Southern California is to be congratulated on this the Twenty-fifth Anniversary of the founding of its graduate school. It is to be congratulated on the record of that school, the 7,500 graduate students who have completed work to gain advanced degrees, and it is to be congratulated on having found and kept such an inspired leader as Dean Hunt.

At its June, 1932, Commencement the College of the Pacific, at Stockton conferred upon me through its president, Tully C. Knoles, the honorary degree of Doctor of Laws. This deeply appreciated honor served to bind me still more closely to the institution which had become my Alma Mater, when, in 1896, Napa College, where I had graduated in 1890, was consolidated with the University of the Pacific.

One day, in the spring of 1936, near the approach of Commencement time, President von KleinSmid informed me in a very casual manner, that the University of Southern California was about to confer upon me an honorary degree. If I responded in a similarly casual manner, my outward appearance belied my inner emotion! I had been at the University for more than a quarter of a century; just the previous year I had served as the head of the general committee on arrangements for the Twenty-fifth Anniversary of the Inauguration of Graduate Studies. I felt deeply the honor to be conferred upon me by the institution that had become so much a part of myself.

On Commencement Day, at Exposition Park, when I was presented to the President for the honorary degree of Doctor of Letters, the great audience before me, beginning with the candidates for doctors' and masters' degrees, rose to their feet to greet me, and remained standing while I was being hooded and handed my diploma. I received the honor with humble gratitude.

Following the celebration of the Twenty-fifth Anniversary in 1935, as a kind of echo, there was a suggestion, quietly expressed, that a portrait of the Graduate Dean should be painted to be hung permanently in the University. The thought was taken up by some of the officers of the Associated Graduate Students, though I afterward became convinced that the suggestion first came to them from Mary Sinclair Crawford, the accomplished Dean of Women.

In any event, the seed thought germinated; and later, under the student presidency of Frank H. Sparks, a movement was launched by the Associated Graduates to make a canvass for funds to underwrite the expense of a portrait. Students, former students, and friends were given opportunity to make small contributions, which they did in large numbers. The artist selected was Peter Ilyin of San Francisco. In the course of time I had sittings in his studio; later the final sittings were completed at the University in Los Angeles.

The unveiling ceremony occurred October 31, 1939 in the presence of a large group of graduate students and professors. Frank Sparks was the master of ceremonies, Val Lehnberg was president of the Associated Graduate Students, and President von KleinSmid accepted the portrait for the University, paying generous tribute to the Dean, who responded very briefly expressing his gratitude, with feelings of humility.

The life-size portrait hangs in the Council Chamber of the Graduate School suite, in Bovard Administration Building.

I have been keenly aware of the practical difficulties implicit in the task of writing the story of my life during the thirty-seven years of active and intimate connection with the University of Southern California as a faculty member. On the other hand, it would be impossible to minimize my relationship to the University — it was my very life from the time I began at age forty till the time of my retirement at the age of seventy-seven.

On the other hand, to seem to write a history *in extenso* of the University with which I was so intimately associated during that long period of development would require inordinate space and endanger a true perspective of the whole.

I have striven to steer a safe course, avoiding the perils of Scylla and Charybdis; but how successful I have been must be left to the reader's charitable judgment. How completely my life was wrapped up with the institution I served, and which is the *Alma Mater* to each of my three sons, may in a casual manner be illustrated by the fact that there appears on my private bookplate the seal of the University on the left center, while over against it, on the right center appears the great seal of California, my native state. My interest was by no means confined to any single department, or group of departments, nor to the College of Liberal Arts, nor even to the Graduate School. I consciously endeavored to identify myself with the entire University and its welfare as a whole, recognizing fully, however, that my own chief responsibilities pertained to certain departments and divisions.

I threw myself into my task wholeheartedly. But my task, as I viewed it, had many ramifications — it reached far beyond the University campus; it called for a life of intense activity and complete dedication. Perhaps I may illustrate this point by quoting from a personal letter I wrote to my four brothers April 21, 1918 — a round robin letter which we called "the budget." I wrote:

> It's a busy week—in fact, as I was saying at the dinner table tonight, I have never seen a time when there were so many truly great tasks to engage my best effort as the present. I wish I could be at my very best all the time, then multiply that little best many times over. No day is long enough for me. I don't mean that I am in panicky haste all the time—such is not the case: I am not working as long hours as I have in earlier years—for it seems necessary to conserve strength, or accomplishments would be even less than they are.

During my incumbency at the University the growth in student enrollment and in the number of degrees conferred was spectacular. During my first year thirty-eight baccalaureate degrees were conferred; eight years later the number was 153. The student body increased from less than 1000 in 1908 to between 4,000 and 5,000 during the year (1920) in which the Graduate School was organized. In 1910-11 eleven candidates received the Master of Arts degree; there was almost a steady increase, year by year, until the early 1930s, when the numbers jumped to above 400. During my final years the total numbers of graduates ran into the thousands. I witnessed these and many other changes and developments in the history of the University. With this history I was closely identified.

As dean my relations with my colleagues on the faculty were happy with scarcely any exceptions; and I can recall only two or three instances that involved really disagreeable relations with individual students. I look back upon my association with scores of faculty members and students numbering into the thousands with pleasurable sentiments and happy memories.

On many an occasion there came gratefully to my mind a slight incident that happened during my earliest years of teaching. While I was a professor at the University of the Pacific at San José, in 1898, I taught a class, once a week, in Pacific Slope History at Stanford University. On one occasion I had some small point to talk over with President David Starr Jordan — I've forgotten completely what the point was. It was then, and there that I learned a lesson about conducting an office that I never forgot. I knew that with his administrative duties, his researches in ichthyology and his governmental responsibilities, Dr. Jordan was a very busy executive. But I did not fail, while sitting alone with him in his office, to notice that he gave individual attention to me and my small matter, revealing no sign of outside pressure, signing no letters, shuffling no papers on his desk, giving me the impression of a man of perfect poise, with unlimited time at his command. I have never forgotten the quiet, masterful manner of President Jordan. Fortunately I realized he had other things to do besides answering my queries — I did not tarry after my errand was completed.

In my long experience as Dean, when a professor or a student sat before me in my office, I gave my attention to him, never showing irritation by thumbing a book, or signing a diploma, or poising a pen in my hand — my business was then with the caller. Of course, more than once it happened that a caller would unconsciously impose and remain too long; but I never found it necessary to ask one to leave or rudely suggest that his time was up. On such an occasion, however, an efficient secretary is a great help. She becomes alert to the situation, comes quietly in from her office to ask if you will meet your next appointment, or lays a little note before you — some very polite gesture that your visitor cannot fail to observe, who then is suddenly reminded that he too has a duty elsewhere!

My secretary, Miss Ruth Bohnett, was a loyal assistant in this and many other ways. She was with me for more than twenty years of my deanship — she came to know my ways and wishes quite perfectly. It is personally gratifying to add that she continued as secretary under my sucessor Dean Emory S. Bogardus, and (after his retirement) under Dean Harry J. Deuel, Jr.

As I contemplate the transformation that came to the University of Southern California during the period of my active service (1908 to 1945), I gratefully recognize that to me was given the unusual opportunity of being a participant in the development of the University during a most important formative period of its history — I saw it a struggling institution of severely restricted resources and financial support but with courageous spirit and faith in the future: when I left it, it had become a recognized metropolitan university, functioning successfully in its rapidly growing community. The words of Thomas Jefferson, written to Skelton Jones in 1808, come to mind. He said:

> I have been connected, as my fellow laborers were, with the great events which happened to mark the epoch of our lives. But these belong to no one in particular. All of us did our parts, and no one can claim the transactions to himself.

For many years after the University had come of age — too long, many of us thought, on general principles — there was no general retirement plan in effect. To be sure, a number of retired professors had been "taken care of," in a very modest — if not precarious — way by a pension arrangement; but this had been on a purely individual basis, and I fear, not always calculated to increase the self-respect of the recipient.

A faculty committee worked on possible plans of retirement through several years, and consulted with a trustees committee. After long study and many conferences, a complete plan was worked out, which was finally adopted and put into effect during the year 1944-45. Personally, I had favored the adoption of a plan all along, though I had no part in drawing up the official plan — under which I was a member of the first group to be retired.

Previous to that I was of course, for a number of years aware that my age was already past that at which large corporations retired their employees. Recognizing this, I had each spring for several years, called personally on the President, when some such dialogue as this occurred: "I thought I should drop in to inquire, how about next year?" "What is your own thought? How do you feel about it yourself?" the President asked. "So far as I'm concerned, " I replied, "I'm in good health: I'm quite willing — in fact, I think I'd prefer — to continue for another year." "Then let it be so," Dr. von KleinSmid said; and that was it.

When my actual retirement came, in 1945, and my title was

changed from Dean to Dean-Emeritus, I was seventy-seven years old. My physical condition was good, though I was aware that my hearing had become somewhat impaired. I felt then, and still feel, that I was fully capable of continuing in active service; but I accepted the situation without a murmur, along with a dozen of my colleagues, and stepped aside — but not to a life of idleness! The actual date of my retirement was September 1, 1945. A farewell reception was tendered me in the Hall of Nations on the fifteenth of August, with Dr. Emory S. Bogardus, who had been announced as my successor to the Graduate deanship, acting as master of ceremonies. Many friends had accepted the invitation to attend. President von KleinSmid's remarks were very generous. Notice of my retirement brought numerous personal letters from a wide range of persons, including Los Angeles Mayor Fletcher Bowron, County Supervisor John Anson Ford, Bishop James C. Baker, Rabbi Edgar F. Magnin, Superintendent Vierling Kersey, President Tully C. Knoles, Dr. Roy L. Smith, Dr. Merle N. Smith, and many others.

The decade since that date has proved to be one of the most interesting of my life. But my new position as Director of the California History Foundation, beginning in 1947, took me away from the University of Southern California and Los Angeles.

I have never been a member of a Greek-letter social fraternity, although all three of my sons were initiated into the University of Southern California chapter of Sigma Alpha Epsilon. My own non-membership was not so much because of any settled opposition to fraternities in general as to the fact that the subject never gained priority in the broad scheme of things in my academic life.

However, during my long incumbency at Southern California I became a member of a number of Greek-letter honorary societies: it is quite unnecessary, I think, to list them here. All such memberships were sincerely appreciated, none, perhaps, more deeply than the invitation to accept membership in the Occidental College chapter of Phi Beta Kappa. In two or three instances I was at some loss to discover any special qualifications on my part: this applied particularly to the Sigma Xi; but I was inclined to think at the time that since my son Lloyd, an engineering major, was to be initiated, the committee generously concluded that it would not be amiss to initiate his father at the same time, as a representative of the social sciences. At all events, I have deemed it an honor to hold membership in each of the societies into which I have been inducted.

The University of Southern California alumni have come to number many thousands; indeed, so numerous are they as to render it virtually essential to hold their reunions by year-groups or department-groups. The annual affairs at some large center, such as the Los Angeles Biltmore Hotel, are a source of keen enjoyment to many hundreds, but they have become so intricate as to preclude the general acquaintance and intermingling characteristic of earlier days or small colleges.

I have always interested myself in the activities and progress of the alumni, which probably helps to explain my own honorary membership in several U.S.C. classes. First, there is the class of '08, the year my own term of service began at the University. Then I was made a member of the class of '12, "for" as one member remarked, "you have now been here four years, and so should graduate as a '12-er." Later I was given honorary membership in the class of '16, and still later one or two others.

But the solidarity and confraternity of '08 has been specially inspirational. Due largely to the devoted personal efforts of one member (Elaine Anderson), held in loving regard by all the others, the class has been maintained through almost half a century as an entity which approaches that of a real family in regard to the individual members in their relationships to each other. This unusual oneness has been achieved chiefly, I think, through the agency of the round-robin letter, whose remarkable success has been assured by the ceaseless vigilance and efficient activity of Elaine.

I have elsewhere referred to subjects I have taught at one place or another. Here let me jot down a more complete list, compiled from memory, with brief explanatory comment. At Johns Hopkins University my group major was in the History-Economics-Politics department, headed by Herbert Baxter Adams, with chief emphasis on history.

At Napa College and the University of the Pacific history was my main but by no means exclusive teaching subject. Having graduated from the Commercial Department at Napa in 1887, I assisted Professor H. L. Gunn, its head, for a year in bookkeeping; and having graduated from the California School of Elocution and Oratory in 1892, I taught students both individually and in class in elocution and coached many in their debating and orations. One year at Napa I had a class of seniors and juniors that was known for want of a better name as the "Plus Class," which met once a week for drill in commonly mispronounced words, in breathing exercises, use of the hands and arms in simple gestures, and the like. From this I probably derived as much personal benefit as any of my students—it was a unique and valuable experience.

Naturally I was called upon to teach many history courses, including Ancient History, European Medieval and Modern History, the period of the Protestant Reformation, the French Revolution, American History, and the History of California—a favorite subject of mine for both teaching and writing throughout my active career. Similarly I have taught a rather wide range of courses in economics—throughout my long period of service at the University of Southern California I was professor of economics. Courses ranged from the principles, for lower classmen, to the department seminar for graduates, and included Public Finance, History of Economics Doctrine, Recent Theory, Socialism, Money and Banking, Labor Problems, Conservation of National Resources, and still others. In sociology there were courses in Principles, Applied Sociology, and Municipal Problems.

My early teaching included, at one time or another, instruction in such varied fields as Word Analysis and English Composition, Penmanship, and Commercial Arithmetic, Economic Geography, Civics and Political Science, Shakespeare Reading, the Bible, and the Liquor Problem. I even conducted a class in Logic one semester; in the Y.M.C.A. night school in Baltimore I taught spelling, as well as commercial subjects. Entirely apart from all this I have had classes in Sunday School with groups all the way from boys of twelve to the Men's Bible Class — which, incidentally, included for some time a dear retired ministerial saint with strong theological obsessions who was not infrequently well-nigh insuppressible! But he was amiable and of Christian disposition.

The range of my teaching seems in retrospect quite fantastic; though of course it will be understood that a good many of the courses listed were either quite elementary or of the stop-gap variety, calling for but little special preparation on the part of the teacher. When it is remembered, also, that the deanship of the Graduate School called for my major effort for twenty-five years, it must appear obvious that I never was — nor did I ever profess to be — a highly trained specialist in any strictly limited field or subject. Had I restricted the scope of my activities and teaching more severely from the beginning, I presume I might have attained to a higher rank as a specialist; but I am not certain such a course would have made me a more well-rounded scholar.

In any event, I am not now disposed to cavil about what

actually happened. I am inclined to think that the totality of experience brought a versatility and an appreciation of other fields than my own that have proved invaluable in my life. And as I observe in some of my contemporaries a tendency toward early and over-specialization, I am frequently reminded of a statement, made many years ago by President Faunce of Brown University, "The truly educated man is a broad man sharpened to a point." I am reminded also of the first sentence of the initial lecture by Woodrow Wilson in his course on Administration at Johns Hopkins University. The date was January 25, 1894. I took down the sentence verbatim in my notebook, which is still a prized possession. He said: "No man who knows one thing knows anything." He then proceeded to point out the need for seeing the broader implications and relationships of things, emphasizing the thought that no man is a good specialist who does not know more than his own set of phenomena.

I have found much satisfaction in my teaching. First and last my classes in the University were of all sizes, ranging from a low of six or eight graduate students to a high of more than 300 lower classmen. The low was reached in the Economics Seminar during war time, when most of the male students were enlisted in the service; the high was in the Principles of Economics class, open to freshmen. Obviously, in such a huge class the lecture method must be employed; but the more detailed work is conducted by quiz masters, each section numbering from thirty to forty students.

For a good many years I continued in charge of the large class in General Economics. But when, with my colleague, Dr. John G. Hill, I left on sabbatic leave on a world tour, in the fall of 1926, I turned the class over to Dr. Elmer Fagan, a brilliant young teacher. Because of my duties as Dean of Graduate School, and my graduate teaching, I did not resume instruction of the class on my return eight months later.

From that time, the Economics Department having become one of the large departments of the University, I limited my own teaching to the courses in History of Economic Thought, Recent Economic Theory, and the department Seminar, four hours of class work per week. Nearly all my students were graduates, the men strongly predominating.

The development of the Seminar was of special interest to me. This was composed of a small group of graduates, most of them economics majors, seldom numbering more than a dozen, once or twice dropping to half-a-dozen. The weekly meeting was a stimulating occasion for all of us. The scientific attitude of mind in approaching a research problem was insisted on, meticulous care was taken in the preparation of bibliographical work, a combination of dignity and informality in presentation before the group was encouraged, and candid criticism on each performance was expected. One of my main objectives was to inspire in my students a feeling of confidence and self-reliance as a preparation for later tasks.

A chief compensation for the true teacher, which I may venture to call a deferred dividend, consists in learning, many years afterward, of some incident, or particular statement, or pointed criticism, that was taken to heart by the student, and made fruitful in his life. During the course of my own long experience many such dividends have come to me; and I think those that have been most genuinely rewarding to my psychic exchequer have been those that surprised me most. I had been totally unaware of the impression being made. Such payments have greatly added to the gratification I now feel for having reached the decision, as a young man, to invest my life in the field of education. It has been a rewarding experience.

Among my numerous associations since my retirement at U.S.C. in 1945, I mention one particularly that has afforded me much pleasure: it is the Half-Century Club, U.S.C., which held its first meeting on the University campus on June 11, 1949, and whose annual metings for their programs and especially for the warmth of fellowship that characterizes them, have become events of high rank.

Membership is limited to graduates of fifty or more year standing, matriculates of at least fifty-five years, and emeritus faculty members and other retired personnel. At the first meeting Arnold Eddy, Alumni Executive Director, presented the following as charter members: Dr. Thomas Nixon Carver, '91, LL.D. 1928, professor-emeritus of Harvard University; Dr. Clyde M. Crist, '98, D.D. 1919, former district superintendent San Diego District of the Methodist Church; Dr. Mary Sinclair Crawford, Litt.D. 1941, dean-emeritus of women; Judge Jesse W. Curtis, '07, LL.D. 1926, retired Justice of the California State Supreme Court; Dr. John G. Hill, L.H.D. 1943, professor-emeritus of Biblical literature; Dr. Rockwell D. Hunt, Litt.D., 1936, dean-emeritus of the graduate school; Dr. Rufus B. von KleinSmid, LL.D. 1948, president of U.S.C. 1921-47, Chancellor since 1947; Dr. Frank G. H. Stevens, '99, D.D. 1919, pastor of St James Methodist Church, Pasadena.

Each year witnesses the formal initiation of newly eligible members; after a simple ceremony membership certificates are presented. "In Memoriam" is also a feature of each program.

I have found the annual reunion and lunch a stimulating, heart-warming experience, all the more affecting to me because of long personal acquaintance with most of the members.

Similar in organization and aims to the Half-Century Club of U.S.C. is the Half-Century Club established at the College of the Pacific, in 1951. As a member of the Napa College Class of 1890, I became also a charter member of this club — it is as dean-emeritus that I am a charter member at U.S.C.

In more respects than one I suppose I might be called a pluralist. I do not regard the true interpretation of history as being economic. To be sure, there may be *an* economic interpretation, but to refer to *the* interpretation as exclusively economic I deem misleading and fallacious: for I find also other factors — politics, ethics, religion as examples — quite as essential to an accurate interpretation of history as economics. Likewise, I cannot pick out a single discipline — economics, politics, sociology — as the master fundamental social science; for I conceive all of them to be essential and interdependent.

My own interest has not been confined to history or economics or political science: all of these fields have engaged my attention both as student and as teacher, though obviously I could not claim a high degree of specialization in the entire group. What I have lost, however, has perhaps been compensated for by an overall view of the larger unity of the social sciences and the oneness of human culture. When in 1908 I accepted a position in the University of Southern California, it was in economics and sociology: from that time my major field was economics, though I never lost interest in history and sociology.

Since economics was my principal teaching subject during a period of many years, I may be indulged certain personal reflections touching that important field of thought. For the better part of my life I have held membership in the American Economic Association. I have had opportunity to meet most of the "major prophets" in the realm of economics — those dominating the scene in the generation now gone. The names of Ely, Clark, Taussig, Seligman, Fisher, Fetter, and Carver readily come to mind.

My own honored teacher at Johns Hopkins University, John Bates Clark, was among the founders of the American Economic Association. He later won recognition as the leading theoretician among American economists. His lectures, presented with a somewhat austere dignity, dealt chiefly with an assumed "static society," knowledge of which was held to be indispensable as a prerequisite in dealing with dynamics. It is to be regretted that he never completed his contemplated work on dynamic society. I came to know Dr. Clark better personally in later years. He was a true gentleman, innately modest, always putting principle above expediency, not lacking in human sympathy and genuine kindliness, a devoted husband and the father of a noteworthy family. I have always been grateful that he extolled "enthronement of character" as the *sine qua non* in social science.

The disciplines known collectively as social science include history, economics, politics, sociology, and ethics, with due consideration for subdivisions and border studies. I have tried to think of their relationship toward each other. Without question they are closely related and highly interdependent. For more than a century writers have been at work on this relationship. Which is the fundamental science? What is it that makes it dominate the others? The "Spencerian analogies," viewing human society as an "organism"? The segmentation of the social sciences? —none of these theories have seemed to me to solve the problem.

Analogy is admittedly an aid in illuminating our social relationships, though it has its limitations. With due modesty, I have likened the circle of the social sciences to an endless cord, whose several individual strands represent the respective social sciences closely braided together, each strand being in direct contact with all the others all the way around the circle. Every strand is essential to the character and strength of the cord as a whole. If this is a true analogy, then the idea that the economist has no concern with any other aspect, as the political or the ethical, is pure fallacy. Every social science has need of every other social science—none can exist and continue to function in complete isolation from the others.

I am unable to think of economics as a natural science, fully demonstrated at every point. The term "science" is admissible, with the reservation that economics (or any other of the group) must be studied in a scientific manner, without personal bias, in an atmosphere of disinterestedness — which is itself no light assignment. Since human society is undergoing incessant change, with apparently increasingly rapid tempo, many "truths" or so-called laws applicable to the days of my youth are not valid in today's dynamic society. If I were teaching economics now it would have to be at numerous points a different economics from what I taught fifty or sixty years ago. Much of the *status quo* of my college days is passé today.

But since economics pertains to human beings, and human beings are the same genus through the centuries, I believe there is and must be an overall objective, valid at all times, which may be expressed as weal, well-being, or welfare. In the absence of the goal of human welfare, economics becomes meaningless. It follows, I think, that the true goal of economics — as, indeed, of all social sciences — is nothing less than the advancement of the general welfare. With coordination of effort the economist works with other social scientists, in a well-ordered federation toward the cooperative achievement of a worthy end, which is nothing less than the common weal and continuous progress of humanity.

From this it follows that nothing is truly economic in a positive sense that is not also socially beneficial. In a broad view, therefore, all economics must be regarded as welfare economics. Not the acquisition of more individual wealth but the advancement of the common good is the ultimate aim and end.

How fares the theory, then, that economics has nothing to do with ethics, is not at all concerned with moral issues? To advocate such a theory involves, I think, not straight or integral thinking but thinking in water-tight compartments — which have no existence in reality. Because of the very nature of civilized man and of the ultimate goal of economics as a social science, it rests, and must rest, upon moral foundations. As there must be two sides to every equation, so every transaction to be truly economic, must be in harmony with the general welfare. I am aware that such a statement is tantamount to disapproval of many practices in contemporary life.

As a long-time teacher of economics and member of the American Economic Association, I wish to make two or three further comments touching upon current trends, as I view them from the sidelines. First, I deprecate what seems to me to be a tendency on the part of many economists toward over-specialization. I find this illustrated in numerous meticulously prepared articles recently appearing in standard journals, some of which, involving intricate mathematical formulation and perhaps strange terminology I cannot even read, but, more serious than that, they labor unendingly about some comparatively inconsequential point or theory. Such a tendency widens the already too wide gap between the specialist and the common man.

I observe, also, a tendency on the part of some to cling to outmoded theory, whether it be *laissez faire*, or high protective tariff, the recurrence of the business cycle, or the iron law of wages. Students are sometimes encouraged to prepare dissertations, after months of research, on topics that might well be forgotten, or left to the historian. They remind me of a man who sits with his back to the road while the world goes by.

Again, partly as a result of the attempt to isolate economics from sociology, philosophy, politics, ethics, and all the rest, I find some of my colleagues indulging in absolutes, when the crying need is for accommodation, adjustment, and resilience. The spirit of intolerance may manifest itself in economics just as truly as in politics or religion. It is as if one proclaimed, "The times may change, but I never change!" Such a person would be worthy of greater respect if he could see the light of a new day, and frankly admit —

> New occasions teach new duties
> Time makes ancient good uncouth.

The age-long economy of scarcity must some day yield to an economy of abundance. Economists must join hands with all other men of good will in preparing for the great social revolution. I thought I saw evidence of the change when a decade ago I stated in an article:[1]

> The unseemly strife for higher wages and shorter hours, exhibitions of the extremes of luxury on the one hand and dire poverty on the other, will have been weighed in the balance and found wanting— they will become anachronistic, no longer to be tolerated in a socially-minded community. Answers to the thundering questions in economic and political life can be found only in the moral realm. They must unflinchingly assert the conviction of right and duty, the principle of mutuality.

When it comes to what men call business affairs I have to confess what may be a weakness in my make-up. I have a strong distaste for such sayings as "Business is business," with its common implications, "Do the other fellow before he does you," "It's O.K. if you can get away with it," "There's no law against it," "Get a-plenty while the getting's good," and others of the same ilk. I think they are degrading to good business and demoralizing to those who adopt them as well as to society at large.

My own tendency has been to go too far in the opposite direction. When a clerk has overpaid me in change I have sometimes caused slight embarrassment in making the correction; but if she short-changes me I'm likely to let it pass. I have never been disposed to drive a hard bargain — with the possible exception of purchasing souvenirs from fakirs in certain oriental

[1] *World Affairs Interpreter*, January, 1947

countries! In renting my house to a trustworthy tenant I had rather ask what I know to be below the going commercial rate than to seek anything above. In a word, it is more tolerable to be imposed upon than it it to impose upon another. And no doubt I have suffered more than one slight imposition.

As a student of business economics I have given some attention to the so-called "business cycle," to the ups and downs of the stock exchange, to such phenomena as the boom, recession, depression, and recovery. But my studies have been quite largely historical and theoretical. Here I must mention, however, one very concrete and practical experience. In 1919 I was asked by the Pacific Electric Railway Corporation of Los Angeles to find out in detail the cost of living in Los Angeles for such an income group as the employees of the corporation over the years 1913 to 1919 — that is, covering the inflationary period of World War I, and to ascertain whether the wage scales (which were furnished me) had kept pace with the increasing cost of living during the period. The corporation desired reliable data in the event of possible labor difficulties. It was a painstaking but interesting task. While the results of my investigation were obviously disappointing to the corporation, my actual figures were not challenged.

My own modest investments have been conservative, far removed from anything like pure speculation. An assured fixed income, though small, is more satisfying to me than the speculative chance of quick profits. As for gambling, it is abhorrent to my moral sensibilities and economically indefensible. The ancient Latin maxim, *"Ex nihilo nihil fit,"* has as its corollary the theorem, any truly economic transaction is a two-sided equation — value for value — while the essence of a gamble is an attempt to get something for nothing.

I have been advised, once or twice, to bring suit to recover damages in case of automobile collision; but so strong has been my dislike for being involved in a court trial that such advice has been politely rejected — though I admit there are hypothetical conditions where I might be quite wrong in refusing to appeal to the courts.

Preparing my annual income tax report, while admittedly comparatively simple, has been among my most unwelcome tasks, imposing a severe test on my personal philosophy to seek enjoyment in whatever I do! I have preferred to err — and who has wholly escaped error? — in favor of the government rather than of myself and I am now morally certain, as I look back over the years, that has happened more than once. The one time when I employed an attorney to assist me, my report came back to me because of the omission of a single item!

Long ago I deliberately foreswore all expectation of amassing a fortune, when I chose to enter the field of education. Fortunately, I have never had any great craving for monetary wealth as such. I have found my life and am satisfied.

CHAPTER TEN

Varied Activities

In addition to a full schedule of teaching hours and teaching a Sunday School class in University Methodist Church during much of the time, I accepted numerous invitations to give outside lectures or addresses before organizations or groups. To illustrate, during the first semester of 1914-15 I lectured at Lennox Methodist Church on "Socialism and the Church," at the Los Angeles Public Library on the "Principles of Economics" and the "Literature of Economics," at the Council of Social Agencies on "Development of the Charity Organization Movement," gave six addresses before the Inyo County Teachers' Institute, and one address before the San Bernardino City and County Institute, addressed the Civic Convention of Southern California on "Colleges and Universities," and the Eagle Rock Congregational Church on "The Church and the Industrial Situation."

On several occasions I have addressed teachers' institutes: of them all I think my experience at the Inyo County teachers was the most interesting. For reasons of health my colleague at the University of Southern California, Tully C. Knoles, had accepted the principalship of the Bishop High School, in that mountain region. He was instrumental in inviting me for the Institute engagement. Bishop is a small town of Inyo County, lying east of the southern Sierra Nevada Mountains, several thousand feet above sea level.

There had been bitter complaints and deep resentment on the

part of the farmers of Owen's Valley because the city of Los Angeles, almost 250 miles distant, had constructed the great Los Angeles Aqueduct against their strong opposition and was piping the valuable water supply of the area entirely away from their alfalfa and pasture lands—which they were very loath to part with, even at good prices. And besides, at the time of my visit Europe was in the throes of the early phases of the first World War, and the agitation in the United States was becoming more intense monthly. I can recall my visit with Professor Knoles quite vividly; and there was no lack of interest on the part of the alert teachers at that particular time and place.

Approximately a score of outside lectures and addresses were presented during the semester—not an unusual number; and with few exceptions they were given without monetary compensation. There was an exception in a certain instance, when I remarked to my brother George, a rather hard-headed business man, "They're going to pay me for that address." "How much?" he inquired. "Twenty-five dollars," I told him. Then he quipped, "Be sure to stop when you have given them twenty-five dollars' worth!"

As for myself, I had deliberately chosen the field of education for my life work, understanding fully that I should never expect to become rich in this world's goods. The "psychic income" derived from a job well done and from words of sincere appreciation has indeed been very rewarding. Still, after all the years, as I look back upon the struggles to maintain anything like a suitable standard of living for myself and my family, it may be— it *may* be—that I should at times have been somewhat more commercially minded. By and large, however, my three living sons all being graduates of the University of Southern California, each having a home of his own and in no great need to look to me for sizable bequests, I do not repine for any lack in this direction, but rather hereby express gratitude for the opportunities to serve that have come to me and for the precious friendships that have been mine through many years.

During the 1910 Summer Session of the University of California at Berkeley, I taught two regular classes in economics — a lower division course in the Principles and and upper division course in Labor Problems. Dr. Charles H. Rieber was Dean.

A minority of my Labor Problems students were graduates. In order to obtain graduate credit, however, each of these was required to present, in addition to regular class work, an acceptable report on an approved topic. I wish to mention the work of one student and what became of it — the young man was Paul F. Brissenden.

He chose as his topic for special study, "The Industrial Workers of the World," a labor organization that was then very active and militant. He attended their meetings in San Francisco, talked to members, and obtained copies of their guiding literature. His class report was satisfactory, and his own interest had become so keen that he further developed the topic into his thesis for the Master of Arts degree. Later he attended Columbia University, receiving his Ph.D. degree in 1917, his dissertation being on "The I.W.W., a Study of American Syndicalism." His completed monograph appeared as a large publication of the Columbia University Press in 1919, probably the most complete exposition of the subject ever made. That is not all. After serving as special agent for the U.S. Commission on Industrial Relations, and in one or two other responsible posts, he became a member of the faculty of Columbia University, rose by stages to the rank of full professor, served in numerous important positions in labor relations and as arbitrator, and recently retired from active duty.

A most pleasant experience during that summer at Berkeley was my personal acquaintance with Dean Rieber. Years later he became Provost of the University of California at Los Angeles, where our acquaintance grew in intimacy and mutual pleasure.

I met him frequently in the "X" Club, to be mentioned later, where his wise and witty discussion enlivened the scene whenever he spoke. Rieber was a choice spirit, a highly esteemed friend. Not every community or every university can boast his equal.

A good illustration of my activities outside the campus walls is seen in California State Conference of Social Agencies, which had its annual convention in Los Angeles May 1 to 5, 1916. That year Dr. Milbank Johnson of Los Angeles was President of the Conference. He was anxious to make a conspicuous success of the meeting, and he really extended himself to that end.

Dr. Johnson asked me to undertake the rather difficult task of heading the general committee on program, appointing Mrs. Carrie Parsons Bryant vice-chairman of the committee. Since the program was to be an elaborate one, ten subcommittees were constituted, as follows: 1) Care and Training of Feeble-Minded; 2) Child Welfare; 3) The Church in Social Service; 4) Corrections; 5) Education for Social Work; 6) Health and Sanitation; 7) Immigration and Housing; 8) Public and Private Charities; 9) Recreation; 10) Unemployment.

Arrangements for such a many-sided program called for much time and thoughtful planning. It is pleasant to recall to mind the very devoted and efficient service rendered by the committee vice-chairman, Mrs. Bryant, and in general the fine spirit of cooperation exhibited by a large number of prominent leaders in social work. Of these I mention Mary J. Workman, Dr. Jessica Peixotto, Judge Frank Murasky, Dr. Emory S. Bogardus, Mrs. Frank Gibson, Rev. Thomas C. Marshall, Dr. Ira Cross, Mrs. Cora D. Lewis, and Mrs. Benjamin Goldman.

The Los Angeles Meeting, with its record-breaking attendance, was pronounced a success. The collected proceedings were published in durable pamphlet form.

It was a great happiness to me to be intimately associated with my personal friend William M. Bowen in the early development of Exposition Park, of almost 120 acres, perhaps most notable of the numerous parks of Metropolitan Los Angeles. Because of his dominating position in the project that eventuated in the realization of this splendid cultural and recreational center, his incessant fight, single-handed and alone for years, I have been — and still am — of the opinion that this park should have been given the name William Miller Bowen Park. It was through his valiant and untiring efforts that old Agricultural Park, with its evil concomitants, was compelled to give way to this significant institution, a commanding resource for city, county, and commonwealth.

For thirty years I served as member of the Board of Governors of Los Angeles County Museum, located in Exposition Park, my connection dating from the beginning of the Museum itself. My special interest was in the development of the History Division of the Museum. During those three decades I witnessed the Museum grow from its infancy into a great, mature institution, featuring the divisions of history, science, and art, that would do credit to any county or any city — and it continues to expand at a phenomenal rate, having attained more than national distinction.

Following my resignation as a member of the Board of Governors in 1947, to accept the post as Director of California History Foundation at the College of the Pacific, in Stockton, the Board passed complimentary resolutions stating officially —

That the Board of Governors officially convey to him herewith the warm and most appreciative thanks of its members for his long, tireless, and faithful service.

The resolutions, dated September 8, 1947 are signed by the president of the Board, Howard Robertson.

While a resident of San José I had become an active member of the Santa Clara County Historical Society. When in 1908 I moved to Los Angeles to take my position at the University of Southern California, it was only natural that I should become interested in the Historical Society of Southern California, especially since I was to teach a course in Pacific Slope History.

After some inquiry I discovered that the Society, which had been founded in 1883, and had issued an annual volume of *Publications* during most years — though with some irregularity — was not then in a flourishing condition. Its meetings, which were rather poorly attended, were being held more or less intermittently, at the homes of individual members, and apparently it had no real headquarters or fixed meeting place. I learned that the burden of responsibility for carrying on the Society rested chiefly — it seemed to me almost exclusively — with Mr. James M. Guinn, who was virtually the factotum.

I decided to do what I could to assist in reviving the Society, and perceived also in the situation an opportunity for the University of Southern California to render a community service.

After conference with President Bovard, an invitation was given the Society to hold its regular meetings in a conveniently located University room. The invitation was gratefully accepted. As a next step, Dr. Bovard graciously accepted the presidency of the Society, which office he retained for several years. In 1916 I was made president; but all the while Mr. Guinn, happy to be relieved of much of the burden, continued actively as secretary, finally to be succeeded by his daughter, Mabel E. Guinn.

The next meeting place of the Society was in the newly constructed building of the Los Angeles County Museum, in Exposition Park. A more central location was desired, however, and for some years the meetings were held in the rooms of the Los Angeles Board of Education. More recently permanent headquarters for the Society have been established at what had been the residence of E. T. Earl, on Wilshire Boulevard.

My incumbency as president continued for a period of eleven years, the longest term of any president. Then, in late 1926, my resignation was accepted, since I was entering upon my sabbatic leave from the University, for a period of eight months. I had no thought of resuming office on my return to Los Angeles, though I did not permit either my membership or my interest to lapse. I have presented numerous papers to the *Publications*, others came from students in my class or seminar, and editorial service was rendered for a number of years.

Even since moving to Stockton and the College of the Pacific in 1947 I have been happy to maintain my membership in the Society — I have derived much pleasure in my few visits to the Wilshire headquarters. I think it only just to say that the Historical Society of Southern California was deeply indebted to James M. Guinn, who by his loyal devotion and continued activity was the dominant factor in its success, if not its very existence, through a good many trying years.

Beginning in 1916-17 I was an instructor in economics in the Los Angeles Chapter of the American Institute of Banking for a considerable number of years. For the first few seasons this work was in the nature of the University of Southern California's extension teaching; but the Institute rapidly developed its own program of studies, attracting to the evening classes a large number of junior officers and clerks of the Los Angeles banks.

I found the young men and young women of my classes attentive and earnest, and was well impressed by the program of studies set up by the Institute. In the course of a few years the Los Angeles Chapter became one of the largest chapters in the United States. The annual banquet was a rather elaborate affair, the speaker of the evening usually being a leading banker or successful business man of prominence.

There is no doubt that this educational program has been of direct benefit to many hundreds of young people who have entered the banking and similar professions. Not a few of the students have reached positions as senior executives.

My own class in the Institute program was in the elementary principles of economics, though for a few sessions I had also an advanced class. I found real satisfaction in carrying on this work; but since it was added to the responsibilities of my regular University position and my family duties, and the down-town classes were in the evening, it was something of a burden. The compensation was a welcome help especially when my own sons were in college. It is gratifying to have had part in the very practical educational program of the American Institute of Banking. My lectures were well received by my students; although at times I thought I sensed a feeling on the part of some of the more conservative senior bankers that certain of my views were somewhat more "liberal" or "progressive" than they unreservedly relished.

This gives me opportunity to remark that in all my teaching I have enjoyed great freedom of thought and expression; but never have I been brought to task by any director, president, or trustee because of my expressed views on any of a very wide variety of economic and social questions. My aim has been to prepare myself as thoroughly as I could, present all sides of controversial issues, then in tactful but clear manner give my students the advantage of my own conclusions. I have always highly prized my freedom in teaching, but along with my freedom has been felt my own responsibility to the institution I served, to my students, and to the larger community.

For a good many years I have maintained membership in

the Order of the Native Sons of the Golden West, an organization composed of men born in the state of California, whose general aim is to cultivate more intimate acquaintance with the history and spirit of early California and to extol its virtues and advance its interests at all times.

The fraternity was founded by Gen. Albert M. Winn in 1875, although he himself was not a native. Each of the scores of chapters over the state is known as a "parlor": the Grand Parlor, headed by the Grand President, with headquarters in San Francisco, is supreme authority.

My own membership is in the Ramona Parlor, No. 109, located in Los Angeles. While I have never accepted office in the organization, I have given lectures and talks on California history both in Ramona Parlor and the Friday Lunch Club at Los Angeles, and have on several occasions appeared before the annual meeting of the Grand Parlor. Among the past grand presidents may be mentioned such men of prominence as Joseph R. Knowland, Clarence E. Jarvis, Edward J. Lynch, and Walter H. Odemar.

The Native Daughters of the Golden West is the sister order, with similar plan of organization, having numerous chapters widely distributed throughout the state. *The Grizzly Bear*, a monthly magazine, has been the official organ of the two organizations.

Membership in two small men's clubs proved a very stimulating experience over a good many years. First, there was the "X" Club, a limited group, meeting once a month for dinner and discussion. The members represented a very wide range of views on economic, social, and political questions — it was expressly so designed. There was no constitution, no regular dues were charged, and the sole official was the secretary.

For some years the very efficient secretary was William J. Ghent, well-known socialist leader, whose reports of our discussions were most vivacious, often real works of art. At the beginning of each meeting a chairman was selected: he introduced the speaker of the evening who had been named at the previous meeting; following the main discussion, each member present was called upon in turn. There was the utmost freedom of speech; and considering the wide range of views held by different members, there was plenty of diversity, with repartee and rebuttal; but the main speaker always had the closing words.

Among the members were university professors, lawyers, judges, business executives, labor leaders, clergymen, and publicists. The extraordinary diversity is best illustrated by mentioning individuals: Russell Ballard, head of the privately-owned Southern California Edison Company, and Dr. John R. Haynes, champion of public ownership and direct legislation; William B. Munro (formerly of Harvard), Pasadena banker, and W. J. Ghent, intellectual socialist; Judge Benjamin F. Bledsoe, fundamentalist Republican, and Samson Lindauer, independent Democrat; David Edstrom, iconoclastic sculptor, and Bob Wagner (later of the movies), *sui generis*; Tom Gibbon, editor, lawyer, publicist; and Ralph Criswell, left-wing city councilman; Dr. Caldecott, Unitarian, and G. Bromley Oxnam (later Bishop), Methodist; Meyer Lissner, reform politician, and Frederick Sears, eminent astronomer; and so on through the interesting roster of members. For several years the meetings of the "X" Club were more than interesting—they were exciting. I shall never forget the time when Thomas N. Carver (guest speaker) almost literally pulverized Ghent in rebuttal, bringing him to a state of daze by his ruthless charge of willful intent to deceive. Ghent, whom we all respected as our brilliant secretary, had no oppportunity to reply to Carver's devastating criticism.

The other club was called "The Twenty (XX)," composed of religious leaders, both clergy and lay, of widely varying faiths and shades of belief. Membership was theoretically supposed to be limited to twenty; but in actual fact it was nearer thirty-five, with average attendance about twenty. It was a luncheon club, with president and secretary-treasurer; but meetings often continued until 2:30 or 3 o'clock. The appointed speaker usually presented a thoughtfully prepared paper, to be followed by volunteer comment by members. Among the many members I recall with pleasure were Bishop Bertrand Stevens of the Episcopal Church, Roy Smith and John W. Hoffman, Methodists, Allan Hunter, Presbyterian, Father T. J. O'Dwyer, Catholic, and Rabbi Edgar Magnin, Hebrew.

Seldom if ever have I enjoyed finer fellowship with kindred souls in higher thinking than in the XX club. I wondered, if these men can meet together in harmony and a spirit of toleration and discuss problems of human betterment without acrimony or even the slightest tinge of malice, why cannot humanity get together for the sake of the common good of all? I cherish the memory of my membership in the X and XX Clubs.

From early childhood days I have been a lover of books. Despite the fact of low salary and the expense of growing family, I managed to acquire a respectable number of books each year. On retiring from the University of Southern California in 1945 I donated virtually all my collection in Economics and related social sciences to the University Library, but retained my growing collection of Californiana, expecting to devote major attention to the history of California and the West during the period of my retirement.

This collection has been steadily augmented year by year, until now it numbers in excess of a thousand volumes. I cannot claim to be a real collector, for the simple reason that I could not indulge in so expensive a luxury. However, I have come into possession of a considerable number of rare and scarce items and not a few copies of special and limited editions. Of

California poetry alone I have accumulated close to 100 volumes.

Particularly prized are books autographed or inscribed to me by their authors. These include — to mention a few from the many — Hubert Howe Bancroft, Cornelius Cole, John Steven McGroarty, Herbert Eugene Bolton, Henry Meade Bland, Catherine Coffin Phillips, and Irene Paden.

When I was considerably younger I took a good deal of pride in reading books through, from cover to cover. But more recently because of limited time, comparatively few books are read from beginning to end. Most of them are used for limited purposes or special reference. It is a matter of some regret that in recent years I read so little of fiction — I do indulge in a good historical novel occasionally. But I have no sense of regret or guilt at having omitted entirely the flood of detective stories.

Because of my particular interest in California history, it must not be inferred that my reading is confined to that field — quite the opposite is true. For years I have been acquiring new books on a variety of subjects, always faster than I can possibly read them. But the periodicals that come to my desk bring perennial interest and often intellectual excitement.

As to the challenging political, economic, and world questions, I have tried to avoid prejudice or hastily formed opinions. To that end my reading includes different and opposing points of view. I am unwilling to trust any one journal to present all sides to every question discussed in its pages — I must consider its sponsorship and the source from which it springs. Several weekly journals devoted to book reviews are a welcome aid in a crowded schedule. Of these I find the *Saturday Review*, with its essay reviews and other features, most stimulating. Membership in such organizations as the American Historical Association, its Pacific Coast Branch, other historical societies, and the American Economic Association brings a flood of official publications. I have been a member of the American Historical Association and the American Economic Association for more than half a century; and with Henry Morse Stephens of the University of California and Max Farrand of Stanford University was a founder member of the Pacific Coast Branch of the American Historical Association, and participated in its First Annual Meeting, in San Francisco, in 1904.

The daily newspaper must not be neglected. Quite regularly I read one morning and one evening paper, often referring to others. I have frequently exercised the prerogative of writing letters to the editor's forum, as indicated in another place.

The mail carrier, in pursuance of his dull, daily routine, affords me daily pleasure, with an occasional disappointment, but now and then a thrill of delight. I am always looking forward to what Uncle Sam's messenger has to offer: the most perplexing feature is found in the too-numerous wonderfully-worded, never-so-urgent appeals from charitable organizations. The causes were never in such need of support, and your name — once on the mailing list — is never omitted from year to year! How to respond to all the appeals is truly baffling. Unwilling to consign them all summarily to my waste paper basket, I have left some letters unanswered for weeks, as the query has arisen, why must so many worthy causes depend upon the contributions of persons like me? If they are really meritorious — how can that be questioned? — why must their very existence be conditioned upon contributions from thousands of individuals of small means?

My maternal grandfather, a pioneer on the Illinois frontier, exemplified an old-fashioned division of labor long since rendered ineffective. He provided his own venison and wild fowl, made his own wash-tubs and buckets, tanned buckskin for various uses, did his own carpentering and blacksmithing. He had to be effective, to survive.

But that was more than a century ago — everything has changed.

That belongs to ancient history. The self-sufficient individualism of his day has been superseded by inter-dependence; old-fashioned division of labor has given way to specialized industry, technological advance, and mass production. With the transformation have come new problems.

And that is not all. When the atom bomb fell on Hiroshima the world entered a new era — the Atomic Age. We find ourselves now in the midst of a universal revolution, whose tempo is far swifter than Adam Smith witnessed in the Industrial Revolution in England at the time of our Declaration of Independence. Every phase of life — economic, political, religious, and any other — feels the impact. Let us take a look at the political.

I like to think of politics as the Aristotelian ideal, the noblest of all sciences, depicted by Macaulay as the most important science, which "most tends to expand and invigorate the mind"; but I have been ruthlessly brought to earth by sordid and baneful exhibitions in the practical political arena. As a believer in the spirit of democracy I accept the principle of party politics; but I have to confess my present inability to find a party with which I could sincerely and permanently align myself. For some years as a young man I joined the Prohibition movement — and I have never abandoned the principle of prohibition: but the time came when I was convinced of the inadequacy of the political party to meet the increasing demands.

Then I became a Republican; but as an admirer of Theodore Roosevelt, hard-hitting champion of the square deal, I espoused the cause of the Lincoln-Roosevelt League. Another dilemma confronted me when Woodrow Wilson, labelled a Democrat, captivated me as a founder of the League of Nations, while certain Republican leaders effectively blocked the entrance of the United States into the League. Still later, it seemed to me the ruling group of the Republican party turned its back upon social progress — which it could not wholly prevent — by repudiating the New Deal, though it embodied many features that I sincerely believed in. I was not happy as a Republican, yet never actually registered as a Democrat.

Then came another third-party movement — the Independent-Progressives. There again was a platform that in my opinion embodied many sound forward-looking principles; but, partly because of a complicated international situation, this movement was unable to capture the imagination of any considerable segment of the American voters.

As a result of my own thinking, and in view of the changing — sometimes drifting — situation, I must confess, as I write, that while I believe in the party system of government, as pertaining to domestic affairs, I find myself in fact an independent. There is a place for compromise and adjustment; there is also, for me, a place for firm moral conviction whether in the field of economics, religion, or politics. We have witnessed too much regimentation of the unthinking. I can at least sympathize with David Starr Jordan when he declared; "I always vote a straight ticket, by weeding out all the crooks."

Discredit (and worse) has too often been cast upon practical American politics by unscrupulous bossism. It is only necessary to mention certain names, like Buckley, Tom Platt, William Herrin, and Abe Reuf, to suggest sordid scenes, not confined to one party, or locality, or decade. My own brother Frank, then a prominent Granger, expressed a widespread feeling when he wrote in a personal letter, dated March 12, 1924:

> It's no wonder that the common people lose faith in our governmental men in charge of running things for us. That's the reason we hate to vote for improvements any more (about 50% goes for graft). Both big parties about equally guilty—as illustrated by Teapot Dome Scandal . . . nearly all of them afraid to go ahead with it much farther. They don't want to know too much.

Instead of subscribing to the dictum that politics has nothing to do with morality I make bold to declare that without morality politics can lead only to the downfall of democracy and to final chaos. The situation is well expressed in a phrase used by Sheldon Amos of England a good many years ago to the effect that the state has not developed "in an ethical intelligence adequate to meet the new demands upon it."

From where I view the changing scene it seems astounding that there are still in our midst so many men—some of them accredited leaders—who are apparently blind to the world revolution that is sweeping our generation. They are "stand-patters" when there's no such thing as standing still, who have been compared to blind unreasoning fossils in a fast-moving world. Like unto them are those who would still uphold the banner of isolationism at the very time they, and all of us, are literally a-whirl in a great world tornado.

We must be willing to learn from all sources. There is no nation that cannot give us instruction at some point, if we but have receptive minds. And this applies to allies and adversaries alike. After returning from a trip around the world, in the year 1927 I wrote in a letter, dated September 18, words that seem pertinent now:

> Have recently heard a good deal about Russia, the Five-Year Plan of industrialization, etc., and I give it as my opinion that the capitalists of America had better watch Russia closely and had better be willing to learn something from her. Some very significant and radical changes in the United States may be in order during the next ten or fifteen years.

As I see it, sweeping changes in our manner of living, as a result of the current revolution, must be accepted, in the light of history and of progress; then they must be accurately interpreted and guided to the end of promoting the welfare of all the people. However it has come about, the United States of America, as an integral part of the world, has been assigned a leading rôle in world affairs, and our responsibilities are inescapable. It is therefore clear that the new American way demands dynamic integrity, independence of mind, and a spirit of world citizenship on the part of our people. While the cardinal virtues of the founders — individual liberty, self-reliance, universal morality — are as binding today as at any time in the past, it is a truism that contemporary life is undergoing many swift changes. "There is nothing so constant as change." It is my business, therefore, to seek to understand the significant changes and to interpret them in the light of the enduring principles upheld by the founding fathers. As a corollary, there is urgent demand for broad-visioned leaders, facing the marvelous future, who can dramatize the transcendent issues and point the way to the multitudes.

The word "if" is a very small word, but "in fact" it carries great potentiality. I do not consider it mere idle speculation to assert that if three United States senators (Borah, Lodge, Johnson) had not blocked the way the United States would have entered the League of Nations, and by assuming its rightful place in the League would have rendered the human tragedy of World War II unnecessary.

However that may be, we have today the United Nations organization, created in our own city by the Golden Gate, with world headquarters in New York. In the swiftly changing scenes of our times this organization cannot be thought of as perfect and static: but, with means at hand for its modification and implementation, it is, I think, our best hope for the abolition of war and the attainment of an enduring peace for mankind.

My grandfather on the Illinois frontier was a good American; but it is now impossible for me to be a good American on his terms. I have in all humility tried to formulate a statement more nearly commensurate to present demands:

"The good American has entered into the rich heritage bequeathed by the establishment and development of our common democracy. He possesses the sterling qualities of self-respect and personal initiative, with the fear of God in his heart and his destiny in his own strong right arm.

"The good American adheres to the tenet that, with good will toward his fellow man, true freedom comes through wisely conceived and justly administered laws. He will not tolerate mob rule; he abhors a state of anarchy.

"The good American exalts the ideals of equality of opportunity, the dignity and essential worth of the individual; and he has a consuming passion for freedom. He has dreamed 'of a land in which life should be better and richer and fuller for every man.'

"The good American ardently loves peace; but he recognizes that the right is even more precious than peace. He will fight to defend and preserve his democracy against every enemy, domestic or foreign.

"The good American is a man of deep conviction, undergirded by a steadfast religious faith. For him the power of moral judgment is a well-spring of human motivation. Religious faith removes mountains of difficulty, sustains the believer in the crucible of fiery ordeal, enables the meek and the humble to walk erect and emerge as man triumphant.

"The good American of today is likewise a good citizen of our one world. His purview and his responsibility comprehend all mankind.

"The good American is characterized by the chastity of honor, the unbought graces of life, the beauty of symmetry, the ever-alluring quest for perfection."

Personally I have always been a total abstainer and firm believer in the principle of prohibition. I cannot doubt there were some bigots in the Prohibition movement that swept the country as a political issue; but, on the other hand, of this I am equally sure — there were many earnest, devoted idealists and practical-minded citizens who were motivated by a faith and hope that national Prohibition would point the way to the abolition of alcoholism and of the widespread and obvious evils of the drink habit. To denounce the entire movement as hypocritical and dishonest, as some do in our day, reveals either a hopeless ignorance of the facts or a naïve and puerile bias totally unworthy and unbecoming a forthright American citizen.

Alcoholism in America is taking a heavier toll today than ever before, and is becoming progressively worse. The many-sided drink problem was never more menacing to the nation than now — and its gravity is not diminishing. As I view the scene, whether in the United States, or France, or elsewhere, moderation is the beginning, but by no means the end, of alcoholism. If Prohibition is not the answer, it is high time for men and women of realizable ideals and clear social vision to come forth with a new and better formula — time is running out.

CHAPTER ELEVEN

COLLEGE
of the PACIFIC

After an exchange of letters with President Robert E. Burns about the possible publication of a small volume pertaining to ghost towns of the Mother Lode country, along came a letter from him dated April 17, 1947, which startled me by propounding the question, "Have you ever thought about the possibility of joining our history staff on a limited basis, doing work particularly in the American or Gold Rush Period?"

Then he went on to indicate he was anxious to get someone to undertake work in that field, who would conduct one graduate seminar, and devote "the rest of his time to writing and digging up ideas." He was acquainted with my long-time interest in the history of my native state and I was not unaware of his more recent interest. In conclusion, he was generous enough to say: "there is no one I would rather have than you. It is an idea. What do think about it?"

In my reply to President Burns I admitted that I was deeply interested, that he had struck "a weak spot in my armor against taking on anything new at this stage." I was then seventy-nine.

Other letters followed. On May 16 he wrote: "We are very much excited about the possibility of having you with us during the Centennial Year. . . . Frankly, we think this is a golden opportunity to capitalize on your long and important work in the field. You would be giving a great service to your Alma Mater and to California."

Naturally I felt compelled to give the matter serious consideration. California history was already my avocation — why not make it my major? Here was a cordial invitation from the president of my Alma Mater — where could I hope to find more congenial employment? I was offered virtually a free hand in the use of my time — why should I hesitate?

On the 19th of May I practically agreed to accept a definite appointment, and added in my letter, "As to tenure, I would hope to remain for the three years, if you wish, with the understanding that in the event of mutual desire, for any reason, any such arrangement could be modified." To that date no specific salary had been mentioned on either side. My attitude had been expressed in a previous letter. "As to compensation," I had written, May 1, "I would have no misgiving on that score; for you would sense the situation clearly." It was not until weeks later, after I had definitely arranged to leave Southern California and move to Stockton, that the matter of salary was talked over by us in an informal chat, and agreement was reached on a very modest basis, to our mutual satisfaction.

Thus when in 1947 I agreed to return to the College of the Pacific, the same institution I had served in San José from 1895 to 1902, my hope was that I might continue to be active for possibly three years, which would include three important California Centennials: Gold Discovery, January 24, 1948; the memorable Gold Rush Days (Days of '49), 1949; and Admission Day, September 9, 1950. Three years were thought be a maximum, but there was also a hope that I might be a witness to the Centennial Celebration of the College itself, in commemoration of the granting of its state charter, July 10, 1851.

No one has been more surprised than myself at what actually happened. Instead of remaining two, or three, years, as I had anticipated, I rounded out my second cycle of seven years at Pacific! It may be that I was close to the sentimental fringe during that second seventh year; for I had long known of the ancient tradition that seven is the perfect number, and that knowledge may have been a factor perhaps subconsciously — in my desire to retire again on the completion of the second cycle. At any rate, I willingly became Director-Emeritus of the California History Foundation in the summer of 1954.

My recent years in Stockton constitute an interesting and eventful chapter in my life. Some account of this period must be made. In one sense, I was alone: I had suffered the loss of my life companion years before, and for a still longer period my sons had been living in their own homes.

In another sense, I was far from alone: I was surrounded by friends from the day my work at Stockton campus began. For many years I had known Tully C. Knoles, as a colleague on the faculty at Southern California, then as president of the College of the Pacific, now as its chancellor. My personal acquaintance with him dates from 1908, when I became a colleague at the University of Southern California. While president at Pacific he was one of the most popular and most successful speakers in California. A man of exceptional ability in the pulpit and on the lecture platform, his readiness in speech, versatility, directness of address, and never-failing humor gave him ready access to all kinds of audiences. As college president — to quote from my History of the College — his long and brilliant administration "stands out like a lofty mountain peak — it has no close parallel in the history of Pacific." Dr. G. A. Werner, for many years professor of political science, now retired, had once been one of my students, and a truer friend one could not wish. Older members of the faculty, like Dean J. William Harris, Dean Fred Farley, and Dr. George Colliver were so friendly that it almost seemed I had known them always. I would probably never have accepted an invitation similar to that of President Burns for any other college, but coming from him, and from my Alma Mater, the attraction was irresistible.

On the eve of my departure from Los Angeles for Stockton I addressed the Luncheon Club of the Native Sons of the Golden West at Hotel Clark, where I was introduced by the Grand President of the state-wide organization. The audience paid me a generous rising tribute both at introduction and conclusion.

Moving away from the house on Brynhurst Avenue, Los Angeles, that had been my home longer than any other, a home filled with all manner of family keepsakes, books, all kinds of articles I had lived with so long, was far from easy — there was something poignant, almost excruciating, about it. But the day of departure came: I was ready.

As understood from the beginning, actual teaching at Pacific was limited to a small seminar in California History, meeting weekly. For one semester, however, I also gave a more popular lecture course on Beacon Lights of California History.

I accepted an invitation from the Adult Division of the Stockton Schools to give a series of weekly lectures in the Philomathean Club House during the spring of 1948, under the general title "California in Review, After a Century of American Control." These lectures attracted rather wide interest and were well attended. David L. Greene, Director of Adult Education, provided a court reporter who took down each lecture in shorthand. Much to my surprise the Honorable Leroy Johnson, Congressman from this district, became so much interested in my lectures, based on stenographic reports — I had not prepared manuscript — that they were accepted by him as "Extension of Remarks" and published in the *Congressional Record*. These were separately printed in pamphlet form for wider distribution. This I deemed a rather unusual personal compliment.

Numerous invitations to speak to service clubs, historical societies, schools, church organizations, and other groups were accepted, an experience that brought me into touch with many communities. Most of my addresses had to do with the California Centennial Celebrations.

One address must be given particular mention. I was privileged to speak to the local Monterey Historical Society in Colton Hall, on the evening of October 13, 1949, exactly one hundred years, to the day, from the time when the delegates to the constitutional convention completed the task of drafting California's first state constitution *in that same room!* That experience was to me one of the most thrilling of all my platform efforts. I felt the sacredness of the place — I was standing on holy ground.

A good second to my Monterey experience came in the autumn of 1952, when I gave the dedicatory address at the new San José High School just half a century after I became principal of that school. To me that also was an unforgettable thrill — already more fully reported, however, in an earlier chapter.

My most fundamental work at Pacific was as Director of the California History Foundation, the development of which was my major function. With the close cooperation of President Burns and Dr. Malcolm R. Eiselen, head of the history department, a prospectus of the Foundation was drawn up and printed. All activities were to be under the control of the Director and Executive Board. In addition, there was constituted a group of sponsors, named by the President of the College. As formulated at a later date the fundamental objective of the Foundation is "the promotion and development of the study of the vital, significant history of California, with particular reference to the periods of the American conquest, the Gold Rush, and the establishment of the Commonwealth." In harmony with this, ten specific purposes and objectives are set forth. The sum of not less than $100,000 as an endowment fund was set up as a goal for the support of the Foundation.

From time to time additional names were added to the list of the sponsors, until the group included at least forty persons from different sections of the state, and beyond, a truly representative body of men and women interested in the promotion of California history.

An important function of the Director of the California History Foundation was the preparation of the program for the Annual Institute. During each of my seven years as Director, the Institute was held, in the month of March. With slight variation the pattern set for the first (March 12-13, 1948) has been maintained throughout.

After a meeting of the Executive Board and Foundation Sponsors on Friday afternoon came the Annual Dinner that evening, followed by a leading address. Two meetings were held on Saturday forenoon, one specially for teachers, the other a general session at which two papers were presented. Then came the Annual Luncheon, followed by brief remarks by several speakers, thus concluding the program.

We were fortunate in securing as speakers a number of well-known authorities in the field of California and Western history. These included John D. Hicks, Robert G. Cleland, John W. Caughey, Joseph R. Knowland, George P. Hammond, LeRoy R. Hafen, Peter M. Dunne, John E. McGloin, Marshall Stimson, Glenn S. Dumke, Owen C. Coy, William G. Paden, Peter T. Conmy, and Herbert C. Jones.

The Board of Sponsors at present is a splendid list of men and women, interested in California history, representative of different sections of the state, including institutions of higher education, Native Sons and Native Daughters of the Golden West, public officials, and private individuals.

The fundamental objective of the Foundation is "the promotion and development of the study of the vital, significant history of California." The city of Stockton, which was the chief commercial capital for the Southern Mines, is ideally located as a center for the study and development of California history.

At the Sixth Annual Institute of the Foundation (1953) there was a joint session for teachers and local historical societies in California, which proved so successful that it was decided to hold a special conference in the interest of local societies at Columbia State Park in July. The program there, arranged under the chairmanship of Harold G. Schutt, met with enthusiastic response: it was spontaneously voted to stage a similar Conference in 1954.

At the second Columbia Conference there was effected the organization, on a permanent basis, of the state-wide Conference of California Historical Societies, and a set of appropriate by-laws adopted. Since it appeared to be the general wish of the delegates that I, as head of the general sponsoring body, be the first president of the new federation, I put aside my personal reluctance and accepted the office. I recalled that just fifty years previous to the date I had been a founding member, along with Henry Morse Stephens and Max Farrand, of the Pacific Coast Branch of the American Historical Association; now I was again to be a pioneer in a movement that promised a useful and enlarging future in the field of California history. The First Annual Meeting of the Conference was scheduled for the historic city of Monterey, June 24-25, 1955.

The College of the Pacific has won an enviable reputation in conducting special tours and developing the subject of educational travel. In this rather new but very promising field, Dr. G. A. Werner was for years the College Conductor of Tours, succeeded, on his retirement, by Elliott J. Taylor, chief of the admissions

department. Mention of this phase is made here because one of
the annual tours during my seven years was the visit to the sites
of the twenty-one Franciscan Missions of California, during the
Easter Week vacation. The party, limited to one bus-load of
registrants, at first occupied seven days, but later was expanded to
the full eight-day period.

As Director of the Foundation, I accompanied the Mission
Party each year during the seven-year period, as a very informal
lecturer and mentor. Most of my discourse was "running" talk
by means of a public address system, while the bus rolled along
the highway. A majority of the members, a very congenial group,
were teachers and students, with here and there an older person
or a young child. I found enjoyment in every one of these trips,
assured that they were both entertaining and instructive to
those who went. Usually a majority registered for college credit,
completing their requirements by submitting acceptable reports
on approved topics. On the last of my tours there were twenty-
nine who thus earned their credits.

On the occasion of the elaborate Centennial Celebration of
the College of the Pacific I expressed myself, in part, in these
words:

> The College of the Pacific has been a bulwark to the common-
> wealth of California. Its history offers a striking parallelism to that
> of the state. As early as 1848, the year of gold discovery, the General
> Conference of the Methodist Episcopal Church took note of the need
> for Christian service in the land of El Dorado: under its direction
> Bishop Beverly Waugh selected two young men of excelling promise
> for work in the Far West—William Taylor and Isaac Owen—who
> arrived by different routes almost simultaneously in California, in the
> gold days of 1849. Both became founders of the state's first chartered
> college. In 1850, the year of California's admission into the Union as
> a free state, Martin C. Briggs and Edward Bannister arrived in San
> Francisco. . . . During the following year, in the midst of California's
> struggle for social order, the year of San Francisco's first great Vigi-

lance Committee, three educational conventions were held by Methodists, and it was decided to establish an institution of university grade. It was on the 10th of July, 1851 that the College was chartered by the Supreme Court of California.... The College of the Pacific has grown up with the state. By its contributions in all legitimate fields of endeavor, intellectual, moral, and spiritual, it must continue to enrich the heritage that California bestows upon all the grateful people.

Elsewhere reference is made to my volume, *History of the College of the Pacific*, 1851-1951, "written in commemoration of the one hundredth anniversary of its founding."

One of my very interesting experiences of recent years was my appearance, December 10, 1953, on the "This I Believe" program of Edward R. Murrow, announced to be released on more than 200 U. S. radio stations and 140 AFRS stations in Europe and the Pacific. The invitation to appear was naturally a surprise to me. Here's how it happened.

I had sent a reprint of my little piece "Zest After 80" (appearing in *Life Today*, April-May, 1953) to my friend Dr. George M. Day, sociologist of Occidental College: he in turn had sent it on to President-Emeritus Remsen Bird of that College, who was a consultant for the Murrow Program. That brought me the formal invitation. I prepared my script, had it recorded at the College of the Pacific radio station, then sent it to Philadelphia for final release in New York. So many persons have requested copies that I have decided to include the brief script in this chapter.

Among the numerous expressions reaching me in response, the letter from Edgar H. Borde, of Engineering Ltd., Port-of-Spain, Trinidad, B.W.I. surprised me perhaps most of all. The faraway writer had heard part of my script sometime later, on the local U.S. Armed Forces Radio Station W.V.D.I., and was so impressed as to write me an air-mail letter from Trinidad.

THIS I BELIEVE
(December 10, 1953)

I am in my 86th year. Never in my long career as an educator have I had more life interests. My own individuality sets me apart from every other human being—I am not entirely like anybody else. I believe that it is only by being my best self that I can make my best contribution in life.

While distinctly limited by my own finiteness, I have been endowed with the power of apprehending infinity, though but vaguely and quite imperfectly. Whether I consider the vastness of astronomical space or the minuteness of the atom and its component parts, I seem to catch fleeting glimpses of infinitude.

I believe in God, all-wise creator of all things. It is not given me to understand him fully, or to limit him in terms of human thought or dimensions; measured by my own finiteness he would not be the supreme ruler of the universe I conceive him to be—God would not be God. By faith, and faith alone, the horizon of my vision, the circle of my thought, may be so expanded as to embrace the idea of the true creator, who holds the scepter of omnipotence.

I believe in the compulsive force of intellectual integrity as a prerequisite to the truth that can give me real freedom: in a moral universe in which one truth cannot be at war with another truth, complete intellectual and spiritual integrity transcends all man-made creeds and formulated opinions of groups or denominations.

I believe that through faith and devoted endeavor I may attain a state of poise and serenity of spirit, even under the most adverse and inhospitable conditions and circumstances. This I deem essential to complete self-mastery.

Being a responsible man, I have always had a continuing sense of mission in life. It follows that as an individual I am not bound to conform in all particulars to the common mores of the community when such conformance violates my own sense of right. The final mandate does not issue from the insidious words, "everybody does it," but is the still, small voice of my own conscience.

I believe that sufficient time will be vouchsafed to me fully to obey every call of duty, since duties never conflict, and neither nature nor providence demands the impossible of me. If I actually have not time for something I'd like to do, then that cannot be my duty. It is only by the absence of inner conflict that I can accomplish all the things I'm called upon to do. Therefore I believe that the full application of my resources is a prerequisite to optimum service — an obvious impossibility if I'm not at peace with myself.

In my heart I have no room for bitterness or vengeance, which are poisonous to the soul—hatred is an emotional liability. I accept the ancient maxim, "The best way to avenge a wrong is not to repeat the offense." I believe this to be a friendly universe, governed by law and order. I cannot annul the laws of nature, but I may injure or destroy myself by doing violence to its established laws. I believe that through faith I may to some degree be a humble partaker of the power, the spirit, and the character of the creator of all things. That, to me, is the essence of manhood.

Not long after the Centennial Celebration of the College of the Pacific at Commencement time, 1951, my faithful friend and colleague Dr. G. A. Werner drew me aside one day on the campus, near the Administration Building, and unfolded a plan that had been forming in his mind regarding the California History Foundation, on the executive board of which he had been a member from its beginning — a plan that brought my name into an entirely new and surprising relationship to the College. He had obviously given careful thought to the matter; but before proceeding to put his plan into actual effect he submitted this question: "Would you be willing to have us create a chair, or professorship, in California History, bearing your name, that is the 'Rockwell Dennis Hunt Chair in California History'?"

Dr. Werner's suggestion took me completely by surprise. After reflection, I replied: "If such a plan is authorized by the President of the College, I can see no valid reason why I should object to it. On the other hand, I would deem it a great honor, which I could not do otherwise than accept with humble gratitude."

Such was the genesis of the plan for a "chair" in the College of the Pacific bearing my name. On the 25th of March, 1952, the Board of Trustees unanimously endorsed the establishment of the Hunt Chair: President Robert E. Burns advised me of the action, concluding his letter in these words: "Establishment of this Chair is a signal honor to the College, and I am very happy to notify you of this formal approval."

In my reply to President Burns' letter I stated:

> I indulge the hope that the establishment of this Chair in my Alma Mater will insure in perpetuity the teaching and otherwise promoting the history of our great Commonwealth, and will be of real assistance in bringing to our College Library a leading Collection of Californiana; furthermore, that the College of the Pacific will become and remain distinguished among institutions of learning in this unique, important field. ... I sincerely trust it will prove as great a benefit to the College as it is an honor to myself.

Of the many congratulations that came to me following this announcement, I quote from two letters. President Fred D. Fagg, Jr., of the University of Southern California wrote:

> Congratulations to you and your friends on the establishment of the Rockwell Dennis Hunt Chair in California History at the College of the Pacific! This enterprise has been thoroughly merited by your outstanding record of scholarship in the field, and your host of friends will delight in this latest recognition of your splendid endeavors in making California history available to us all.

President Cloyd H. Marvin of George Washington University wrote:

> I congratulate the College of the Pacific upon the Hunt Foundation. I think that they could not have honored themselves in a better way, and I am most happy that they honored you in honoring themselves.

For the support of the Hunt Chair the goal was set at $100,000 as an endowment fund.

As briefly as I can I must tell of another honor that came to me while I was Director of the California History Foundation.

Reasons for this bestowal I am unable fully to account for. It involves the story of a full-size portrait in oil.

First, let me state that one of the citizens of Stockton for whom I had developed the warmest friendship was Stuart C. Gibbons, president of the South Calaveras Grove Association. I had been made Honorary Chairman of the Association, an honor in itself that I have thought — though I had no actual proof — Mr. Gibbons was chiefly responsible for. Mr. and Mrs. Gibbons invited me to their home for the evening of July 23, 1953, there to meet also their friends Mr. and Mrs. Hugh Rice. During the evening Mr. Gibbons referred to Mrs. Rice as an artist and remarked, in lighter vein, that he thought he had found a subject for her. A little later we all drove over to the Rice home, where Mr. Rice displayed, one after another, a number of his wife's paintings.

The purpose of the visit finally dawned upon me! Nan Rice was the artist and I was the potential subject for a portrait — the maneuvering of Stuart Gibbons had been most skillful. Would I consent to sit for a portrait, with the understanding that it would be the property of the artist and that I would be under no financial obligation? Really, if the artist and my friend Mr. Gibbons wished it, I could think of no valid reason for declining so generous an invitation.

Sittings were arranged at the home of the artist. In due time the portrait was completed. In the meantime it became possible for my three sons to see the painting — they were naturally interested. On the 8th of November the artist opened her house to a large number of guests, and my newly completed portrait occupied the place of honor among her paintings.

The inevitable question arose, where shall the painting hang? The answer seemed almost equally inevitable: if anywhere in Stockton, it must be at the College of the Pacific — such was the commonly expressed opinion. Finally, Mrs. Rice agreed that in case it should thus be disposed she would willingly donate to the College one-half the regular purchase price; and to guarantee its acquisition my three sons underwrote the purchase of the portrait.

The formal presentation to the College was set for the evening of March 19, 1954, as a feature of the Sixth Annual Institute of the California History Foundation. Mr. Gibbons was master of ceremonies, the artist took her appropriate place, and President Burns accepted the gift for the College. A particularly gratifying feature to me was that among the 150 persons present for the unveiling were my three sons, their wives, and at least a dozen other relatives. It was announced that the portrait would hang permanently in the California Room of the new Library Building.

The seventh and final year of my active service as Director of the California History Foundation was for me extraordinarily eventful. More honors came to me during the course of that year, I honestly believe, than during any other single year of my entire life. I think some of my good friends have concluded that I would prefer to have them express their kind thoughts toward me while I was still living amongst them, with my active interests and questing spirit, rather than to have them reserve all their sentiments for an appreciative obituary and sacred inscription upon my headstone.

If that is the case, their reasoning was correct. More than a few times, along the way, I have been pained to observe the absence of praise or just recognition for good men during their lifetime, who were earnestly striving for the common weal, contributing to the community life, but whose real virtues were not proclaimed till the day after death, or at the memorial service weeks later. I have thought, why not prize the music before the bird has flown? Not that I object to the roses on the casket — but orchids to the living may be even more beautiful.

On the reverse side of the coin, to speak metaphorically, I

have seen men of achievement, in a few cases, treat the honors that came to them with almost total lack of appreciation, almost contemptuously, as if to say, "Well, I earned it, didn't I — so what?" Such a blasé attitude of ingratitude is, I think, as unworthy of a man as the lack of recognition of the special merit of another while, or because, he is yet living.

Again, the recipient of high honors may sincerely feel his lack of worthiness, but he should at least show by word and demeanor that in accepting the accolade he is truly grateful and at the same time of humble spirit. Failure to express appreciation of an honor or award sincerely bestowed reveals a dearth of some of their finer graces of life.

Some months before my eighty-sixth birthday my faithful friend, Stuart Gibbons, in a casual manner requested me to hold the evening of February 3, 1954 open. I of course had no idea of his real purpose at the time. Nor was I admitted into the secret until very close to the actual date, when it became necessary to advise me of the plan.

Then it was revealed to me that a birthday party had been arranged for me in the Empire Room of the Hotel Stockton. And, only a few days before the actual date I learned that I was to be honored at the birthday party by being publicly proclaimed by Governor Goodwin J. Knight, as "Mr. California."

The evening program, following the sumptuous dinner, was participated in by the Mayor of Stockton and its City Council, the Chamber of Commerce, the Grand Parlors of the Native Sons and Native Daughters of the Golden West, while the Honorable Joseph R. Knowland of Oakland officially represented the Governor, who had sent his personal regrets at being unable to attend. Mr. Gibbons, who was in general charge of the program, read telegrams of congratulation from the Chief Justice of the Supreme Court Earl J. Warren, U. S. Senators William F. Knowland and

Thomas Kuchel, Chancellor Rufus B. von KleinSmid, and others.

The high point of the occasion was reached when Mr. Knowland, for the Governor, presented me with a beautiful scroll which reads —

> In recognition of his outstanding contribution to California life through his teachings and writings and of the many years he has devoted in service to his native state in various capacities, I hereby name

DR. ROCKWELL DENNIS HUNT

MR. CALIFORNIA

> *Goodwin J. Knight*
> Governor of California
> Stockton, California, February 3, 1954

[*Signed also by*]
  Leslye A. Hicks
    Grand Pres. N.D.G.W.
  Philip C. Wilkins
    Grand Pres. N.S.G.W.
  J. R. Knowland
    Pres. California Historical Society

The official signature of the governor was affixed to the Proclamation at a later date in his executive office at Sacramento, in my presence, and the great seal of the state was affixed to the document.

Such an honor, totally unlike any previous experience, unique in the history of California, was almost overwhelming. I made such grateful response as I could in the presence of the 130 friends who had gathered for the occasion. I deemed it fitting to outline the traits and characteristics of the true Californian, referring to him as long-lived and versatile, a prudent conservationist, and I said finally, "The true Californian is virile, abounding in life, the spirit of youth singing in his heart, as his boasted State, though now well into her second century, is still young and strong and unafraid, pressing ever onward and upward to higher and better things."

In the presence of my friends I concluded my remarks with these words:

> I pledge my faithful allegiance and undying affection to my native state, "Land of Heart's Desire," "Terrestrial Paradise," "California the Golden." Long may she flourish as a shining beacon on a hilltop, giving light even to the ends of the earth. And with the lengthening of days may she never cease to grow in wisdom and in virtue. May we, her grateful children, enter fully into our precious heritage from the past, ever increasing in nobility of thought and deed, because of our dedication and consecration. My California—I shall never cease to love thee, for thou art mine!

To render the proclamation still more impressive and greatly to aid to the honor bestowed, the California Legislature later unanimously adopted Senate Concurrent Resolution No. 5— "Relative to Congratulating Dr. Rockwell Dennis Hunt on his being named 'Mr. California'." The text is as follows:

> *Whereas*, Dr. Rockwell Dennis Hunt, scholar, educator, and author has been proclaimed "Mister California" by Governor Goodwin J. Knight in recognition of his outstanding contributions to California; and
>
> *Whereas*, Dr. Hunt so richly deserves this title in view of the many years he has devoted to educating the sons and daughters of this State, and in view of his magnificent achievements in setting forth the dramatic history of California for all to see; and
>
> *Whereas*, Dr. Hunt, born in the City of Sacramento in the year 1868, early established his brilliance as a scholar, having earned his Bachelor of Philosophy Degree from Napa College in 1890 and his Doctor of Philosophy Degree from Johns Hopkins University in 1895, and has had conferred upon him the honorary degree of doctor of laws by the College of the Pacific and the honorary degree of doctor of literature by the University of Southern California; and
>
> *Whereas*, Dr. Hunt's long and devoted service as an educator dates from the year 1891 with his becoming a professor at Napa College

and has included such positions as principal of the San José High School, professor of history and political science at the University of the Pacific, member of the faculty of the University of Southern California for 37 years, and, for 25 years, Dean of the Graduate School of that university, and

Whereas, Doctor Hunt, through his authorship of numerous books and articles on the history of California and Californians, has made an invaluable contribution to the greatness of our State and to the spreading of its fame throughout the world; and

Whereas, Dr. Hunt continues to add to this remarkable career of service and study by serving as Director of the California History Foundation at the College of the Pacific; and

Whereas, the people of California are truly indebted to this native son for services outstandingly rendered; now, therefore,

Resolved, by the Senate of the State of California, the Assembly thereof concurring, That the members of the Legislature welcome this opportunity to congratulate Dr. Rockwell Dennis Hunt on his being proclaimed 'Mister California' and commend him for the long and distinguished record of contributions he has made to his native State; and be it further

Resolved, that the Secretary of the Senate is hereby directed to have a suitably engrossed copy of this resolution delivered to Dr. Rockwell Dennis Hunt.

The resolution, adopted by the Senate March 18, 1954 and by the Assembly March 31, 1954, is signed by Harold J. Powers, President and J. A. Beeks, Secretary of the Senate, and James W. Silliman, Speaker, and Arthur A. Ohnimus, Chief Clerk of the Assembly.

I am happy to make grateful acknowledgment to Senator Verne W. Hoffman from the Twentieth Senatorial District, for he it was who introduced the resolution, and to Mr. Stuart C. Gibbons of Stockton, whom I must designate chief instigator. Being a native of Sacramento, capital of the state, I had long made the claim that I was neither a northerner nor a southerner but a native of the entire state! I had never dreamed of such a validation of my claim as came to me when on my eighty-sixth birthday I was proclaimed by the Governor as "Mr. California."

When I returned to the College of the Pacific in my eightieth year to become Director of the California History Foundation, Dean Bogardus, my successor at the University of Southern California, suggested, "Now you are a freshman once again." Three years later I contributed an article to the Southern California *Alumni Review* entitled, "Now I'm a Senior — and Glad of It." This brought from Dr. Bogardus a new statement: "May your 'senior' year be your best so far, and may you be laying plans for post-graduate years, at least three of them." I did continue three more years, though they were not all planned in advance.

For quite a while I felt myself as somewhat a stranger on the Pacific campus, as if I might be viewed as an obtruder, at times a bit uncomfortable because of self-consciousness as I passed the throngs of young undergraduates, wondering if they thought me an interloper. But gradually the feeling of aloofness — which really stemmed from a trait of my own personality — wore away, and was finally supplanted by a wholesome sense of belonging.

That I was in truth living in a different world may be illustrated by two or three incidents. One day on the campus I was modestly accosted by a young lady student — the following conversation took place: "Are you Dr. Hunt?" On making due acknowledgment: "My grandfather told me he was one of your students when you taught at San José." "What was your grandfather's name?" "Mr. Griggs." "Ernest Griggs?" "Yes, that is his name." "I remember him well: he became a Methodist preacher." "Yes, grandfather retired as a clergyman years ago — he is still living in San José."

Not long afterward I made it a point to call on Griggs in his home where we enjoyed a friendly visit together: he was a

Pacific alumnus of the Class of 1899. Not very long afterward I learned that he had departed this life.

Another of my older students is Chris L. Petersen, who, as I write, lives with his wife on his lovely hillside ranch near the town of Calistoga, at the head of Napa Valley. On several occasions I have enjoyed their hospitality there. Chris, an alumnus of the class of 1900, now in his eighties, is the father of seven sons and daughters, all grown to maturity, and is the proud grandfather of at least nineteen grandchildren and ten great-grandchildren. When he announced the birth of his first great-grandchild, I suggested that the *pater familias* bring him to the college reunion in June, 1951 as Exhibit A! And I was Chris Peterson's teacher!

In 1953 I was requested to have a part in the funeral services of Mrs. N. M. Parsons of Oakdale. She had been Helen Beck, one of my students at old Pacific, in San José, graduating in 1902. She married another of my students, Marvin Parsons, alumnus of 1902, and their seven sons and daughters have now reached middle life. The family holds the record for attendance at the College of the Pacific, since both parents and all of the children are graduates, having amassed a total attendance for the family of fifty years. Running second to the Parsons was the family of Dr. and Mrs. Knoles, of seven children, all graduates at Pacific — but the parents cannot claim that distinction.

Incidents and observations such as those just noted might readily be multiplied — they all tend to bring me to the conclusion that, while not myself a forty-niner, nor even a centenarian, I must be a patriarch in my commonwealth, though I would dislike being called "venerable," and the term "aged" would be still more unwelcome.

It is always difficult to evaluate the imponderable — quite impossible, I would say, in many cases. For example, how is the influence of a sermon, or a poem, or a serious book, to be measured? One may have a certain "feeling," or possibly make a shrewd guess, but I know of no scientifically contrived standard that can be applied to reach accurate quantitative results.

Fully aware of this difficulty, I still may venture the personal opinion that some of the most valuable and widely influential work I have accomplished, or service rendered, during my seven-year period with the College at Stockton was in the form of the printed page, that is, in my books and articles. When something is actually in print, it assures an element of permanency that cannot otherwise be guaranteed. For years I have had the desire to see the best products of my thinking and my researches put into print: when the book or article finally appears in suitable format, then I can say, that is now done!

During my seven active years at the College of the Pacific six books of my authorship were published. Concerning them a single paragraph about each will suffice. First, there was *California Ghost Towns Live Again*, a small volume, with Foreword by President Robert E. Burns, whose brief chapters afford easy reference to the area of the Southern Mines, or "Mother Lode Country" with its mining centers in gold-rush days. Most of the lively centers became "ghost towns" following the decline in gold mining: but much interest again centered in them in connection with the California centennials, 1948-1951.

Another small volume, *California Vignettes*, also published in 1948, brings together nineteen short pieces that had been written at different times, most of them having previously appeared in the Los Angeles *Times* or other periodical. The little book is intended as a humble tribute to my own pioneer parents and as an expression of my love for my native state.

California's Stately Hall of Fame was published in 1950. The rather large volume contains 104 biographical essays of notable

Californians, besides an introductory essay, a carefully selected bibliography for each character, and complete index. With only two or three exceptions, portraits accompany the respective essays. I may confess that the preparation of this book required considerable temerity on my part: for who am I that I should dare to select the list of Californians meriting inclusion in our Hall of Fame? I fortified myself at one point by stating that no person living at the time of the writing could be given a place. My simple claim was that the list "is broadly representative of California's fascinating, many-sided history."

In 1951 a companion volume to *California Vignettes* was published under the title *A Vintage of Vignettes.* This is a collection of twenty-one short pieces written at various times over a period of almost sixty years, including my graduating student oration at Napa in 1890, and a concluding selection, "Eighty is Just a Number." Some of the pieces reveal my deep interest in universal principles of morality.

The *History of the College of the Pacific* was written "in commemoration of the one hundredth anniversary of its founding." I had urged the preparation of such a volume as an appropriate feature of the celebration, but was reluctant, for what seemed obvious reasons, to undertake the task myself. It was only after it was pressed upon me, that, because of my student days and graduation at Napa College, my seven-year period of teaching at San José, my long association as an alumnus, and my current position as Director of the California History Foundation, that I was the logical person to write the history, that I finally consented to undertake the rather formidable task. Having reached the decision, however, I entered upon the work wholeheartedly; and with the cooperation and encouragement of kind friends I was able to produce the volume in time for the Centennial Celebration, in 1951.

California in the Making is the title of a volume published in

1953, being a collection of twenty-three of my historical essays and papers that had appeared in various publications over a long period, thus brought together to render them more accessible to the reader. Practically all of the chapters are concerned with events and personalities of the American period of California history. I am of the opinion that a true perspective demands major emphasis on the period following the acquisition of California by the United States from Mexico.

My other books, which made their appearance previous to the six just enumerated, are listed in order of publication in the appendix.

By this time it must be apparent that most of the books I have written deal, directly or indirectly, with the history of California. I have a strong affinity for the state; was born in its capital city; my parents were pioneers in it; my wife was a native daughter, and all four of our children, as well as my four brothers, were native sons. I have been in all fifty-eight of our counties, looked upon the more than seven natural wonders of the commonwealth, camped in the heart of the Sierra, spent my early boyhood on the Hunt Ranch, lived in our largest cities and visited the ghost towns of an earlier day. Perhaps the reader will understand my affinity for California and agree that I have not chosen unwisely when I chose *California the Golden* as a favorite book title.

In addition to the books, something like 200 articles of mine, some of them very brief and unimportant, have made their appearance in various periodicals other than newspapers, in which a still larger number of pieces have appeared. A partial list of titles of published articles appears at the end of this volume.

An experienced administrator of my acquaintance recently remarked, "I just can't write." My reply to him was, "I just can't stop writing!" The force of my reply will be more apparent when I add that I now have in mind at my age, at least four or five more books that I would like to write, but not all of which I can hope ever to complete.

To illustrate this remark, I would like to complete a book for children — most of the material is at hand — on the boyhood days of the five Hunt brothers on the banks of the Sacramento back in the 1870's. This story from real life would be for the boys and girls of today a description of how the children of real pioneers lived and what they did on a ranch in early California.

Another project, one that has intrigued me for a long time, is the preparation of an attractive California birthday book, which should be a beautiful volume, artistically and appropriately embellished, with quotations in poetry and prose from California authors. At the end should be an appendix briefly identifying each author quoted.

A third book, one that may actually be completed soon, would be a volume on significant firsts in California. I have now a considerable collection of data: the subject, I think, holds real fascination. This should not be a mere dictionary of dates, or a skeleton cyclopedia: it should possess readable quality along with essential factual material. In its entirety the volume would embody important segments of the history of the commonwealth.

For the most of the books I have written, appropriate dedications have been made. First of these appeared *California the Golden*, published first in 1911 (later, in rewritten edition, a required state school textbook), dedicated to our two older sons, Paul Adams Hunt and Lloyd Freeman Hunt; *California a Little History of a Big State*, a book for young children, published in 1931, is dedicated to our first grandchildren, Dorothy-May Hunt and Paula Theresa Hunt; I was happy to dedicate *John Bidwell, Prince of California Pioneers*, published in 1942, to "My Pioneer Parents"; *California Vignettes*, which appeared in 1948, is dedicated to the memory of my wife, "N.S.H."; and to our youngest son, Clarence Stuart Hunt, is dedicated *A Vintage of Vignettes*, published in 1951.

Of the other volumes, *California, the State Everybody Loves* (1935), is dedicated to the San Francisco Branch of the National League of American Pen Women; *California's Stately Hall of Fame* (1950), bears the dedication "To the Commonwealth of California, My Native State"; *History of the College of the Pacific* (1951), to "The Founding Fathers"; the dedication of *California in the Making* (1953), reads:

To the
COLLEGE OF THE PACIFIC
with which
The author has been identified
as
Student, Teacher, Director, Historian
through
Many Happy Years
with
Steadfast Loyalty and Sincere Affection

Most of my writing in the field of economics and the social sciences has been in the form of articles and essays. In the quarterly periodical *World Affairs Interloper* alone, edited by Willet L. Hardin, at the University of Southern California, nearly a score of articles have appeared, beginning in 1933. Some of the topics discussed are "Economics of Welfare Today and Tomorrow," "In Praise of Democracy," "The Moral Foundations of Economics," "In Search of Human Welfare," and "Quest for Plenty." All are intended to have international significance; taken together they might be ample material for another published book.

As an avenue of expression, also in a small way as a factor in the formation of public opinion, I have on numerous occasions written letters on current issues that appealed to me, for the public forum of newspapers. These might be referred to in a general way under the heading "We, the People." Portions of three letters will afford a hint as to their scope and nature. Concerning the agitation for loyalty oaths I wrote the *San Francisco Chronicle*:

> It is passing strange that our legislators, both in Sacramento and Washington, should spend so much time and energy in this matter of loyalty oaths ... I think they would be better advised to grapple with global changes and soberly recognize the place of world leadership thrust upon our nation, with the heavy responsibilities thereby imposed. Why spend endless fruitless endeavor trying to trap a mouse while a pack of ferocious wolves is at the gate of the sheepfold? ...
>
> The big changes that have taken place in recent years cannot be wished away; nor can our petty industriousness in our own little yard stem the tide of vast changes sweeping in from abroad. We must lift our sights to gain a true perspective and reach a world view. ...

In the same paper I had this to say regarding liquor and politics:

> The allegation that "too many governmental decisions have been reached at cocktail parties" seems to be quite generally admitted. Then what?
>
> The answer is, it's time for a change. There has been a great outcry against the unmitigated evil of drunken driving. ... But by what logic can one claim that driving an automobile while under the influence of alcohol is dangerous and against public policy, and at the same time defend drinking by those who are legislating for the general welfare? If drink makes the driver muddleheaded, by the same token does it not make the lawmaker muddleheaded? ...
>
> I applaud the stand of Governor Theodore McKeldin of Maryland, who lets it be known that he not only personally abstains from alcoholic drink, but that he never serves liquor in the Maryland executive mansion.

After an inspiring visit to the South Grove of the Calaveras Big Trees, recently acquired by the state and designated as a State Park, I had this to say in the Stockton *Record* and several other papers:

> I have seen the glory of the Grove. And what a sight for the eye of

mortal man! No adjective can express the majesty of the mighty trees, symbol of strength and immortality....

With President Stuart Gibbons and a group of ardent associates, ... I have just visited the South Grove, ... with stops at the "Agassiz," the "Palace Hotel," and other towering masters of the forest. I saw them as the shining sunlight played upon the delicate sheen of their clear reddish pink columns. There they stand—simply standing there in their gentle power, defying the storms of the ages.

But other trees there are in nature's grove—thousands of them— adding to the richness and variety of the forest. Chief among these I place the sugar pine, my favorite of all the pines.... The great round stately shaft of this princely tree always inspires; and never have I seen such an abundance and profusion of the gracefully suspended cones, high up above the beautiful dogwood and the delicate plant life carpeting the soft soil—altogether a vision of ravishing beauty when silhouetted against the azure sky.... It was a glorious day— how could I ever forget it? Never had I been so enamored of the trees of my native California.

Since my early student days I have always had an urge — sometimes almost a passion — to write things down, and in later years to get them into print. Vanity, perhaps, in part; but always a desire for permanency — to write *finis* after an article, or a book. As the old Scotch schoolmaster said: "Get it down. If it stays in your head it'll never be anything." Or as Hubert Howe Bancroft groaned, in the midst of his overwhelming task: "Whoever has lived, laboring under the terrible pressure of *cacoethes scribendi* without promising himself to write a dozen books for every one accomplished!" There's much yet to be done — I'd like to have an honorable part in it.

As I look back over the long list of articles I have contributed to different periodicals, some of them very slight and inconsequential, I feel that the most presumptuous of them all was what I titled "Ninety-Five Theses for These Times," which appeared in *World Affairs Interpreter* for the spring of 1943, four and a quarter centuries after Martin Luther affixed his epoch-making ninety-five theses on the church door at Wittenberg, thus signalizing the beginning of the religious revolution known in history as the Protestant Reformation.

I realized that it was bold to the point of audacity for me to employ such a title; but two considerations led me on: for many years I had been a great admirer of Luther's character, one of my favorite fields in college teaching being the period of the Reformation, and I felt impelled to emulate his method, though in a modified manner. The other consideration was my firm belief in the interdependence of the so-called social sciences and the necessity for moral and spiritual undergirding throughout.

My theses, or propositions, were arranged under ten sub-heads, as follows: Historical, Economic, Political, Social, Psychological, Educational, Moral, Religious, Rôle of the United States, and Synthesis. They were formulated as a result of my own study and reflection—a series of propositions to be defended, but not to be thought of as dogmatic or necessarily definitive. The final section includes nine propositions. Of these I reproduce three here:

> There can be no single, immediate solution to the complex world problems. Special study by experts and men of good will must be given to each main group of questions and to the possibilities of applying their findings to the well being of society.
>
> The pursuit of purely selfish ends to be achieved through strife between individuals or factions, blocks, or fronts, whether in private business or in public life, must be superseded by the practical application of the spirit of mutuality, of the common good of all.
>
> There is ample ground today for faith in the ultimate triumph of the principles of social justice, the exaltation of human freedom, and the enthronement of character.

Not infrequently I have been asked the question, "Which of your books have you found the most pleasure in writing? Which has been the most satisfying to you?" The question can hardly be answered categorically. But I may honestly say that from a personal point of view, none of my books brought me more pleasure in the writing than the biography, *John Bidwell, Prince of California Pioneers.*

Two special reasons go far in accounting for this preference; first, my great and sincere admiration for Bidwell's character; second, my own personal acquaintance with this remarkable California pioneer of 1841 during his last years. When we sat together on the piazza of the Bidwell Mansion on Rancho Chico and he told me of the very early days of California while I diligently took notes, history was made audible to me.

Even before his death in 1900 the General knew I had become interested in writing his autobiography; he had thought of providing financial aid to make this possible. But in the end I was pleased that the book, published years afterward, had not been subsidized by either General Bidwell or his wife, Annie Kennedy Bidwell. I was happy to write freely and independently, without the slightest financial consideration from the family. It was deeply gratifying to put on record the story of John Bidwell, Prince of California Pioneers.

On my retirement in 1945 as dean of the Graduate School and professor of economics, I presented the bulk of my collection of books on economics and other social sciences to the University, having had my book-plate affixed in each volume.

The book-plate, drawn by Anthony Euwer, bears a composition design, distinctly Californian. When I explained to the artist the main features I wished to have included, he remarked, "I have never tried to place so many things in a book-plate before." At the top of the drawing is the old English crest of the Hunt Family, including the motto, *"Semper Fidelis."* The mountain peak symbolizes Mt. Shasta, my favorite mountain, from whose base meanders the Sacramento River through grassy meadows, and above whose shoulders appear a soaring eagle and an airplane.

Other natural features represented include the giant sequoias, a spray of California poppies, a mountain quail, and two deer under an oak tree, with large ferns at their feet. Below, on the right, is a clipper ship — since my father came by vessel to California by way of the Isthmus — and on the left the caravan of covered wagons — since my mother came on a "prairie schooner." Near the bottom is a six-horse stage coach, typifying the method of travel in early days. Indicating my interest in world affairs there is a globe of the world, just back of which is a row of books suggesting my chief fields of study: Economics, Politics, Religion, Sociology, History, Philosophy. Finally, at the left center appears a copy of the seal of the University of Southern California, while opposite to this is the great seal of the state of California.

My collection of Californiana and Western Americana includes more than 1,000 volumes, of which about 100 may be classified as rare or special editions, and some hundreds of pamphlets. I make mention of a few books, which to me have special sentimental value. My copy of *The Annals of San Francisco* (published in 1855), a beautiful morocco edition with gilded leaves, still bears my father's autograph, in pencil, "D. R. Hunt, Oneida Valley, Sacramento Co.," with a further inscription, "Presented to P. J. Hunt [my uncle] by D. R. Hunt, Hamilton [New York] March 23d, 1866." My copy of the *Memoirs of Cornelius Cole, Ex-Senator of the United States from California* (published 1908) is inscribed to me in the Senator's handwriting: "To Prof. R. D. Hunt, with cordial greetings, From C. Cole, scribe. Nov. 2d, 1910," followed by these words: "Should you deign to cut the leaves you may observe some errata of the printer, and a few oversights of the author." My personal acquaintance with this great pioneer enhances the value of the volume to me. I have a copy of H. H. Bancroft's *Retrospection* (published 1915) on the fly-leaf of which the author wrote: "Dr. Rockwell D. Hunt, with the kind regards of Hubert Howe Bancroft." My copy of

Sierran Pan and Other Poems, by the second poet-laureate of California (published 1922), bears the author's inscription, "To Rockwell D. Hunt, from his friend of many and many a day, Henry Meade Bland. Nov. 26, 1928." Below this the poet wrote:

> No matter where the high way tends
> Be sure the Journey never ends.

CHAPTER TWELVE

MOUNTAINS

More than once I have been asked, "What is your hobby?" No better answer has occurred to me than: "The Mountains of California." As a very young boy on the Freeport farm, I knew practically nothing about mountains: I could see the great Sierra Nevada range far off to the east; but I was a complete stranger to the snow-crowned peaks.

That has long since been changed. For most of my life the mountains have been among my best friends. I cultivated their acquaintance through camping trips, the first being when I was a boy of twelve. My experience in the mountain camp I deem to have been of such significance in my life as a whole that something more than casual mention of it must be recorded here. But quite obviously it is impossible to attempt anything approaching a detailed narration of my numerous trips.

My first real camping trip, memorable since it was the first, occurred when I was a mere lad. A family group, with father at the head, in charge of the horses and wagon, and mother as camp cook—her chief utensil being an old-fashioned "Dutch Oven," started north from Napa, in the summer of 1880, continued through Lake County and into Mendocino County, in the region of Mt. Sanhedrin, a dozen miles north of Potter Valley, until we came to Mr. Garcey's ranch, at the base of a perilously steep grade of about two miles. It was all interesting to me—everything seemed so novel. But I remember especially my first primitive fishing for mountain trout and gathering a can-full of pine nuts. I was considered too young to handle a shot-gun.

On the second trip, however, in July, 1885, I did considerable shooting, but killed no game larger than the grey squirrel and the jack rabbit. But I also shot my first rattlesnake. Again it was a family party, but with partial change in personnel. In Berryessa Valley we came to the ranch of Caleb Gosling, a friend of the family, where we camped for two or three days under some large oak trees. Games were played in the evening with the Gosling girls; but I was too shy to get full enjoyment — a condition that made me feel rather "sheepish."

Passing through the town of Monticello we made camp in lower Pope Valley. For part of the way, the road was terrible, simply execrable! — no work had been done on it since the winter storms. But father was an excellent driver. Passing through Middletown, along Clear Lake, and on to the north, we came to Seth Dunham's ranch, near Cummings, and there camped, where we were given free access to his berry patch and peach crop. Points that were especially attractive were Eden Falls, Bloody Chasm, and Jeff Davis and Lincoln Rocks.

Returning home, we went by way of Napa Valley, passing through the towns of Calistoga, St. Helena, and Yountville. I had begun to feel well acquainted with the mountains of Napa, Lake, and Mendocino Counties.

I must say something about my first visit to Yosemite Valley. This was in June, 1892; and it was seeing the marvels of Yosemite at their best. We were three brothers — my older brother Mark, younger brother George, and I, all young men of vigor and spirit. Mark, in addition to having charge of the horses and wagons, was made chief cook; George and I filled in wherever needed.

After we passed Elk Grove, Galt, and Woodbridge, the first night's camp was at the Treadway ranch near Lodi, where the evening was pleasantly spent in their home. Orvis, Sylvester,

Belle, and Susie — all these young Treadways had been students at Napa College. The second night we camped in the yard of the fruit farm of Daniel S. Stuart, near Oakdale. This was even more delightful for me, for here was the home of my Nancy, in whom, by that time, I had come to have a very special interest!

We passed through Chinese Camp, crossed the beautiful Tuolumne River, came to the long, steady pull of two miles up Priest's Hill — George and I of course walked up all the steep grades. It was the morning of June 18 when we caught sight of El Capitan and Ribbon Fall and entered the Valley: and a wonderful week it was that followed.

We pitched our tent near Royal Arches, not far from Three Brothers. Being three we gave the place the classic name *"Camp Tres Fratres."* We even had souvenir cards printed, with names and date, June 20, 1892, at the little print shop. Our first view from Glacier Point is unforgettable — the lovely Valley below, the towering mountain just across, Vernal, Nevada, and other captivating waterfalls at their very best, in plain view. Then commanding South Dome, and beyond, there stood Cloud's Rest, Liberty Cap, and the snow-crowned Sierras to complete the picture.

Grand, also, was the view from Sentinel Dome. We felt wonderful! Climbing up into the lonesome Jeffrey pine tree alone there on Sentinel Dome, we sang the Doxology and gave the college yell for dear old Napa! Then we did not walk down — we ran! It was an easy trail of about a mile and a quarter to Glacier Point, with a few patches of thin snow. When we reached McCauley's little hotel, I looked at my watch and found that we had covered the distance in seven and a quarter minutes. "Come in and register," urged the inn-keeper: "that beats the record from Sentinel Dome."

Homeward bound, we had dinner at Tamarack Flat, passed Gin Flat and Crane Flat, then pitched our tent at Crocker's.

After that last breakfast in the mountains, George and I took the one large-size left-over flapjack, and with hammer and ten-penny nail, fastened it securely to a large pine tree, leaving it there for the wood-peckers to work at during the following winter! Mark had done a good job as chief cook. At five o'clock in the afternoon of July 1 we were back at the Freeport farm, almost sorry to be home so soon.

It would be unforgivable not to mention my short camping trip of 1893; for that was shortly before my departure for Baltimore to enter Johns Hopkins University as a graduate student, and — what is particularly memorable — a member of that particular little party was none other than Nancy Stuart, after we had exchanged our vows as lovers. The others were my brother Mark, his wife Susie, and their little boy Ray. Again Mark was the driver, in full charge of the horses and spring wagon. The cooking was better than ordinary — Susie was in command. The tent was for Susie and Nancy: Mark and I slept under the stars.

It was a visit to marvelous Lake Tahoe, which must always rank high among the Seven Natural Wonders of California. There were not so many visitors at the lake in 1893. Our camp at Tallac, at the edge of the lake, under the tall pine trees, was a quiet, restful place: there was no need for hurry while she and I sat, alone, out at the end of the little pier, while the silver moon cast its soft beams all about, and we two dreamed of days and years ahead. There was no need for hurry then!

What we saw multitudes have seen by now. The one event I remember best was our climb to the summit of Mt. Tallac, by Nancy, Henry Tillman (who had joined us at the Lake), and myself. We had a single pony, which Nancy and Henry took turns in riding — I walked all the way. The sight from the mountain-top was entrancing.

Too soon the trip was ended; but forgotten never. I must make preparations for the new adventure in Baltimore, leaving California in time to spend a week in Chicago, viewing the great Columbian Exposition, in 1893.

It was in the summer of 1910 that I took my longest hike: this was in the San Bernardino Mountains, and it lasted two weeks. I had joined the faculty of the University of Southern California in 1908, and to that time had found little opportunity to be in the mountains.

The party consisted of Professor A. Harvey Collins of the University of Redlands, Professor Shepardson of the Los Angeles State Normal School, Mr. Shirey, a business man, and myself, with our son Paul, then fourteen years old. It was his parents' hope that the experience would strengthen Paul's lung and prove beneficial to his health. At Mentone we packed three gentle burros we had hired to carry our luggage and provisions. Soon we were on the way up the slopes of Mt. San Gorgonio — "Grayback," as it is commonly called — the highest mountain of Southern California.

Never had I seen the stars so brilliant as from our first night's camp at High Creek — we seemed to be in a different world. The ashen gray of the mountain side, under the light of the stars was a weird sight to behold.

Within a twenty-four hour period I was at the summit of Gorgonio three times. Failing to find the side trail leading down to Dry Lake on the north, we too hastily decided, after a careless look at the rocky slope down to the lake, which was in full view, to break our own trail down the steep treeless mountain-side. Then our troubles began. The loose shell rocks made the footing insecure, and the pitch was so steep as to make tacking, or switch-backing, necessary. I went on ahead to break a path for the others with the laden burros. The main problem was to keep the pack animals upright.

Soon a distress signal came from Collins, whose burro had taken a fall, causing the professor to execute a plunging football maneuver to prevent the poor creature from rolling down hill. I started back in haste, but found I could not run up that steep mountain side at an elevation of 11,000 feet. We got the burro onto its feet and started again. Within an hour, a second burro lost balance and toppled over.

By that time we had completely lost sight of the lake below us, and the loose rocks were larger and larger as we descended. Twice the amount of time we had thought sufficient was already gone, and the way ahead looked more and more forbidding. We began to wonder just where we were, and what next? Some of the rocks were now as big as street-cars, and there were deep crevices between them. Here and there was a scrub pine, clinging to the rocks, its branches able to rise only a few feet above them. And the afternoon was all but gone.

Then came the crisis. The third burro lost footing, plunged headlong over the rock and turned almost a complete somersault. A broken back was probably prevented by the stout oaken crossbars of the pack saddle. "No use," we agreed; "we stop right here for the night." And that is what we did, all the more melancholy since we had only a quart of water in the canteen and knew not when or how we might obtain more.

How we spent the night, where there was not a square foot of level space for a bed, while the disconsolate burros stood, each on the top of a huge boulder, must be left to the imagination. About one o'clock I tried to get some sleep. Then the moon came up, making the mountain-side almost as light as day. About four o'clock a burro began his canary aria, with raucous vocalization, *fortissimo, accelerando, molto, molto!* Sleep? There was none to be had!

Slight exploration in the morning revealed to our delighted surprise that we were within seventy yards of a running brook of clear water, just over a slight ridge; also that from the ridge placid Dry Lake was in plain sight, less than a quarter of a mile away! As if by magic our troubles had vanished.

Then came the most amusing incident of the entire hike. The burros were led to the brook under the natural assumption that they were famished for water. Professor Collins was so sure it was water — and not feed — that his burro most needed that when the poor "critter" began to crop the luscious grass in preference, the learned professor inflicted a light blow upon it with a willow bough in a spirit of impatience! But he learned a lesson from the humble burro — he found that it knew best what it wanted! The second most amusing thing was at the expense of Professor Shepardson, most of whose students in Normal School were demure young ladies. He had cultivated a gentle modulation of voice in addressing them: naturally he applied his gentle, modulated voice to his burro, named "Cuba." Now pack animals are proverbially as slow as the traffic permits. When Cuba was inclined to lag behind, Shepardson mildly expostulated with rising inflection, "Cuba, Cuba, a little faster"; but to no effect. The professor tried once more, with a little more firmness, and falling inflection; "Move along, Cuba, Cuba." Still no effect. Then the polite, soft-hearted professor forgot his politeness and broke the rules of elocution and voice culture, as he fairly stormed with high stentorian voice that would do credit to the roughest muleskinner, "CUBA!" Cuba understood — and moved.

It was a good hike. We did a little fishing, a deal of climbing, visiting cosily situated Dollar Lake, the three summits of Mt. San Bernardino, Big Bear Lake, and other points, finally returning by another route and down Clark's Grade to our starting point, and then to our respective homes. It remains only to be said that because there was no razor kit, when I was greeted by Nancy at the door she refused to kiss me until I had shaved — which was not long afterward!

It was in August, 1916, that I made my first acquaintance with the mountains of Tuolumne County, as a guest of my brother-in-law Arthur ("Doc") Stuart, who had established a well-equipped camp at Cow Creek, adjoining the Ranger's headquarters for that area (Camp 31 on the Stanislaus Forest Reserve). From Stockton, Cow Creek is reached by way of Knight's Ferry, Jamestown, Twain Harte, Long Barn, and Strawberry.

The camp, called "Camp Sunshade," had its full quota of saddle horses and pack mules. Everything was arranged for comfort and relaxation — snug little cabins, excellent beds, ample supply of good food. The creek, fairly well stocked with trout, flowed right by the camp. It was a rare treat to spend days and nights at Camp Sunshade; and the master of the camp loved to entertain his relatives and friends there, but had nothing to sell.

Doc was eager to be off on the trail, mounted on "Blaze," his favorite horse, with binoculars and his trusty "meat-in-the-pot," up, up to Cooper Meadow, Ground Hog Meadow, and into the granite heart of the mountains. "Up there in the granite," he said, "you come close to the 'Old Man'; you're not tempted to cheat or graft, up there; there's no bell-hop with hand out for his tip; up there you're mighty near to the Creator."

Our week's camp in the higher altitudes began August 21, the party consisting of five persons, including cook and caretaker, each on his horse, with a total of four pack mules. We were equipped with pneumatic beds, but no tent — provisions were ample. There was time for everything — no hurry: *mañana, mañana.*

I did some fishing, with fair success, but did not succeed in bagging a buck. Varied experiences on the trail and in camp were met. Omitting all others, I must tell of one. Our camp that night was almost surrounded by steep mountain slope, with uneven terrain, fairly well forested. After carefully hobbling the horses Doc turned them loose to browse, believing they could not get far away from camp. In the morning they were not to be seen anywhere. A wider search failed to reveal their whereabouts. Then Doc himself, his good humor having deserted him, joined in the search and hiked laboriously up the mountainside. Finally, the horses were found, hobbles and all, at an old closed gate, so they could go no farther, several miles from camp! Doc had not thought it possible for his horses to make such a climb, with hobbles! He was infuriated — even threatened to take his six-shooter and kill his leading horse. However, he quickly became normal again when his son Everett quietly said, "The only trouble with you, dad, is that the horses have got more sense than you have."

The August thunderstorm in the mountains is an experience in itself; but we were also favored with a heavy hail storm in Louse Canyon.

Up to that time I had not become a coffee drinker: but when I joined my comrades in a cup for breakfast one morning, Doc remarked, "That's fine, Rocks; I believe if you'd stay out with us for a month, you might learn to swear."

My first visit to Cow Creek and the Tuolumne mountains came to an end with the month of August; but there were to be others; and for that I had reason to be glad.

Four years later (August 27 — September 9, 1920) I was again the guest of my brother-in-law Doc Stuart in the Tuolumne Mountains. Nancy was with me.

We became familiar with places like Bull Flat, Bumble Bee, Emigrant, Buck, Huckleberry, and Tin Can Lakes; we rode down the steep, rough trail to Hell's Half Acre, and through Louse Canyon; visited Coffin Hollow, Piute, Poison and Yellow-hammer Meadows; from many vantage points we viewed Granite Dome, Grizzly Peak, Haystack Mountain, Birth Rock and many another noble pile of Sierran granite.

During one of our side trips into the granite I had the thrilling experience of being in three separate mountain thunder storms within a twenty-four hour period. It was grand and glorious — and awesome. I have tried to describe the finale of the heavy artillery of the crashing thunder as "the decrescendo of retreating and distant roaring like the tumbling down of a vast avalanche of granite, booming, reverberating, and grudgingly settling into position, as if gathering its forces for a fresh onslaught."

One morning back in camp, after fishing for trout in Cow Creek, I accosted a young man with his rifle coming down the trail, carrying something in his red bandana. Surmising he had shot a deer, I asked him, what luck? "I didn't get a shot at a buck," he replied, "but I got forty rattlesnakes." "Forty!" I wondered. Then he explained he had found a den of snakes in a huge rock pile with its many crevices, and stated that he had killed several large snakes, and the others were baby snakes, many of them not yet born from the parents' bodies. He opened his bandana and displayed a mass of the tiny baby snakes, some of them still alive and wriggling. I was amazed. Then I remembered I had seen snakes' eggs in early boyhood — these were born directly from the mother's body: one mother yielded eight babies, he said. I was mystified. Then I learned something that was new to me. After returning home, I reported the experience to Dr. Samuel Rittenhouse, our professor of zoology, who informed me that there were "oviparous" snakes and "viviparous" snakes, and that the rattlesnake falls into the latter class.

I suppose every mule possesses its own idiosyncrasies. One of Doc Stuart's mules, called Miss Slim, had a well-marked trait that I have not seen in any other. As everyone knows, most of the higher mountain trails are very narrow; hence the riders and pack-mules must proceed single-file. It is usually desirable on certain rough trails to have the mules in a string hitched together by a strong rope, which assures steady travel and mutual support. But still another reason applied to this particular mule. For when she saw alongside the trail a cow in the pasture with her young calf Miss Slim seemed irresistibly urged to break rank, make for the cow and if possible drive her away from the calf which she herself tried rather pathetically to fondle or coddle between her own legs. I leave it to the mule expert to explain the phenomenon — call it hidden intuition, supressed instinct of motherhood, or what you will. I have at times thought of attempting an article on "The Idiosyncrasies of the Mule," but have never quite had the boldness to make the start!

It had been about twenty years since I had shot a deer, and that was near Seth Dunham's ranch, in the mountains of Mendocino County. Another chance came in the Sierra Nevada, in Tuolumne County, in 1918. I wondered whether it would again give me a thrill to bring down another buck after that lapse of time. I found out on Friday morning, August 16, 1918. It did.

I was enjoying an outing with my brother-in-law Doc Stuart at his well equipped camp on Cow Creek. In preference to going with Doc and Clay (his "buckaroo") to prospect Huckleberry Lake, I set out early and alone from our improvised camp on foot, in search of venison, ascending in a general way the canyon down which cascaded sprightly Cherry Creek.

For two or three hours I continued quietly up the mountain, at about a mile an hour, without catching sight of a buck. It was getting a little late to expect to find a deer feeding, when I stopped a moment, maybe sixty feet above the creek, looked across the ravine where there was a patch of green underbrush, and became suddenly excited as I clearly saw, a quarter of a mile away, a young buck that had been browsing. Immediately stepping behind a tree for concealment, for he had not seen me, I quickly thought out a plan of procedure.

I concluded it would be foolish to risk a shot from that

distance. In just a moment the deer made one or two easy jumps and disappeared from view. I surmised he had taken his "lay" for the day. Then it was I decided to make a grand sneak on him. Studying the rugged mountain side beyond the creek I located two definite objectives, the first a good-sized "tamarack" pine, one-third of the distance up from the creek-bed, the second a low clump of junipers another third up. I would make my way to these points.

The climb up the steep, rough granite, rifle in hand, was slow and difficult. I used every precaution to avoid making noise. My old diary tells what happened:

> At each objective I peered carefully in the direction I supposed the buck to be, but everything was quiet. Then I saw a granite rock a rod or so ahead, favorably situated, and determined to reach that objective. This done, I was looking eagerly about the brush near the two trees ... when I saw, standing in full view and about forty yards beyond where I had been looking, the buck, head high in air, looking in my direction. Within a few feet from him stood, in similar position, a smaller deer, probably a spike buck. I did not hesitate a second, but at once took aim at the larger deer and fired. One shot did the work. Immediately, I saw him pitch forward, I said to myself, "I've got him!" After one jump the smaller deer disappeared—I cared nothing for him. Saw the buck attempt to rise, but he fell back and slid down the little gully a few feet. I clambered up to him, saw him gasp once, then proceeded to "stick" him.

> The bullet could not have been better placed—through the lungs, just back of the shoulder, near the heart but not touching it. After taking out his entrails I secured heart, liver and kidneys and tied them up in my red bandana. Then I started a fire on a rotten tamarack nearby as a mark (the smoke to be a guide), and set out for camp for pack mule, placing "ducks" on the rocks, etc.

About 2:30 P.M. the cook and I reached camp with my young buck. When Doc returned he saw the fine forked-horn suspended from a tree; shouted "Rock's got a buck!" That evening we had a great supper — buck liver and bacon, raw onion, "cow-grease" (butter), "sore finger dough-gods" (bread), "French bog oranges" boiled potatoes, coffee, and prunes. Then off to bed by the great campfire. A résumé of our camp bill of fare, à la Doc Stuart, would include "sore finger dough-gods," "bog oranges," "condemned milk," "cow grease," "buckaroo stew," "embalmed horse," and "smoked hog."

But while in search of deer that morning I did not fail to observe something else. Let me mention three things that interested me. First was a beautiful male mountain quail guarding a big flock of little ones. When I came suddenly upon him he gave a quick slight note and in a few seconds every baby quail was perfectly hidden, while the parent bird remained perched on his granite boulder not more than twelve feet from me, risking his life for his young family.

At another place I almost stepped upon a fine porcupine, that appeared to be very tame, seeming not to care about getting out of my way. I threw stones at him just to see him clamber over the rocks.

Most beautiful of all was the scene that greeted my eyes at a well-shaded spot on the border of Cherry Creek — the loveliest, most queenly group of tiger lilies I have ever seen anywhere. Four stalks of them stood together about six feet tall, bearing respectively 19, 19, 18 and 17 blossoms, buds and seed pods. It was a regal, almost miraculous display of the superb work of nature, perhaps never seen by other human eyes. Other lovely lilies were standing round about, doing obeisance to the incomparable quartet.

Certain days stand out above others like Shasta above the surrounding mountains. Such a day was Tuesday, June 26, 1923. Nancy, our son Clarence, and I were enjoying a visit in Yosemite Valley. A part of the brief entry in my diary for that day runs as follows:

A perfect, wonderful day. After breakfast motored to Mirror Lake for sunrise—about 7:30. Brilliant reflection. Hiked on Tenaya Trail, then to river and up the beautiful cañon. Climbed up the tilted granite for view of beautiful waterfall, where river plunged into bowl-shaped pool and dashed up and out 40 to 60 feet. Lunch in shady place. Then back to auto and drive to Happy Isles—entrancing place amid rushing rivers for picnic and quiet.

Then took trail for Vernal Fall—...the mist and trail real sport—a good drenching coming and going. Wonderful cascades. Next on trail to Nevada Fall. Entrancing scene of surpassing beauty—gorgeous rainbow near base—what could be more lovely?

Decide to go to see the bears at garbage feed.... Full moon in perfect sky. Drove in near base of Yosemite Fall—queen of them all! ...to camp in time to hear the stentor call and see the brilliant Fire Fall from Glacier Point.

One of the best days ever for enjoyment of the wild beauties of nature—and California!

There existed between the Hunt brothers a strong fraternal bond. This applied with particular force to four of us, since my oldest brother Major married young and was away from the home center during much of my later childhood and youth. Our bond of brotherliness was strengthened and cemented partly by a round-robin letter — we called it the "Budget" — which we maintained for many years. For some time all five of us contributed, then for a briefer period after Major's death, in 1927 the remaining four, and for several years after the death of Frank, in 1929 we were three — Mark, George, and I.

Another bond that helped to preserve the family feeling is seen in the outings we enjoyed together in the mountains, though Major was not so situated that he could participate. I recall, for example, the summer of 1928, when we four brothers went by automobile over Tioga Pass, when the highway was far from today's perfection. Among other places we camped in Tuolumne Meadows, near Lake Tenaya. From an elevated point we obtained a different but attractive view of Yosemite, looking across and down upon Glacier Point and other features, from the east.

One of the most enjoyable outings we three younger brothers had was that of August, 1929, at Camp Number 80, of the Southern California Edison Company, in Vermilion Valley, on the bank of the beautiful, well-stocked trout stream. It was through the courtesy of the Edison Company, and that of my son Lloyd, an electrical engineer in their employ, that the beautifully located camp was made available to us.

First, we were guests at Big Creek Power House. There D. T. Redinger, District Engineer, took us on an instructive excursion through different power plants, then by Shaver Lake to Huntington Lake, where we were assigned a cottage as the Company's guests. At the hotel we were shown every courtesy by Mr. Williams, the manager.

The ride to Camp 80 on the specially equipped automobile over the narrow private road through the solid granite with its many curves and steep grades, was itself a rather thrilling experience. Saddle horses were ready for us to complete the trip to the actual lovely camp, at the base of Vermilion Cliffs. Never had we been in a more attractive, better equipped mountain camp.

No lack of trout there; and they were ideal for breakfast when served as we knew how. The "griddle-cakes" (no more flapjacks) that Mark prepared were masterpieces of four dimensions — the fourth being substantiality. On the esthetic side, I found about camp perhaps a dozen varieties of wild flowers, including Clarkia, larkspur, aquilegia, buttercup, aster, goldenrod, musk, and mimulus, with beautiful tiger lilies near-by. Among the birds were observed the crested jay, wood-pecker, black-headed snow bird, quail, hawk, and eagle. We had unusual opportunity to watch the eagles, as they soared aloft, so gracefully — indeed, this gave special pleasure to my brother George with his binoculars. Of the smaller animals there were numerous chipmunks, pine squirrels, and prairie dogs. Besides the willows along the creek the trees included two or three kinds of pine, the rugged juniper, quaking aspen, red fir, and some hemlock.

With the sunset glow striking the greenery and the bright-hued rocks and crags across the valley, the Vermilion Cliffs display marvelous coloring. And our situation was perfect for its full enjoyment. The luxury of Camp 80 was to us a unique experience. I am willing to forget my painful retreat from a too-near approach to a hornet's nest, even the intensely cold night spent without bed clothes at Mott Lake, and to remember the total delightsome stay in that lovely camp, in Vermilion Valley, as the guest of the Southern California Edison Company.

It was while we were in our mountain camp in July, 1931 that we three brothers (Mark, George, and I) enjoyed the experience of catching the beautiful golden trout, found only in a very limited area. Entering the high Sierras from the east, we proceeded on horseback over Bishop Pass, finally reaching our camping place on the Middle Fork of Kings River.

There was something of a thrill in serving ourselves those golden trout for breakfasct; but if we had been blindfolded we would have been unable to detect any difference from the more common rainbow variety. Little difficulty was experienced in catching the limit of the golden beauties. Our hikes on Muir Trail were another pleasurable experience of our outing in 1931. After about a fortnight, our man, as per previous arrangement, appeared on the scene with the saddle horses and the happy outing was soon at an end.

On several different occasions, I have got close to the heart of the Sierra — it is always inspiring. May I borrow some lines from one of my little *California Vignettes*:

The storm king displays his power in reverberating thunder, while his sceptre flashes dazzling lightning; anon old Sol shoots his super-ardent rays with a directness and intensity not to be denied; at night the starry heavens display the unspeakable glories of the firmament. The trees of the forest stand about in mysterious and awe-inspiring silence, or sway to the breezes in dignified and soul-entrancing rhythm. The snow-fed brook that harbors the golden trout has here the gentle murmur of its quiet ripple, yonder the thunderous roar of rushing waterfall.

Such an experience was mine on the 16th of August, 1935. We three brothers, with Pete Garn as a congenial guest, had packed in on horseback from Onion Valley over Kearsarge Pass and dangerous Glen Pass, and made camp on the South Fork of Woods Creek, between two lakes. That frosty morning I set out alone to climb to the rim of Ray Lakes Basin. I was richly rewarded. At the base of bold Finn Dome, on the super-solid base of pure granite, I was granted a wonderful view — each side seemed grander than the other. To the west I at first saw four lakes, then seven, then twelve, at one time. The eastward view was of equal splendor. I could look directly down to the camp I had left; and my brothers could see me in the heights — they signalled to me by flashing the sunlight from a mirror. I felt myself away from and above the vicissitudes of the troubled world. Time seemed to pause as I made my way slowly but safely back to camp. I had acquired something that none could take away.

Another series of outdoor experiences of more recent years deserves to be recorded. These were family outings that I was happy to sponsor. In addition to the enjoyment of grand natural features of California and beyond, my thought was that the bringing together of my three busy sons and their wives for such occasions would serve as a means of cementing more closely the family ties. I had observed many instances of families gradually drifting apart and was eager to prevent the possibility of any such misfortune in my own family.

Beginning in the summer of 1948 we enjoyed a happy outing in Yosemite Valley; the following year our family group, numbering eleven persons in all, paid a visit to Yellowstone and Glacier National Parks. Each succeeding summer we have had a family outing, though with more or less incomplete personnel, and have thus enjoyed the Canadian Rocky Mountains, going to Banff and Lake Louise and as far north as Jasper, then the Grand Tetons and Jackson Lake, the lovely Avalon Bay of Santa Catalina Island, and the Sequoia and Kings Canyon National Parks. These recent summer outings have enabled me to see sublime works of nature and at the same time to enjoy the closer fellowship of my own family.

Why do people leave their comfortable homes and go to the mountains in ever-increasing numbers? Why does the government establish parks, and monuments, and great forests? What is it that gives even the desert and the wilderness more and more charm?

To some it is the opportunity to hunt wild game in the season that lures them to the mountains — there's something instinctive and virile about it. To a larger number it is the elusive trout of the mountain stream that tempts them. But wild life in the heights is attractive also to nature lovers who have no intent to kill. The hidden lily, the delicate fern, the wonderful snow-plant, the iridescent humming-bird, or the regal eagle — to discover them in their native haunts itself brings its reward. And who does not now carry with him a camera into the mountains in order that what he sees may thus be taken home for subsequent enjoyment?

Then there's a naturalness in the mountain camp that finds no counterpart in city life. The good fellowship around the evening campfire, with the hours of delightful communion under the stars — it's not to be found in the club or the drawing room. There's a freedom, an exhilaration in the mountains that nothing else can give. They bring you into quick touch with sublimity — and who does not yearn in his heart of hearts for the sublime?

With me it is the grand ensemble of many features that has attracted me to the mountains. I have seen mountains in other lands — and they too are great and wonderful; but the mountains of California are *my mountains*. I too am a Californian! I have lived with my mountains and I have found them good. Their various phases through the hours of the day and the cycle of the seasons, always the same in their primeval grandeur, their challenging heights and alluring vistas all about — they have enriched and ennobled my life.

CHAPTER THIRTEEN

EDUCATIONAL TRAVELS

During much of my lifetime, travel in other lands than my own was not for me. And this was chiefly because Nancy and I were preoccupied with raising our family of sons, helping each of them to acquire an education and to become established in life on his own. Not that we would not have enjoyed visiting other parts of the world; but with our limited resources and income, together with home obligations, travel abroad was not practicable.

It was not until 1926 that I actually saw something of the world beyond my own country; and then the trip was made possible by my sabbatical leave from the University — the first such leave that came to me. The experience introduced me in a practical way to the educational mission of travel. It brought intimacies of contact with peoples and conditions previously strange and distant; it brought near many problems that had seemed far removed; it widened horizons and kindled a spirit of cosmopolitanism. It taught me certain first lessons of travel — that it stimulates the inquiring mind and the understanding heart, that it enlarges the vision of tomorrow, and that it brings increase in spiritual stature, while helping one to make worthy contributions to mankind.

Since the world trip of 1926-27 I have enjoyed other travel under favoring conditions, with such results as to lead me now to present in the present chapter a brief summary of different trips, each of which has meant an added experience of value to me, and the totality of which has been a significant enrichment of my life.

My trip to Alaska was in August, 1951. It was one of the tours conducted under the auspices of the College of the Pacific, where I was Director of the California History Foundation, and was escorted by President and Mrs. Robert E. Burns. To me it was in most respects like a short tour to a foreign country.

The congenial party numbered about thirty persons. My special traveling companions were Myrtle Showler, my niece of Sacramento, and my long-time friend Dr. Emory S. Bogardus, who was also my roommate. The trip from Sacramento to Seattle was my first extensive airplane flight. At Seattle we boarded the steamship *Aleutian* for the attractive "Inland Passage" to Alaska.

Omitting any description of numerous interesting views and experiences, which have been common to many thousands, I shall confine this report to a few points that were of more special interest to me.

The very vastness of Alaska is itself impressive, with its area of more than 586,000 square miles, or almost four times the area of California, the second largest state, but with a total population of less than 130,000. It is impossible for me to believe this great territory will remain so under-developed indefinitely, or that its population will remain so small. Something more is in store.

Among Alaskan industries three in particular are deserving of mention, which, I think, are destined to undergo much development and expansion; these are the canned salmon industry, farming, and paper pulp. The fundamental bases for this development are seen in the very extended ocean front and river systems, the wilderness areas of land that may be cleared for farming and made comparable to beautiful Matanuska Valley, and the illimitable forests of conifers that may be made to yield tremendous harvests of paper pulp. Besides these three there are other resources of considerable potentiality, such as water power, a variety of minerals, and wild life. Even tourism can be greatly developed by the application of more of the spirit of true enterprise and the use of more attractive advertising.

The two natural objects that impressed me most on the trip were the Columbia Glacier and Mt. McKinley. The stupendous ice wall of the glacier, three miles across, from which icebergs of all sizes — some of fantastic design — were constantly being born is a magnificent spectacle, overpowering. And you have not seen North America's greatest mountain peak if you have not looked with wonder upon Mt. McKinley! Our first view was from a point eight miles out from the hotel at Fairbanks, on a perfect day, August 12, 1951. I jotted down in my diary these words:

> A never-to-be-forgotten sight. Conditions exceptionally good. Many later views of the mountain—most complete and wonderful mountain view I ever had.

Alaska is a land of magnificent distances. Fortunately, its people are already air-minded. Through much of its vast area slower methods of transportation, including the steam railroad, may be directly overpassed in favor of the swift airplane for both passenger and freight service.

A ride on the Alcan Highway today gives a good hint of what is in store for the touring motorist of tomorrow. The superhighway, with its increasing numbers of tributaries, will become a great artery bringing the distant Territory into more and more vital relation with the great southern empire. With improved roadbed, which must be suited to the seasonal changes of temperature, the hundreds now traversing the highway will become multiplied thousands.

Two side trips must be mentioned: that to old Fort Yukon, an hour's flight from Fairbanks, located some eight miles above the Arctic Circle, with its small population of native trappers; and the visit to Sitka, the old Russian stronghold, with its St. Michael's Cathedral and other features which told of an earlier day.

Even a casual study of Alaska from the global standpoint reveals its highly strategic location in world affairs in a critical time. What this may lead to within the next generation or two of supersonic speed cannot be fully revealed or appreciated at present. At least we find here another strong justification for the acquisition of Alaska by the United States.

The question of statehood for Alaska was in everybody's mind. My own impression was that a large majority of the people favored statehood and that much of the opposition came from representatives of certain special interests. Perhaps no one knows Alaska better than former Governor Ernest Gruening, whose valuable book has been published since my visit to the Territory. To a greater extent, I think, than most of us are ready to admit, Alaska holds the future for the United States of America.

I found my trip to Alaska in August, 1951 so enjoyable and informative that I was encouraged to enroll for the College of the Pacific Tour to Mexico, scheduled to start from San Diego on the 21st of December of the same year. The party was escorted by Mr. Elliott Taylor of the College, an experienced and competent guide. My longest airplane trip up to that time was the flight from Tijuana, across the border from San Diego, to Mexico City.

I had been across the border before, both at Tijuana and Mexicali; but this was my first visit to the heart of the Republic of Mexico. I found much interest in the country; and I must set down a few personal recollections of the more salient features, which are rendered more vivid in my memory by reference to the entries in my diary. But I have no intention of imposing a travelogue upon the indulgent reader.

The Catholic Church has a powerful hold upon the people of Mexico, an overwhelming majority of whom are of Indian blood. The church building is almost invariably the outstanding structure of any Mexican town. Its doors are always open. Many people, mostly women, enter, often in early morning with or without their babies; they humbly kneel, fervently pray, arise and depart in quiet, with the utmost personal decorum. To throngs, the richly decorated church is the nearest place to heaven on earth. It means much to many people.

One other observation: if cleanliness is next to godliness, might it not be more emphasized in and about the churches, where, too often, squalid conditions around the entrance are seriously lacking in cleanliness and sanitation?

Substantial progress has been made in recent years in improving the schools of the country; but the actual conditions I saw indicated that educational opportunities are still decidedly inadequate; and most of the school buildings throughout the country — very insufficient in number — present a strange contrast to the beauty and grandeur of the churches. Even in Mexico City, I learned, many thousands of the people had no actual schooling at all. I wished that the relatively few leaders of true social vision might be multiplied many times, recognizing, however, the progress actually being made, under difficult conditions.

A majority of our party went to see the bull-fight on Sunday — "why go to Mexico," some asked, "if you don't see the bull-fight?"

But from what I had read and heard about the sport, I formed an unfavorable impression about it, and found that I was far from alone in inclining toward an attitude of disapproval. Should I go and actually witness the spectacle? When reports came to me in the morning that there was some kind of "racket" connected with handling of tickets, and a certain amount of "scalping" was being practiced, I decided against going. I found that there exists a rather strong moral revulsion against the age-long sport, as now conducted, and that it may some day be declared illegal and forbidden.

To the student of history and antiquities the most impressive feature in Mexico is found in its wonderful ruins. These evidences of antiquity are to be found in several different localities, and no one would venture even now to prophesy what wonders may yet be uncovered.

The ruins of Monte Alban are said to date back to about 500 B.C. Some of the human figures seem to be of Mongolian origin, others of Egyptian, still others Negro. Much is yet to be discovered regarding the rise and fall of succeeding civilizations — Zapotecan, Aztec, Toltec — of that great country, whose more recently uncovered ruins have been compared with those of Peru. The museum exhibits, including exquisite objects of gold, jade, obsidian, rock crystal, copper, with large pearls and articles made from shells — these must be seen to appreciate their beauty.

The Mitla Ruins are likewise marvelous for their extent, for the huge hewn rocks, handled by sheer manpower, and the King's Tomb, entered by a long, low, narrow channel carved in solid rock. After paying a visit to such antiquities as these and many others in Mexico and other parts of Latin America, one feels something of the fascination of those handmaids to human history, archaeology, and anthropology.

Perhaps nowhere can the restless North American experience the placid "Mexican Mood," so needful in today's stressful living, to better advantage than in the picturesque town of Taxco, with its quaint, uneven, cobble-paved streets, its commanding ornate church tower, and its out-of-this-world *fiesta* for every occasion.

The most sensational exhibit of any natural phenomenon I was privileged to see in Mexico was without doubt Paracutin, a real volcano in active eruption. That was an experience long to be remembered!

To reach the selected point of observation we changed automobiles for the last thirty-five miles over the very rough road, with its narrow, precarious log bridges, etc.; then after putting on overalls, jumpers and broad-brimmed straw sombreros, came the final hour's ride in the dark on horse — or mule-back. I had a sure-footed "calico" (pinto) mule, which served me well. Each animal was led by a native boy along the strangest kind of trail, covered with a thick layer of volcanic ash, the trail sometimes almost touching the red-hot mountain side, from which fragments of rock were constantly falling. The warmth from the heated walls being pushed out from the intensive inner heat was easily felt. That was an unforgettable ride, and I did enjoy it.

The outlook was a good safe place, directly across from the unobscured crater of the volcano, and the moon was shining to heighten the spectacle. I tried to think of adjectives to describe what I saw that night: the best I could remember had been preëmpted by Hollywood — "super-colossal," and the like — they had to be discarded as totally inadequate to describe Paracutin. After a deep-throated roar and rumbling reverberations out came such fireworks as no Fourth of July had revealed to me. Red-hot rocks of all sizes were hurled from the maw of the mountain, hundreds of feet into the air, some higher, some lower, then falling in glowing showers upon the slopes of the volcano and rolling, tumbling down until coming to rest, thus building up the new mountain. Time after time, with unnatural rhythm, came the unrestrained emissions, following the deep cacophony of sounds, giving forth a strangely lurid light softened a bit by the pale moon overhead.

The memory of Paracutin is the more prized now because, while the volcano had been active less than a decade when I saw it, it ceased to be active not long after my visit. I am happy to have witnessed this marvelous spectacle of nature.

Mexico is a land of contrasts. The bustling, highly dynamic capital city, with its modern skyscrapers and powerful motor cars speeding about with apparent abandon, is in striking contrast to every other city in the Republic — not to mention the innumerable Indian villages. There is evidence of progress in the country, to be sure; but there is the inertia of the ages yet to be overcome. While there is a very small percentage of highly cultured families, as there was back under the Diaz régime, constituting a real intellectual aristocracy, the great masses are still densely illiterate; at the present rate of educational progress, decades if not generations will be required to attain to satisfactory levels.

I was impressed with the desirability of liberating the prevailing religion of the Mexican people, and in the country districts its more complete separation from superstitious practices, a survival from ancestral times. All in all, however, I found evidences of recent genuine improvement and of a sincere desire to cooperate with neighbor nations in the struggle for a brighter day. We of the United States may well find a sermon in the grace and civility of the cultivated Mexican, in his appreciation of civic art, and in his serenity of spirit, sorely needed by our on-rushing people.

Guatemala is a very small Central American country, with but one large city (Guatemala City), and that not very large when measured by our North American standards. But the land of the *quetzal* has loomed rather large even internationally during the current decade of world history. I think I gained a slightly better understanding of this because of my visit to that country in June, 1953. It was a brief visit, but one can see much in so small a country even in a single fortnight.

I was privileged to go with my close friend and associate of many years, Dean Emory S. Bogardus. Any trip means more in such company. I can refer here to only a few of our enriching experiences, with an observation or two of more general nature.

If horizontally very small, Guatemala is vertically, that is historically, very large; for the archaeologist has already uncovered impressive works of great antiquity. Some scholars believe that the early Mayas, or their predecessors, made their appearance as early as four or five milleniums before the Christian era. I became convinced that the remote past in Guatemala will be a subject of intensive investigation for a long time to come.

And the fact that much of the expensive archaeological work, as well as the establishment and maintenance of splendid museums, has been done by the powerful United Fruit Company poses a very complex politico-psychic-ethical problem, since the United Fruit Company itself has been under attack in many quarters and was only recently made defendant in government charges of monopolistic practices. It was scarcely a matter of surprise that while many Guatemalans believe the strong corporation has been of great benefit to the people of the nation, there are others who are reluctant to express their private opinions.

Hernando Cortez, conqueror of Mexico, was greatest of all the *conquistadores* of North America; and his prowess was matched by his ruthlessness. The same spirit was exhibited by his chief lieutenants, especially in the case of Pedro de Alvarado, pitiless conqueror of Guatemala. I found that even to this day there is among the people, perpetuated by tradition, a deep feeling of hatred toward him because of his inhuman methods. Seldom has the world seen such complete and wanton destruction of a civilization as that wrought by the *conquistadores* like Cortez and Alvarado.

In some parts of Guatemala the Indians of today are believed to be direct descendants of the ancient Mayas. Indians constitute a large majority of the country's population. Most of them are quite content to have a small piece of hilly land where they can produce their corn and beans and be left alone. Many of them have never seen even the most primitive plow; but they are adept in the use of huge hoes. They live as their ancestors lived centuries ago.

The markets are extremely interesting to the visitor. Of these I must mention two. Market day at Chichicastenango is a sight to behold, when 3,000 men, women, and children arrange themselves in what appears to be a solid mass on the public square in front of the great stone church; but there is constant circulation as buyers and "window-shoppers" wind their way good-naturedly through the crowd where all manner of merchandise is displayed for sale. About mid-afternoon the break-up of the market begins, and before dark the people and their paraphernalia have disappeared.

Even more intriguing, if possible, is the market at San Francisco de Alto, at an elevation of 9,200 feet, literally on the summit of the mountain. During the early morning hours of Friday, market people can be seen on the roads and trails converging from all directions on this strange market place, laden with all kinds of wares, the women always carrying their goods on their heads, often with their babies securely bound to their backs. Livestock, including goats, sheep, pigs, and poultry, constitutes a conspicuous part of the merchandise. One of the most amusing sights of the entire trip, to me, was that of an Indian leading, or driving, an entire litter of ten or a dozen little pigs to this market. I marveled at his dexterity in handling these shoats, driving or guiding them up the devious paths, with people and packages all around, to the mountain top at San Francisco de Alto.

Religion plays a large part in the life of the Guatemalan, and a weird, strange type of religion it is — or so it seemed to me.

While the Catholic faith, generally speaking, predominates, it is a decidedly modified type of Catholicism, in some regions of the country. In Chichicastenango district, for example, while the Indians cling to the brilliant rituals of the religion forced upon them by the Spanish conquerors, nothing has been able to cause them to abandon the faith, or superstition, of their ancestors. The Catholic church has made important concessions to the "pagan" tradition; otherwise, it is thought, the Quiche Indian would not have remained a Catholic. As Muñoz says, "He has really accepted — not the Christian faith as we understand it — but the glittering rituals of its church." Even the strange incantations and magical ceremonies I witnessed in the church on market day constituted a form of worship and supplies another exemplification of the truth of the universality of religion alluded to by Plutarch nearly 2,000 years ago.

I came away from Guatemala with the impression that, though three-quarters of the people were said to be non-communistic probably a similar percentage had no real conception of the meaning of either communism or capitalism, as we are accustomed to use the terms. Nor did they care, as our guide remarked, "This is a democracy — let them alone." But in our restless, dynamic age no person, or group, or nation is "let alone" — all are subjected to pressure, often many pressures, from outside. The sojourn of even a fortnight in the little, attractive, evergreen country of Guatemala proved to be a rewarding experience.

One reason why I decided to accept the kind invitation of Dr. Emory S. Bogardus to make the trip with him to Latin-American countries might be called sentimental — I would be far away from the home place on Brynhurst Avenue, Los Angeles, where my family had lived so many years, on the first anniversary of the loss of my precious life companion — I felt deeply that I did not wish to be there, alone, on that anniversary day. As it came out, I was on that particular day on board the *Reina del Pacifico,* on the Pacific Ocean, *en route* from Mollendo to Balboa and Panama. Yet the first entry in my diary for May 16, 1939 is: "Even before daylight my mind reverted to sad scenes of one year ago, at the dear home place, 5143 Brynhurst Avenue, Los Angeles. However, I did not dwell upon this, but busied myself with Bryce's *South America* and Calderon's *Latin America.*"

When I went to President von KleinSmid's office to consult him about a three months leave from the University, I introduced the subject with the supercilious question, "Do you think the Administration Building would still be standing here on my return if I should be away three months?" The President's reply was ready: "If it is not, I will help you set it back on its foundations!" Dr. Clarence M. Case of the sociology department, one of my most esteemed colleagues and trusted friends, had agreed to spend necessary time in looking after the Graduate School office during my absence, and my experienced secretary knew the routine quite perfectly. And besides, our travel plans called for my return to Los Angeles in ample time for me to resume my responsibilities in connection with the commencement activities. The day of our departure on the "Goodwill Tour" came, Wednesday, March 15, 1939.

The first leg of the journey was by train from Los Angeles to New Orleans on the "Argonaut." Three days later we were on board the S. S. *Del Norte,* where I found a huge, beautiful bouquet from my special friends and students Frank and Abbie Sparks. The cruise on the *Del Norte* proved to be the longest I have ever had on water. She was a rather slow vessel, and there was no stop until we reached Rio de Janeiro, on the sixth of April.

The regular passenger list numbered not more than thirty persons — it is always interesting to look over the roster on shipboard. Of our list approximately one-third were specially trained young men, including one Ph.D. from California Institute of Technology, who were on various assignments relating to fresh discoveries and development of petroleum in different Latin-American countries. After the passage of a good many years, my impression is that the history of the oil industry in the lands south of the United States will reveal even greater contributions by American scholars, scientists, and technicians than we or our southern neighbors have suspected. The development and conservation of natural resources, including petroleum, constitutes one of our greatest industrial and social problems. A sincere application of the Good Neighbor Policy, and, of still more recent origin, of the Partner Policy, can go far toward crystallizing the solidarity of the Americas and ultimately achieving the kind of world unity for which thoughtful men everywhere are yearning.

The small number of passengers on the *Del Norte* made it but natural to become somewhat acquainted all-around. To me it was a pleasure to enjoy the acquaintance of Señora Matilde de Cabrera, a Mexican lady of high quality, whose husband had owned seven farms in Mexico, and who impressed me as a person of unusual refinement. She had been living in Southern California several years and was then on her way to Argentina in the hope of satisfactorily investing her funds, salvaged from the sale of sheep, where the rate of exchange seemed more favorable than in the United States. Señora Cabrera stated that in connection with the disturbed, revolutionary years preceding, all her farms had been seized by the government and that she had practically no expectation of receiving any substantial compensation. I am not fully advised as to later developments, but understand that conditions in general in Mexico have materially changed for the better.

Since Dr. Bogardus and I had not crossed the equator, up to that time, we were much interested in the initiation into the Order of the Deep. Fortunately, for us, because of our years and academic positions, we were generously permitted to be on-lookers from the upper deck at the actual ordeal to which each neophyte was subjected, including the profuse use of raw eggs, the ship's paint, castor oil, and ammonia water. Luckily, all took their medicine like good sports and at the end plunged into the swimming tank without a casualty, as "Neptune" stood by, ready for any eventuality. I look upon my O.D. certificate as a kind of honorary degree!

On this trip we found time for considerable reading. Our book list included Carleton Beale, *America South* and *The Coming Struggle for Latin America*; Thomas Mann, *Joseph and His Brethren* and *The Coming Victory of Democracy*; Lloyd Douglas, *Disputed Passage*; Calderon, *Latin America*; Bryce, *South America*; and two or three others.

One of the pleasantest experiences of this trip was the meeting of valued friends at several chief stopping points. Even before our ship came to anchor in the wonderful Rio de Janeiro harbor in a heavy rain on the 6th of April, we saw our devoted friend John B. Griffing on a small tug, he having come out to meet us. Mr. Griffing was director of the Agricultural and Technical School at Viçosa, 250 miles in the interior.

He introduced us to Dr. Hugh T. Tucker, then eighty-one years old, who had been in Rio fifty-two years as missionary leader and representative of the American Bible Society. We could not possibly have had a more resourceful or more devoted guide than Dr. Tucker. I dare say his equal for our purposes could not have been found in all Brazil. It is with extreme gratification that I am able to state that this consecrated Christian leader, honored in two hemispheres, is still living, in retirement in Pennsylvania, well advanced in his nineties, as these lines are penned. I am quite convinced that he has done more for the social uplift of the great city of Rio de Janeiro than any other individual of any race.

Rio is a beautiful city, possessing in exceptional degree its appeal to the esthetic, with its broad double tree-lined avenue, its wide sidewalks with their curious designs in concrete, its attractive modern buildings, and its rows of majestic royal palms, the loveliest palms in all the world.

Of the many places visited, the Positivist Temple had for me an interest all its own. There it stood, a substantial, well-built structure, sanctuary of a religious science based upon the positivist philosophy of such thinkers as August Comte and Lester F. Ward. But when we were there it seemed to be actually functioning not at all, while the masses of the people flocked to the Catholic churches, and many had accepted Protestantism. I was forcibly reminded that a vital religion demands something more than science, or intellectuality, or technical knowledge; it must have a place for symbolism, it must appeal to human emotion, with a touch of what is called mysticism. It must appeal to the heart as well as to the brain; it is somehow linked to the infinite, must be sustained by faith.

Even a short stay in Brazil — what a vast, potentially rich country it is! — convinced me that the world will yet receive great contributions from the far-flung areas yet wholly un-developed. My visit to a typical *fazenda*, with its coffee plantation, what I learned about the necessity of developing a hardy breed of cattle that can withstand the parasitic attacks of the tropical wilderness, and by means of patient research produce superior strains of cotton, and tame the great areas of rubber trees — these are simply intimations of future advances, well begun even now. Much in the life of the natives is still distinctly primitive. Never had I seen so many ox-carts trundling along the narrow roads. And I learned the meaning of the old saying, "If cart doesn't 'sing' ox won't travel" — the loud squeaking of the huge wheels served notice to any distant cart to locate a turn-out place in the road to facilitate passing.

It was delightful to note the recognition and distinction accorded to Dr. Bogardus by leading Brazilian authorities in the social sciences. On being introduced to him one (C. Delgado de Carvalho) said, "I have known you through your writings for twenty years, Dr. Bogardus; I am most happy to meet you personally." On another occasion we were taken for a call on Fernando de Azauedo, who at once brought forth from his revolving book-stand two of Bogardus' books.

Before reaching Uruguay I had already heard of the fine spirit of freedom and friendliness in that small but fascinating country. I was fortunate to have a cordial letter of introduction to Herbert Coates, a prominent Methodist layman and leading international Rotarian. During our stop for a single day in Montevideo he was our host and a prince of a guide he was. His friendly and generous spirit enabled us to see much of that beautiful city and confirmed us in the feeling that Uruguay exemplified the real democracy in a way and manner not surpassed by any nation we visited.

On the 19th of April we reached Buenos Aires, largest city south of the equator. Here again we were welcomed by a former student and as true a friend as one could wish — Dr. Fred Aden, of Southern California's class of 1915, President of Ward College. He met us at the pier and took us into his own home for the delightful week we spent in Argentina. That was indeed a rare privilege for both of us. There were five children in the family, three daughters and two sons, all native Argentineans, with both Spanish and English as their native tongues. I have never seen a more ideal Christian family than that which made the home of Fred and Meda Aden, with a mutual affection of parents for children and children for parents that was beautiful to behold.

Colegio Ward impressed me as a striking example of what can be done for human betterment by American capital in another country. It is a distinctly Christian institution, its thirty-acre campus located at Meija Ramos, less than a dozen miles from the center of Buenos Aires, whose controlling board and president are Protestants, and three-fourths of whose students come from Catholic families. It is there that the Adens, sincerely respected and loved by the people, have invested their lives since early maturity in fruitful endeavor, coming to the time of retirement in 1955, with signal honor and distinction.

I can remember yet the superfine beefsteak I enjoyed at the superior restaurant; also the abundance of fruit and profusion of lovely flowers of Argentina in the month of April. All this, with the rapidly advancing industry, intense political activity, and agricultural development, supplied excellent groundwork for a better understanding of the motto I saw conspicuously displayed at the *Museo Social Argentino* — "*Por Una Argentina Mejor*."

Our chief reason for preferring the train to the airplane in crossing over to Chile was that we could thus see the countryside, with its farms, fine horses and cattle, to better advantage. The train service, however, was a little disappointing, especially since the passengers had to be transferred at Mendoza to a fleet of Fords for a long ride over dirt-and-rock roads because of a serious washout of five years before.

Late at night, April 24, our train reached Santiago, after an interesting ride over the rugged Andes affording a good view of Mt. Aconcagua, highest peak in the Western Hemisphere.

Here, again, one of my former students, Rafael Elizalde, found us and contributed to our pleasure in his native land.

Two or three items regarding the beautiful capital of Chile attracted my special interest. First, I learned that the city had a woman mayor; then I greatly admired the charming, graceful manner with which the traffic officers directed the automobile traffic at leading intersections. With his perfect poise and mastery of his position, with his baton in hand and impeccable gestures, the officer might have been mistaken for a great maestro conducting a metropolitan symphony orchestra. How could any driver fail to respond to such directing!

But after all, I was struck, not only in Santiago but in different Chilean cities, by the apparent paradox of the most advanced social legislation and the low standard of living of the masses.

In Santiago we became acquainted with the special pioneering work of A. E. Turner of the Y.M.C.A. Here was a devoted man who dreamed dreams and performed modern miracles. Among the institutions that were contributing to the uplift of the old port city of Valparaiso I must at least mention *Escuelo Popular* and the Technical School for Girls.

We found Antofagasta, in northern Chile, a drab city of 55,000 people at the base of barren mountains, where I was told, "The only way to get wet is to drink beer." I remained dry! Water must be brought in some 250 miles. Not a blade of green grass was to be seen in the cemetery.

May Day was being celebrated, which gave me opportunity to see the labor demonstration. The parade was long but not very impressive; there were many cheap banners and placards, with portraits of Marx, Lenin, Stalin, and others, and slogans like "Down with Fascism and Imperialism," "For the Popular Front," and "Union of the Three Americas for Democracy."

The trip through Bolivia *en route* to La Paz brought us to elevations exceeding 13,000 feet, through wide table-lands where primitive farming was carried on by the Indians, who presented colorful scenes, especially the women, often barefoot, with their high white hats and bright-colored shawls. Sheep, llamas, and donkeys were everywhere. In color, variety, and traveler interest I doubt if anything on the entire trip was more fascinating to the camera-minded tourist than the markets set up on the pavements along the streets of La Paz.

The ride on the steamer across Lake Titicaca, while interesting, was rather cold and was marred by the rude demand by a Peruvian officer to show passports in the middle of the night, immediately on crossing the border into Peru. More high mountains — the railroad reaching elevations above 14,000 feet.

The old city of Cuzco was reached on the evening of May 6. Naturally we must see the pre-Inca ruins, some of the most remarkable in the Western Hemisphere. In my diary appears the entry:

> Impossible to describe in a few words. Masonry walls, caves, waterways, symbolic seats and altars—with endless traditions and hidden meanings, as well as unanswered questions. Sat on the throne of Inca King; looked down upon the vast enclosed amphitheatre where youths were playing football and Indian was leading his laden llama. In the distance stood Mt. Husangati (lofty snow-covered peak). Vastness of the marvelous works a real surprise.

The side trip to view the famous ruins of Machu Picchu is unforgettable. Quoting again from my diary:

> A wonderful trip through the wooded Andes, and opportunity to see some of the greatest works of antiquity on the Western Hemisphere. The ruins...became known to Dr. Bingham (Yale) in 1911, who had charge of excavations, wrote up details. Parts include: nobles' homes or chambers (with King), the Sanctuary, rooms for workmen, cemetery. Adjoining is a series of about sixty terraces.

The good ship *Reine del Pacifico* took us to Callao, and on the 15th of May we paid a brief visit to Lima, the most important event there being a call at the University of San Marcos, oldest in all the Americas.

Our three-day stop in the Canal Zone was filled with interesting and instructive events and experiences, largely through the hospitality and many courtesies of Judge Edward Tatelman, resident magistrate, who had been a student at U.S.C. In this account I can only outline a few of the things that happened.

We were fortunate in being received by Governor C. S. Ridley and General Consul Wang, in receiving a call from President Mendez of the University of Panama, enjoying a fine boat ride up to the old French canal, inspecting the control house at the Gatun Locks, and we were recipients of numerous other kindnesses. But no single experience of the entire trip gave me quite the same thrill as that I felt on the 19th of May, 1939, while riding on the paved highway with Judge Tatelman and Superintendent of Schools Ben Williams. At a certain point the Judge turned to me and startled me by saying, "Right here, Doctor Hunt, is where your father passed over on the Cruces Trail in 1850." I was totally surprised!

But I suddenly remembered I had told the Judge, years before, of my father's coming to California, in 1850, by way of the Isthmus. Immediately I almost shouted: "Is it possible? I wish you would stop right here!—I want to get out!" I did get out, saw the sign "Cruces Trail," at the right, the trail leading into the jungle, with an old Spanish cannon marking the spot. On the other side, a few rods distant, was the historic Chagres River. I took some quiet steps on the old trail, picked up a handful of pebbles and thrust them into my pocket. I had walked on the ground where my father had walked nearly ninety years before. It was holy ground.

At the conclusion of our Good Will Tour of Latin America I prepared a very brief report, in the form of a letter, which was signed by Dr. Bogardus and myself, and presented it to President von KleinSmid. My account of this trip in these pages may be concluded in the words of three of our recommendations to the President, after our visits to Brazil, Uruguay, Argentina, Chile, Bolivia, Peru, Panama, and the Canal Zone.

Renewed emphasis on various phases of Latin American topics in connection with the University's teaching program. This may apply more particularly to such departments as the Social Sciences, International Relations, Spanish, and Archæology.

Encouragement to specially qualified members of our faculty to spend the sabbatic leave in special study and research in selected portions of South America, at the same time making desirable contributions by occasional lectures and conference discussions.

Development, along conservative lines, of the practice of exchange professorships, and particularly extending invitations to carefully selected professors from South America to join our Summer Session faculty.

During the earlier years of my life, as already noted, opportunities for travel were extremely limited. My first trip away from home for an extended visit was in 1887 when I was nineteen years old. That was the summer with my chum in Siskiyou County, California.

I had never been beyond the boundaries of my native State until, in 1893, I went to Baltimore as a graduate student at the Johns Hopkins University. It was many years after that when I had my first trip abroad. This was an extended trip, in 1926-27, of such significance in my life that it is reported at some length on the following pages.

I had been a member of the faculty at Southern California for almost a score of years before my first sabbatic leave — during most of those years such a thing had never been heard of at the University. But in 1926 my friend and colleague, Dr. John G. Hill, Professor of Biblical Literature, interested me in the possibility of a world trip. As I thought of it, it appeared more and more feasible: our sons had grown to manhood and were on their own. Mrs. Hunt's health at the time made it unwise for her to undertake such a trip; but she expressed her more-than-willingness for me to go.

President von KleinSmid readily consented to the plan. We would leave in November, after the work of the semester had been organized and in normal operation. My colleague Dr.

Emory S. Bogardus agreed to serve as acting-dean in my absence, and my secretary Ruth Bohnett was very familiar with office details.

A younger man, E. Dow Hoffman, a Methodist preacher, wished to go with us: so there we were, the three H's—Hill, Hunt, Hoffman. Some wag turned it into "Heaven, Hell, Hades." Then a curious student asked the embarrassing question, "which is which?" On the first page of my diary I wrote: "being the tallest, I have an 'awful' reputation to live up to!"

With the aid of a trusted travel agent our plans for a trip around the world had been worked out in considerable detail; but we had decided against associating ourselves with any organized tour, preferring to maintain a degree of independence and mobility not possible in a regular guided tour. In this respect, our preliminary decision proved to our satisfaction to have been thoroughly justifiable.

The trip began on Tuesday, November 16, 1926, at Los Angeles Harbor, at high noon, with many friends at the pier to wish us *bon voyage*. After a few days in San Francisco, we were on our way to Hawaii, my first experience on shipboard in mid-ocean.

A traveling educator must be prepared for almost any kind of call for service. One of my first came when Bishop Titus Lowe of the Methodist church, a fellow passenger, approached Dr. Hill and me the day before Thanksgiving and in episcopal manner rather casually stated, "One of you is to give the Thanksgiving Day address—the one getting the long straw is elected." We "drew cuts," and unluckily I was elected. I chose as my topic—from which I departed *ad lib*, "The Harvest of the Past."

During the eight months I was away from home I must have given talks, lectures and addresses numbered into the dozens. I addressed audiences, little and big, not only in English but—through interpreters—in foreign tongues, including Chinese, Japanese, Korean, Indian, and Turkish. One of the most novel and interesting occasions was that at a regular missionary meeting in a village in northern India where the district vernacular was spoken; the one where it was most difficult to know just what to say, was to a crowd of poor Koreans, including many children, at an unheated Y.M.C.A. center near Seoul, at the Christmas season, with snow all around.

In Hawaii we were given good opportunity to observe the racial elements, the educational progress, religious opportunities, and the development of the two principal industries — sugar and pineapples. Our friends saw to it that we were entertained as well as instructed during our week's stay there.

While we were *en route* to Japan on board the *President Lincoln*, the sea became very rough. At one point the ship "lay to" for more than an hour to tighten the hatches and take other precautionary measures — she was losing time. For a while the pitching of the vessel was so severe as to give new and realistic meaning to an expression I remembered from childhood days — "shiver my timbers." I wondered if we were being hit by a monsoon. We encountered heavier seas than I had ever seen.

Before leaving home I had accepted an invitation to give a lecture at the University of Commerce of Tokyo almost immediately after arrival there. I had been preparing this lecture on the voyage from Hawaii. But stormy weather brought such delay as to render the date impossible; appropriate radio messages were sent. I was greatly cheered to receive on shipboard two radiograms of welcome, one from Mr. Harai, a Japanese student, the other from Hugh Cynn, my Korean student. The lecture was postponed till the following day.

At the Yokohama pier we were met by Professor Hoashi of Waseda University, who had been a student of Dr. Hill; and almost before the ship came to rest young Hirai appeared on deck, greeting us and offering his services.

A feature of our tour that added very greatly to both our

pleasure and our profit lay in the fact that at most of the ports and chief centers we visited, some one or more of our former students would be sure to meet us, as pleased to greet us in their far-away homes as we were delighted to see them and accept their assistance in furthering us on our way. At Honolulu there were Dr. John Hedley and Neil Locke; here at Yokohama were Hoashi and Hirai — and numerous others, later in Korea, no one could be more helpful than Hugh Cynn; in China, my devoted student and friend, I. T. Chow, and Herman Liu. Others will be mentioned in due course; but even to give the names of all would now be quite impossible. There seems to be no bond quite like that between teacher and pupil.

We were invited into private homes; meetings were arranged for us; dinners were given in our honor. In Tokyo, Dr. Hoashi arranged a dinner attended by about thirty alumni and students of the University of Southern California; in Kyoto Dr. Terao arranged a real Japanese dinner, with its strange but interesting menu. In Kyoto, also, we were fortunate enough to receive an invitation to lunch with the governor of the province in the old Myaka Hotel. With one of the leading men of all Japan, Governor Hamada, were the Mayor of Kyoto and a professor from the University (who served as interpreter) — a highly privileged occasion for us. Two incidents must be briefly related.

I had been asked to be spokesman. Being well aware of the feeling of Japanese resentfulness because of the American immigration act of 1924, I was anxious to avoid any expression that might be out of harmony with our government's policy. As we became seated, the Governor remarked: "So you gentlemen are from California: we Japanese know about California — it is a beautiful place." Not to be drawn into any conversation that might become controversial, I pointed to the snow-laden trees about the Hotel grounds and replied; "Yes, and you too have a lovely country: look at these beautiful trees, their branches so gracefully bending under their burden of snow." There was no discussion of Japanese-American relations!

As I saw in the sideboard an assortment of liquor glasses and reflected that we three were total abstainers, but remembering that the Japanese were accustomed to offer drinks to tourists as a matter of courtesy, I wished to avoid any possible embarrassment, then ventured this remark: "As your excellency knows, we have in the United States a prohibition law. We Americans feel that it is our privilege, as well as duty, to abide by this principle while traveling in other lands also; therefore, we trust it may not be deemed a discourtesy or lack of appreciation if we decline any liquor that may be offered us." "In that matter," the Governor replied, "you are quite right. We in this country hope to learn many things from your experience in America." No liquor was served, either to us or to themselves.

I should not fail to mention that we met many Christian missionaries in different countries visited. One of the most experienced, for example, was Miss Denton, who had then been in Japan thirty-six years. We found the missionaries to be men and women of true devotion, self-sacrificing in character, though in some instances, perhaps, lacking the breadth of vision and thoroughness of training in certain respects that would greatly have enhanced their usefulness. Of men like Mr. Phelps, chief officer of the Japanese Y.M.C.A., who received us into his own home in Tokyo, it would be impossible to speak too highly either of their devotion or their statesmanlike ability.

Hugh Cynn, of Seoul, who had been one of my students in Los Angeles, is another man of the highest character and ability. He was our principal guide and friend in Korea, where he was then head native secretary of the Y.M.C.A. We were in his home for the family Christmas celebration, where we partook of a Korean feast. I remember vividly my private conversation with him regarding the very distressing situation due to complete Japanese domination. At heart most of the patriotic Koreans were wholly unreconciled to the strict Japanese rule. After an hour's very earnest and candid discussion, Mr. Cynn's conclusions could be reduced, doubtless in over-simplified form, to three forceful propositions: 1) The Japanese have brought to Korea some very substantial improvements, in the form of good roads, public buildings, and the like; 2) the Japanese in Korea are gradually becoming richer and richer; 3) the Koreans themselves under Japanese rule are gradually becoming poorer and poorer.

When our ship approached Tientsin, on the 30th of December, introducing our visit to China, we found my faithful friend and student I. T. Chow on the pier awaiting our arrival. No one could have been more attentive to our wishes during our stay in Peking than he — at the time a teacher in Tsing Hua College. He invited us to his home, treated us to a typical Chinese dinner, and went with us to many of the historic spots of the city. But nothing was more entertaining than the vaudeville show where, at a certain place on the program the little orchestra, noting our presence in a front box, undertook to play "Yankee Doodle" in our honor, probably as comical as anything we heard on that eight-months tour! On more than one occasion it was pleasing to note the delightful humor of the Chinese.

One of the greatest personalities we found in China was Dr. Chang Poling, president of Nankai University, undoubtedly one of the foremost educators of the entire nation — tall, large, digni-fied, with urbane manner and distinguished appearance. I felt highly complimented when he accepted Hoffman's invitation to pose with me for a snapshot.

A very personable Chinese educator was Herman Liu, whom we had met in Honolulu, then as a fellow passenger on shipboard. Democratic in spirit, versatile, with fine sense of humor, he was an excellent companion. For years he was engaged in Y.M.C.A. work, later becoming president of Shanghai University.

Early in the struggle between China and Japan, the report reached me that he had suffered martyrdom.

On this world tour I carried with me my portable typewriter, and found considerable use for it. As we traveled along, mostly on shipboard, I prepared a number of short articles for the Los Angeles *Times*. A smaller number of longer articles I sent to the *California Christian Advocate*, under the general title "Hands Across the Sea." I recall that I also sent one or two pieces, dealing chiefly with alumni, to the *Southern California Alumni Review*. I desired to share some of my experiences and observations with a larger number of persons.

In Manila the young patriots were insistent in their demand for complete, immediate independence of the Philippines. Chiefly through the courtesy of Dean Bocobo of the School of Law, we enjoyed the lunch with the heads of the University of the Philippines, President Palma presiding. Dr. Palma then asked me to address the student body that afternoon. In my impromptu talk on the Westward Movement in American history, I brought the story almost to the Spanish-American War, but sensing the Filipino emotion on the subject of freedom, I discreetly saw to it that my time was up before coming to the question of the immediate independence of the Islands! Some disappointment was expressed that I had stopped short of their goal.

Probably the most noteworthy incident in Manila was my personal interview with Governor-General Leonard Wood. That is a pleasant memory today. The General had been subjected to severe criticism because he would not then advocate absolute independence. He told me most convincingly of his real love for the people, that he sincerely wished for their best welfare, but deeply felt they had not yet reached the necessary experience and political maturity for national liberty. Therefore his judgment would not permit him to yield to their impetuosity. General Leonard Wood was a great American statesman. It was a privilege also to become acquainted with Vice-Governor Gilmore, who was in charge of the educational system. Among the others we met and who extended special courtesies were Rev. Sam. Stagg and family, Dr. O. W. E. Cook, pastor of Union Church, and Bishop Mitchell of the Methodist Church.

It was near Singapore that I eagerly watched a family of monkeys scamper across the road — the first I had ever seen in the wild. More important, I visited a rubber plantation and saw the source of much of the world's supply of native rubber. Within the next few days we saw much attractive scenery, including a touch of the real jungle — a novel experience to Californians. Our long motor trip out of Penang took us through a great stretch of fascinating tropical country.

It was at Rangoon that I first met Dr. E. Stanley Jones, who had already in 1926-27 won a secure place in the confidence of the people of India and neighboring countries. On our first visit to Judson College, a Protestant Institution, the principal, Dr. St. John, invited us to remain for Jones' address to the student body. We sat behind him as he spoke to those fine young Burmese students, who showed him the highest respect and gave him their undivided attention. That evening we went to hear Dr. Jones' final lecture of a series; his audience was large, and there was a deeply earnest spirit. It has been my privilege to meet this devoted religious leader on several subsequent occasions. I came to regard him as one of the greatest missionary leaders of the generation.

Six weeks were spent in India, which I found, on the whole, the most depressing of all countries visited. But I am far from claiming that I understand India even now. I saw many things; but what I learned may be compared to a few grains of sand picked up from a vast desert. Even in the short period since I was there in 1927, however, I am impressed that more real progress toward Western enlightenment has been achieved than during the entire preceding century.

Anticipating a long journey while in the country, we called on Bishop Fisher and found him most helpful with suggestions, names of missionaries at different railway stops, and friendly overtures. We stopped overnight several times at missionary stations or schools, which proved of great advantage to us, both as to the information we desired and in the matter of expense. The missionaries were as pleased to see us as we to see them. Mr. Clemes of New Delhi took us to one of the small Indian villages (of which there are thousands), giving us a fine opportunity of seeing just how a gospel meeting is conducted, how the villagers were impressed with clear intimations of their standard of living.

Our trip took us through Benares, Lucknow, to Delhi, then through Jaipur on to Bombay, and next across to Madras. It was at Jaipur that we had the good fortune of meeting Dr. Charles M. Andrews, eminent Yale historian.

The visit to the Taj Mahal at Agra was of course a high point of the trip. A brief quote from my old diary will reveal the impression made on me: "The acme of India! Paragon of perfection! Vision of loveliness! We lingered about the masterpiece, and left with reluctance." In the evening, under the light of a full moon, we looked upon the famous Taj Mahal under the most ideal conditions.

Again, in Ceylon we were treated to an interesting ride through coconut groves, rubber plantations, and countryside of rich foliage, including native cinnamon and clove trees. The city of Kandy has a charm all its own. During more recent years the Ceylonese have come to think of their island as a sort of "Asian Switzerland," that is, a neutral in time of war, a charming place to live, and a mecca for increasing numbers of tourists. It has its beaches, its inviting mountain resorts, and extensive production of spices and rubber; its shops and attractive haunts for tourists are a delight to more and more visitors from other lands.

Passage through the Suez Canal proved to be a unique experience — the slow, quiet passage, the vast stretches of sand and desert on either side, with here and there an oasis, with its inevitable clump of palms. The passage naturally brought to mind the whole question of British-Egyptian relations; and now in retrospect the more recent problems arising out of changed world conditions.

At Cairo, as at so many other centers in our travels, we were met by a former student — this time "Bunny" Burns, the Y.M.C.A. secretary, whose wife (Iola McCrea) was an alumna of Southern California. Their generous assistance added much to the pleasure of our visit in Egypt.

Of course we did the conventional things, saw the wonderful sights. But two incidents were perhaps not quite ordinary. The night after our climb to the top of the greatest pyramid, we were robbed of our wallets and some other possessions while sleeping soundly in our room on the fifth floor of the English Y.M.C.A. Building. (Of course no unfavorable reflection on the Y.M.C.A. is intended.) Fortunately I had then less than $25.00 in currency; but Dr. Hill had just cashed $300.00 in travelers' checks — all gone! Reports to the Egyptian police and the British police brought no results whatever.

The other incident was our visit to the pyramids and the sphinx by moonlight. With the Burnses we prepared a simple supper amid the ruins of an ancient temple, the principal article of food being what we at home would call "hot dog." It was a memorable experience. The immensity of our surroundings was most impressive. The dim outlines of the monumental structures seemed to suggest something of their true antiquity. But we were brought down to date by the slinking figure of a half-naked native, furtively watching from the shadows our every movement in the hope that he might recover some fragments from our meal.

Jerusalem was our headquarters from March 26, 1927 until the day following Easter, April 17. It was a busy time: there was much to see and to learn. The sacred places and biblical aspects made special appeal to Professor Hill, though I, too, was interested.

Out of the ordinary was our visit to the Hebrew University, then in its beginnings, on Mt. Scopus. Chancellor Magnes was our personal guide. We noted the fine forty-five acre site, with its panoramic view of the Jordan Valley, the Dead Sea, and the mountains of Moab, as well as of the city and environs of Jerusalem. There was then no student body, but a group of resident professors and researchers were at work with the library collections and in other preparatory tasks. We found Dr. Magnes a man of fine social quality, earnest purpose, and rather unusual versatility.

As I was in my room on a Sabbath morning preparing for church, many church bells in Jerusalem began ringing. After having witnessed evidences of the strife existing in the Holy City between different Christian sects, the ringing of the different church bells seemed to creak an unhappy discord; instead of harmonizing and reinforcing each other their harsh clangor seemed to voice unholy strife. This was seed for sober reflection. How can the Prince of Peace, I thought, come to his own, and establish universal brotherhood among men with fierce competition, almost amounting at times to open hostility, in the heart of Jerusalem herself? I made this entry in my diary for March 29, 1927:

> Wouldn't it be Christlike if all sects could here break down their differences, dismiss their special guards, and serve the common Master with simple faith and brotherly love?

Zionism had already become an absorbing question when I was in Palestine. I spent the better part of a week in an intensive study of the situation and prospects. I visited the Jewish headquarters in Jerusalem, where the executives and staff of secretaries were feverishly busy, talked with Dr. Arthur Ruppin, economist, Col. Kisch, senior executive, and others. I sought out several middle-class Arabs — all were interested in the threat of Zionism; everybody talked about the Balfour Declaration. My most enlightening interview from the side of the Arabs was with Moussa Kazem Pacha, veteran head of the Arabian Council and most prominent leader in Palestine. He showed excellent poise, had seen much strife, was not greatly perturbed by the threat of Zionist movement, pointing out that, after all, Palestine was only a small island in a great sea of Arabs, who could unite in case of necessity. The plea of the common people was that they had been in the country for more than 1,000 years, that it was theirs and that they belonged there just like the hills and the trees. They wanted to be left alone, and cared nothing for new methods of farming or doing business.

One entire day, from 7:45 A.M. to 8:45 P.M., I spent in inspecting Zionist activities, having at my disposal as guide a well educated young British Jew, Z. Shwartz, and automobile. I visited numerous institutions, two or three farms, a winery, an orange grove, nursery, experimental station, maternity home, etc. We lunched in Tel Aviv, also called on President Block of the Council. Everywhere I was shown much courtesy, and could not fail to be impressed by the earnestness of the Zionist workers and the progress in their various activities.

My brief experience in the country has afforded me good background for understanding the immense difficulties and perplexities with which statesmen and politicians have been confronted during the years since my visit.

Hill and I remained in Jerusalem long enough to witness the elaborate Easter celebration, with elaborate ceremonies at the Church of the Holy Sepulchre. Next morning we were off for Nazareth in a Buick, with guide and driver. A side trip took us to Damascus, thence to see the marvelous ruins of the Temple of Helipolis at Baalbeck.

Next stop was at the American University, at Beirut, on the shore of the Mediterranean. After a visit at this institution, having already seen a similar one in Cairo, and later to see Robert College in Turkey, all supported by American gifts, I gained the impression that to sustain such a series of educational institutions in the Near East for the training of young men of many nationalities is one of the most unselfish and fruitful benevolences for which American funds could be used in foreign lands. American contributors could be charged with no ulterior purposes — they were interested in human understanding and cooperation.

While at Constantinople (Istanbul) I could not fail to notice that the Turks were in the midst of a renaissance — New Turkey was emerging, and rapidly. Our stay was prolonged to a second week because Dr. Hill had become ill and was hospitalized in the American Hospital.

I had pleasant interviews with Trade Commissioner Nash and Admiral Bristol, American Diplomatic Representative. At the consulate Mr. Allen argued for a free trade policy. Probably my most interesting interview there was with the President of the Chamber of Commerce, through a competent young interpreter. One question the president asked me I remember quite distinctly. "How do you explain," he asked, "that you Americans are able to export raisins from California, and market them in my country, when we in Turkey are producing good raisins, with higher sugar content than yours?" After a moment's thought I replied: "In marketing any product two things must be kept in mind: in the first place, the product must be of good quality — I admit your raisins are good, since I have already sampled them; secondly, the methods used in putting them up, or packaging them, is also important. I have seen large open sacks of raisins

displayed in the front of your shops, with flies walking over them
and therefore not in sanitary condition. The careful housewife
will naturally prefer the clean, attractive packages of California
Sun-Maid Raisins, perhaps even daintily tied with baby ribbon."

We were in Italy — Rome, most of the time — in the middle
of May. My diary tells of the train trip from Brindisi to Rome:

> Reminded all along of the chorus "O Italia, Beloved"; for the
> countryside, with its hills and fountains, its fields and fruits — all
> flooded with spring sunshine — was the most lovely and attractive of
> all lands visited. And this is the loveliest season — the trees are
> gorgeous, crops good, wild flowers in profusion.

No need to describe the glories of the Eternal City here. The
visit was of real educational value to me. Mussolini had been
in power but a few years: people were wondering whether he
would be able to hold out. There was evidence of pomp and
officialism on the streets and in the aerial display overhead.
Interest amounting to real excitement was shown when the
announcement came that Lindbergh had landed in France after
the first flight across the Atlantic.

I was impressed by the magnificence of the interior of St.
Peter's Church, had opportunity to see the Pope (Pius XI) at
fairly close range, whose entrance was heralded by the fanfare
of trumpets, and to observe various religious services. But on
Wednesday, the 25th of May, a novel experience fell to me, as
outlined in my diary:

> While boarding a street car, a young man with newspaper who
> seemed to block the way, was suddenly seized by a husky man and
> accused of trying to steal my pocketbook. His protest was of no avail.
> I was asked to follow the officers (I motioned to Dr. Hill to come)
> while they took the accused to the police office—at least seven of us in
> all in the auto. Very prompt work was done, photos produced, etc.,
> and I was asked to sign the statement prepared by secretary. The
> young man was held for trial, and the man who nabbed him handed

me his card (Ereole Nardini). I thanked him cordially for his prompt action, shook hands, and agreed to send him a post-card on reaching N. Y.

Perhaps the most amazing thing about the episode, if not of my entire trip, was that in the morning paper in Rome I was reported as being a wealthy American tourist, and that this young man had attempted to rob me of a *large sum of money*! Never before had I been accused of having a large sum of money!

Of all the master paintings I saw in some of the most famous galleries of the world perhaps the most perfect and satisfying to me was the "Madonna of the Chair." It would be quite impossible for me to express the wonder and admiration I felt for the marvelous array of masterpieces in the Uffizzi Gallery.

The natural scenery of Switzerland I found beautiful beyond description — the foliage, the meadows, the streams and waterfalls, then the snow-capped mountains.

Much of the time in Paris was spent in seeing the things tourists are expected to see. I wondered if the figures and achievements of Louis XIV and Napoleon Bonaparte were not made conspicuous beyond their deserts. A tour of the battlefields of the First World War and of the many military cemeteries helped to a more sympathetic understanding of the French attitude toward the German power.

Our first day in London was Saturday, June 11, 1927, so cool as to render an overcoat quite comfortable. Three weeks were given to our stay in England, a period packed with special interest.

I turned aside to King's College to hear a lecture by Professor E. R. A. Seligman of Columbia University on installment buying. He had just completed for General Motors a monumental study on the subject. When Seligman lauded the benefits of installment buying I thought I could notice a slight lifting of the eyebrows of Professor Gregory and some of the other British listeners. And later I remembered it was not long after that when the unprecedented crash befell the New York Stock Exchange in 1929.

Dr. Hill and I were fortunate to be in London at the time of the Centenary Celebration of University College. We were duly accredited delegates from the University of Southern California by virtue of appointment by President von KleinSmid. On the 23rd of June, equipped with proper academic costumes, we repaired to the Great Hall, where the King and Queen made their formal appearance, with official attendants, all the people standing. The Convocation was ceremoniously opened, the Centenary duly inaugurated. The royal party filed out by the central aisle and side door. On the lawn tea was served and there were many presentations to their Majesties. When at length the royal carriage conveyed the King and Queen away, the dignified Dean of the Medical Faculty, with whom I chanced to be conversing, his hat removed, ejaculated with obvious emotion that amounted to reverence, "There they go, God bless them!"

One other function that I was privileged to attend was a formal dinner for a small group at the home of Lord and Lady Loch at Lennox Gardens. Despite my democratic way and prohibition sentiment, I found real interest in this special occasion and with animation entered into a discussion with Lady White on conditions in China, where I had so recently been.

As the time of our departure from London approached, everything else was overshadowed by the thought of preparation for starting home. On the 29th of June we sailed from Southampton on the *Olympia* for New York, which was reached on the evening of July 5th, and were met at the pier by Dr. Hill's daughter Gladys.

After spending a few days in New York, I paid a visit to Florida, as the guest of D. Walter Morton, who had succeeded me as dean of the College of Commerce at the University of Southern

California and was then in charge of the J. C. Penney Farms in Florida. A few days later I was again on the train, this time bound for Los Angeles and home *via* New Orleans. Awaiting my arrival, July 15, at the station were my sons Lloyd and Clarence. The final entry in my diary reads:

> Glad to know the big trip is at an end, after a world of interesting and broadening experiences. Now for work.

A short time after my return I formulated some lessons taught by a world tour. Stripped of all discussion and illustration they are these: 1) He who would have friends must show himself friendly. 2) The world is weary of war and yearns for a way out. 3) The West is in the East to stay. 4) Under divers names and symbols the spirit of Christianity is found in many of earth's far countries. 5) A United States of Europe is so imperatively demanded by conspiring forces as to render some such arrangement inevitable. 6) The war-weary world, suffering the birth-pangs of new renaissance, calls loudly for capable leaders of passionate soul.

CHAPTER FOURTEEN ## S OME
LIFE DECISIONS

Recollections reaching back over more than four score years and reflections growing out of many and varied experiences and observations have conspired to produce a blend that reveals much about my life as a whole, with its focus on the here and the now. From my present vantage point I can discern a series of life decisions, some of them momentous — not all of them of my own making, to be sure — that had a determining influence in shaping the course of my life and career. While there is nothing magical about them — and I would vigorously combat a philosophy of fatalism with reference to them — they seem to me to be so significant, more than merely coincidental, that I would like to review them in summary for whatever light they may throw upon the pathway of my life. I cannot hope, however, that this summation is to be complete, nor am I competent to measure quantitatively the effect of each or indeed any decisions.

In the series first came the decision of my parents to move from the Freeport ranch to the town of Napa, where there were far better educational advantages and opportunities in the religious life. This was chiefly the result of my mother's firm purpose of giving her sons a better chance. If the family had remained on the ranch it seems most unlikely that I would ever have completed a college course and virtually impossible that I could have had an educational career. For my life this was truly a vital decision.

It was while I was a student in Napa Collegiate Institute that the institution was by the trustees changed into the four-year Napa College. At the moment the change was rather seriously disappointing to me as a youth, for I was then near the point of graduation from the Institute; but, being well established in my studies and of studious habits, it proved to be quite natural for me to continue; my parents were entirely willing. Thus it was that the change of status of the school afforded me the unanticipated opportunity to earn my collegiate degree, though it was unlikely that I would ever have gone through college except for the change in the local situation. The change that first brought disappointment proved to be a real blessing in disguise.

My decision at the age of seventeen to unite with the Methodist Church and dedicate my life to Christian service was far-reaching. As told on previous pages, I became active in the field of church work, and in varied capacities I have striven to serve my community while serving the church, believing sincerely that my church membership enabled me to render a higher type of service.

I should add that I have never placed strong emphasis on special theological teachings or denominational distinctions; religious dogmatism repels me. Under other environmental conditions I might readily have become a Presbyterian or a Congregationalist, though by and large Methodism has a stronger appeal. My inclination has been to minimize such differences in a spirit of broad toleration characterized by true devotion to the main cause, as I have understood it.

What the course of my life would have been without the religious factor, dating more specifically from the year 1885, I have no means for knowing — mere speculation on the subject would be idle. I can only state now, it would certainly have been vastly different; for religion has been a vital force, an inseparable part of life itself — it has been ever present with me and in me.

My decision to enter the field of education as my calling in life has already been referred to. In retrospect I deem this, along with my religious avowal, to have been one of the most important — and, as I view it, most significant — of all my life decisions. But before this major question was settled I spent a year after graduation at home, engaged principally in study and systematic reading, under the general guidance of my highly esteemed college president, Dr. James N. Beard. This proved to be most fortunate for me. For because of that year of informal study, during which my time was free because I did not teach, I was enabled, unexpectedly, to complete my requirements for the Ph.D. at Johns Hopkins University in two years, whereas, a minimum of three years of graduate study was normally required, and I had originally expected to spend only one year in Baltimore. I think it more than doubtful if I ever would have won my doctorate if a third year of residence had been demanded of me; but when I discovered a possibility of completing in two years, I deeply resolved to make the most of the opportunity. Without the coveted degree many inviting doors which I have been privileged to enter would never have been opened to me.

The decision to apply for a high school teacher's certificate, with no specific objective in view at the time — which proved to be a mere formality because of my doctoral diploma from the Hopkins — proved to be fortunate; for when I was unexpectedly invited to become principal of San José High School, I was already fortified with the legal credential. My six years' experience as principal brought a deeper understanding of the problems of secondary education, which I could not otherwise have achieved, while affording me opportunities for a richer, fuller life as an educator.

In the rapidly developing phases of work and divisions of study at the University of Southern California there came a time when I found myself holding two deanships without ever having planned it thus. President George F. Bovard well knew I did not wish to hold the double position permanently. When I was asked which deanship I preferred to retain, I replied without hesitation, "the Graduate School," notwithstanding the virtual certainty that the College of Commerce deanship would soon command a higher salary. I sincerely felt that for me, with my own aptitudes and personal tastes, to be dean of the Graduate School was to hold the most desirable position in the entire University, not even excluding the presidency itself.

My retirement at the University of Southern California was delayed year after year until I had reached the age of seventy-seven years. It came at length, in the summer of 1945, in harmony with the general plan of retirement that had only then become effective by action of the board of trustees. Having been accorded the opportunity of continuing in service up to that time, I had elected to remain. As matters came about, I deem this to have been personally a fortunate decision; and I may now add the honest opinion that some of the highest service I was able to render the Graduate School, and the University as a whole, appertained to the final decade of my deanship.

I have thus brought into a single group a number of vital decisions the total influence of which upon my life and career is plainly incalculable. Still others might readily be added to the list, such as that to postpone marriage until after having won my doctor of philosophy degree, another to relinquish the principalship of San José High School to accept a position in the University of Southern California at a serious financial sacrifice, and still another to leave my retirement, in my eightieth year, to undertake the directorship of the California History Foundation at the College of the Pacific in Stockton.

To live actively and fruitfully calls for many decisions. One of the specific principles to which I have striven to adhere — the more consciously the older I have grown — is an earnest endeavor to attain and preserve serenity of spirit. Without poise and a serene spirit complete self-mastery and inner peace are impossible. Applying this principle to decisions along the way, it is a grave mistake, having once decided a personal question to the best of my ability, bringing to bear upon it the light of my own conscience and judgment, to look back continually upon it with regret or remorse, or even with questioning whether the decision was after all the correct one. To face the future in the fullness of my powers I must not waste my energies upon the irrevocable past. To be at my best, of unavailing inner conflict there must be none — the future demands my all.

I have profound admiration for the immortal words of James Russell Lowell, in "The Present Crisis," from which I gratefully quote:

> Once to every man and nation
> Comes the moment to decide,
> In the strife of truth with falsehood,
> For the good or evil side;
> Some great cause, God's new Messiah,
> Offering each the bloom or blight,
> And the choice goes by forever
> 'Twixt that darkness and that light.

Then later in the poem appear these lines, indelibly impressed upon my mind, which I have found frequent occasions to repeat, brought vividly to my mind many years ago when I found them quoted by Wendell Phillips in his masterful oration on "The Scholar in a Republic":

> New occasions teach new duties,
> Time makes ancient good uncouth;
> They must upward still and onward,
> Who would keep abreast of truth.

CHAPTER FIFTEEN

EDUCATION
NEVER ENDED

When I reached the age of sixty-five the United States was in the midst of the most serious financial depression it had ever experienced. The year was 1933; the depression was introduced by the 1929 debacle on the New York Stock Exchange. With this grave condition in mind, and because sixty-five is a widely recognized stage in a man's life. I wrote out on my birthday a statement of several pages on "Thoughts on Becoming Sixty-five." This statement is before me now. Touching the financial situation and unemployment, this, in part, is what I had to say:

> I have been given to reflecting much on the anomalous conditions obtaining during this year of grace in the United States and the unaccustomed posture of events throughout the world. For more than two years I have somehow had the feeling that the present depression is not merely a phase of just one more business cycle.... I have come to believe that there is something distinctly unique in our grave situation, more particularly because of its world-wide character, following on the heels of the World War.
>
> I am strongly inclined to believe that we are, even in America, undergoing now a real revolution, already well begun; though by so saying I do not allege that it is or must necessarily become a violent or bloody revolution. It impresses me rather as being a revolution of thought on economic and political subjects.... I fancy it may appear to another generation that we have not only come to the end of an era in human history but that we are this very day well advanced in a

new era of vast unfolding problems of infinite difficulty but holding aloft an inspiring hope.

Just in front of me as I write is the monumental two-volume Hoover Committee *Report on Recent Social Trends,* and alongside of it the compendious *Report and Recommendations of the California State Unemployment Commission....*

Then my statement reviews some of my life principles — total abstinence from alcoholic drink, the use of tobacco, and profane and obscene language, confessing my "monumental ignorance" of card games. Then I continue, perhaps a bit on the defensive:

> I am by no means an ascetic. I delight in recreation and crave more of it. I do not allow a summer to pass without seeking the more intimate acquaintance and deeper communion with the mountains of California, my native state. Travel under favorable conditions affords me great enjoyment....
>
> Life today has a thousand facets and withal is intensely interesting.... There is no lack either of entertainment or instruction: indeed there is challenge and there is inspiration all around.... Thrice happy am I in seizing each new day with avidity and expectancy.

During the years since I thus expressed myself on the current revolution, I have seen no reason to change my view. Indeed the events of the past two decades — the atomic age, miracles of transportation, phenomenal advances of automation — have but fortified and strengthened the view that we are witnessing a revolution of far greater tempo than the Industrial Revolution of England, that is confined to no single nation but is stirring the peoples of all lands.

I find that I wrote out a personal statement, also, on the day I became seventy-six — this I called "The Spirit of 76." And because of my life-long proclivity for saving things, this document also has come to light. Here is one of my early paragraphs:

> But first I must enter dissent from any dogma to the effect that three score and sixteen years are synonymous with old age. The very

spirit to which I refer and of which I write is a living refutation to any such fallacy. It may be that some are old at seventy-six, or even sixty-seven; but I'm writing about myself, and I deny the allegation!

Regarding my decision as a young man to make education my life work, I may insert this paragraph:

For more than half a century I have been connected with educational institutions, as teacher and administrator, with the rare privilege of instructing thousands of young men and women; and now it is personally gratifying to be able to say, with all candor, not only that I have no regrets regarding my choice of profession but also that I do not believe I could have made a wiser decision if I had then been possessed of all the experience of the past half-century. I would do it again! Such a feeling of satisfaction is undoubtedly a factor in "the spirit of 76."

Closing paragraphs of my statement reveal something of my "extra-curricular" activities during 1943-44 as well as my attitude toward life in general. I said, at the age of seventy-six:

Tonight I am looking forward as well as backward. My interest is keen in the domestic scene and in the world situation.... Never has there been such need, such opportunity for contributing to worthy causes everywhere in the round world. As ration board member, membership in such organizations as the Commission on the Organization of Peace, the United Nations Committee, the Los Angeles Commission on the Church and Industry, it is constantly stimulating and challenging.

There is always more to be done than I can do. I'm glad of this, but for several years have kept my resolution not to hurry....

Life is interesting, and exciting enough for one of my years. Life is worth living to the fullest — it is fun to be alive and to work in such a world; and if by my work I can help to make it just a little better, so much the more fun! By now I think you can see by "the spirit of 76" I am 76, but deny being old! The calendar tells at best only a half-truth!

The attainment of four score years marked a real event in my life. There had been an important change — not so much in myself as in what had happened to me. I had retired at the University of Southern California in 1945, at the age of seventy-seven — well beyond the usual age of retirement, but still too early in my own case, I inwardly thought — and had become Dean-Emeritus of the Graduate School.

It was in my eightieth year that I accepted the cordial invitation of President Robert E. Burns of the College of the Pacific to be Director of the California History Foundation, at Stockton. In the midst of my first year's active incumbency, while I was also giving a course of lectures on California history for the Adult Education Department of the Stockton Schools that my birthday came, February 3, 1948. Not only was I honored by the memorable family party at Glendale, an account of which follows, but there was recognition by my large class at Philomathean Hall, and otherwise, in Stockton. With me life had begun anew at eighty.

I wrote down these words: "My 'passion for creativity' finds scope and opportunity commensurate with my strength and ability." I was again absorbed in work that I enjoyed. This sentence appears in some of my notes: "My time is as fully occupied as I wish; but I decline to be 'fussily busy.'" Then it was that hope and encouragement of friends led me to look forward to having a small part in the great state centennial celebrations of 1949 and 1950, and perhaps even of the Centenary of the College itself, in 1951.

A single paragraph from my statement on becoming an octogenarian may be inserted as an indication of my thinking at that time:

> I am not so busy but what I have time for observation and reflection. As a student of history I have to confess my contemporaries have largely failed to learn the lesson of perspective and to profit by the sermons of the past; as a teacher of economics I could wish that my fellow economists had more strongly undergirded their message with

the strength of ethics; as a Christian I yearn for the practical application of the principle of the Golden Rule to the lives of men and of nations everywhere. Never, it seems to me, was there greater need.

My eightieth birthday was made the occasion for a small dinner party that was to me a memorable event. It was at the lovely Oakmont Country Club, near Glendale, in Southern California, where Lloyd and Dorothy have held membership for years. Twenty persons were present. While it was essentially a family party, a few special friends had also been invited.

Following the rather elaborate dinner my youngest son Clarence offered brief remarks, closing with a toast to his father, a copy of which was afterward requested, and which is reproduced here: "I am greatly honored to have the rare privilege of addressing you at this anniversary gathering for the 80th birthday of my father. I propose this toast: To my father, on the 80th anniversary of his birth. A true pioneer of vigorous and rugged stock, whose health and sturdiness may be likened to the great Sequoia; with a character as clean and pure as the waters of the crystal pools in our great mountains; a man of unimpeachable integrity, with a knowledge and understanding as rich as the resources of the great state that bore him; with a vision and perspective as broad and far-reaching as her vast coast-line. May God grant him many more years that those of us who know and love him, as well as all who may come in contact with him, may be the better for having shared his gentle wisdom and kind philosophy. To my father!"

Each person present participated in the informal program. My special friend Dean Emory S. Bogardus presented me with an inscribed copy of Lee Shippey's book *It's an Old California Custom*, after having written on the title page these flattering words:

> To Dean Rockwell D. Hunt:
> A pioneer among California's great pioneers.

A discoverer of gold in the hearts of the people.
A researcher for nuggets of wisdom in California
    history and in human experience.
An exponent in his own life of the highest type
    of Christian faith and character.
A loyal friend forever and a day.

> Emory S. Bogardus
> February 3, 1948.

At eighty I read in Dr. J. R. Miller's *Year Book* these words: "For eighty years Moses had been in preparation for his great mission as leader." Then the thought occurred to me — I am now eighty: does Dr. Miller's allusion carry a meaning for me? Am I prepared for a new task at four score years?

A partial answer to this query may be found in a rather whimsical little article I contributed to the S. C. *Alumni Review* for February, 1948, under the caption "80 Is Just a Number." In this piece I pointed out that, after my thirty-seven years of service in Southern California, having had a hand in many of the developments of what has become a great metropolitan university, I by no means lost the feeling of being a member of the university family when I became Dean Emeritus of the Graduate School. Furthermore, having accepted a most congenial position at my Alma Mater, the College of the Pacific, I confessed that my passion for "creative activity" found scope and opportunity commensurate with my continued excellent health and my ability.

I resolved then — a resolution gladly renewed today — that, so far as lay in my power I would keep myself *alive* until death, seeking to make practical in my daily living the principle of the Golden Rule, heartily repudiating the theoretical man to whom George Bernard Shaw referred, "Died at thirty; buried at sixty."

My education has never been completed: it never will be —

and that is the glory of true education. Admirable is the simple
epitaph of John Richard Green:

> Here lies John Richard Green
> Historian of the English People
> He Died Learning

My own reward for investing a life in educational securities
is twofold: in the first place, the adventure has helped me to
enrich my own being through perennial development of the
powers with which I was endowed; and secondly, it has afforded
me large opportunity to direct and inspire others — I know not
how many — toward better living on higher levels. Employing
an expression coined by that rare American economist Frank
Fetter, my "psychic income" has been, and continues to be,
large beyond computation.

To set down all the memories and reflections that come trooping
to my mind would be to fill another volume — even then the
account would not be complete. Nevertheless I am constrained
to record here a few of my thoughts touching aspects of education,
as viewed from the vantage of the years. The word "problem," like
"inhibit," has been greatly overworked in my time; yet I must
employ it myself for the want of a better — I feel certain problems
have to be mentioned.

One of the most acute, as I view the scene of more and more
children and youth in schools of all grades, pertains to regimentation and routine, when the individual should be the real subject
of our instruction. And as I am concerned about the absence of
individuality, I also deplore the tendency in overcrowded schools
and large universities to become more and more impersonal.
It is the easiest way — granted: but it is not the best way. I hold
that the larger and more complex the institution becomes the
more assiduous and unremitting must administrators and teachers
be in combatting the tendency. The suppression of personality

and the absence of the personal touch are too great a price to pay — they go a long way toward defeating the finer purposes of education.

I have already alluded to the evils of too early and too narrow specialization: as Woodrow Wilson paradoxically declared in his first Johns Hopkins lecture to my class, and as President Faunce of Brown University put it in his terse phrase. Even greater than the need for technically skilled experts is, I think, the need for liberally educated men who have made themselves masters in a limited area after equipping themselves with some knowledge of the problems of the race, full-orbed men who must ever be our chief reliance in passing on the torch of civilization from generation to generation.

The offspring of fragmentized, compartmentalized knowledge is seen in "shredded men." When fields of study become hermetically sealed compartments, barring entrance to all but the elite who possess the jargon password, their superspecialists are forgetting that the true university is concerned with the universal, and that all disciplines — history, literature, science, politics, psychology, and the others, are but interrelated and interdependent strands braided together into the golden cord.

I am, of course, aware that what I am saying now is not anything new. On the basis of very limited knowledge and almost total inexperience, I thought I sensed something of the difficulties involved when, as early as 1892 I presented my "master's oration," "Demands Upon the Modern Scholar." Here are brief excerpts from my student effort:

> A narrow specialism is dwarfing to the mind and dangerous to scholarship. . . .
> The scholar is a god-imaging man, in whose intellect is the world incarnate. He is equipped with the armor of the ages. "The universe is rifled to furnish him.". . . is he not also related to the great Present and the greater Future? . . . The modern scholar, once equipped, has,

and ought to have, immediate and positive relationships.... The scholar has a first place in the republic. He may seek riches, but always as a secondary good.... in order to do one thing well, he must be able to do more than one....

The true scholar is a lover of truth and the friend of man. Whatever his specialty, he owes it to the world to be a philanthropist, for he occupies a vantage ground above the world; and to be a teacher, for intellect is the rightful possession of the ages.

More recently I have further developed this thought, among other places, in an essay entitled "Shredded Men and Desiccated Society,"[1] from which I quote briefly:

> Excessive use of overtechnical terminology, or a kind of sublimated jargon, is another easily besetting sin of not a few social scientists, who might profitably give heed to weightier matters of the law. This savors of dilettantism, which is but "the intellectual equivalent of sport." ... If the respective and respectable social sciences are closely interrelated, as I have alleged, then the speech and terminology should at least be intelligible to anyone informed in any of them. In this regard let us have more of the open shop, or — to use a noble phrase that now awakens melancholy thoughts — "open covenants openly arrived at." How can we break down the hated caste system if we ourselves are addicts?
>
> Our economic life and our political life are but aspects of our total living together in society: they are not lives or things apart, but are integrated into the totality of our being. It follows that between them harmony must prevail if peradventure we are ever to assure the optimum of existence for the people.

As an educator recently expressed it, the market place has moved in on the university. The transcending functions of a university, in bold summary, are: to conserve known truth, to extend the boundaries of knowledge, to disseminate knowledge, and to inspire trained men to serve mankind. Referring to the overall goal of education at every level, Nicholas Murray Butler, as spokesman for his generation, declared:

---

[1] *Sociology and Social Research*, Vol. 37, No. 2 (November-December, 1952).

Diverse as our intellectual interests here are, and various as our daily tasks, there is one aim which the faculties and schools, all teachers and scholars, have in common—the building of character.... We are all concerned, first and foremost, with the forming of those traits and habits which together constitute character.

Of all the basic institutions of American society none is better fitted to adapt and adjust itself to a dynamic and changing world, and to point a guiding finger to the wise course of such changes than the university, *provided* the university is left unhampered to exercise its precious *Lehrfreiheit*. No institution of economic, political, or religious character can equal it in adjusting itself smoothly and uniformly to inevitable great changes brought by the introduction of new knowledge and improved technique. But if it is to function at its best the university's freedom must be sacredly preserved. To render highest service to humanity and make its rightful contribution, the university must cling tenaciously to its birthright — freedom of thought and freedom of teaching, for that freedom is the apple of its eye.

One additional thought impresses profoundly — imperative need for educating for world citizenship. With virtual annihilation of distance at the dawn of the atomic age, the rearing and the equipping of world citizens are matters of utmost urgency. Adequately to meet the present situation I would go so far as to hold a prime requisite to be a critical re-examination of our educational system, with a special view to its revision and enrichment in the light of America's new rôle, which brings its correspondingly heavy responsibilities.

Each of the four seasons in California has its special, distinctive charm. Nature is bountiful here all the year round.

But I have found spring the most charming and delightful of all. It is in early springtime that the smiling meadows are the

ROCKWELL DENNIS HUNT AT 85

greenest, the trees on the rolling hills and hidden vales in between the most gorgeous, clothed in their fresh foliage of varied, indescribable tints, the profusion of wild flowers spring up and bud and bloom in the genial sun, adding a subtle something to every rustic scene that quickens the heartbeat of the true nature lover.

Intimations of the coming springtime are seen in the first golden buttercups that love to greet the sun, and the opening of the baby-blue-eyes on the half-shaded walls of the shallow barranca, where the live oaks display their bright, shiny foliage. Near the coast the tender-leaf trillium is modestly blooming in the shadows of the towering redwood, and along the creek-bed are the swelling buds of the pussy-willow. Further down is seen the first splurge of California poppies adding their brilliant golden tint to the grassy meadow. Then on beyond, in the cultivated farm lands are the acres on acres of orchards transformed into colorful masses of beauty by their fructifying bloom. After days of ravishing sunshine comes the gentle April shower to add new impulse and a fresh start to all growing things.

Early today, during my morning walk, I saw a brilliantly colored goldfinch dextrously balanced on a fiddle-neck stock, enjoying his breakfast — the first goldfinch I had seen this year. I thought, if there's anything lovelier than a goldfinch on a fiddle-neck, it would be a pair of goldfinches side by side on the same stock.

It is in the springtime that I love the winding mountain road, the impetuous stream scampering down the precipitous gorge, birds building their nests along the way, with here and there a graceful gray squirrel venturing forth, and perchance a bonny little fawn.

Early in the year 1948, having just attained my four score years, I pleasantly recall I found unusually keen enjoyment in the spring of the year. Since then, with each recurrent winter, my active mind has queried, may I hope to witness yet another delightful California springtime? With gratitude I confess, I have been spared to enjoy another, and still others; every one has been an unspeakable blessing, for which my deepest soul bows low in reverent thanks to the God of all good gifts, acknowledging "The earth is the Lord's and the fullness thereof." In the rebirth of the delightsome springtime is there not an intimation of immortality?

CHAPTER SIXTEEN

VITAL REFLECTIONS

Since California as a state in the Union was not yet eighteen years old when I was born in the capital, it is somewhat startling to realize that I have almost literally grown up with my native state.

The changes that I have witnessed are so many and so bewildering as to suggest the question, has anything at all remained the same? Yes, some things remain unchanged: marvelous natural features like Mt. Shasta, Lake Tahoe, and Yosemite; the giant sequoias of the Sierra Nevada and the towering redwoods of the Coast Range; the unmatched thousand-mile coast line along the Pacific — these have not changed.

The people have changed — and multiplied. There is no longer the early preponderance of men over women; I have lived through the exciting days of Kearneyism and demand for Chinese exclusion, culminating in the exclusion act of 1882 and subsequent acts, likewise the clamorous days of anti-Japanese agitation, coming to final focus in the act of 1924; these, and still other phases of California's racial problem, including reference to Filipinos, Negroes, and — in lesser degree — Hindus, or Indians, have appeared in my time.

When I was born California's total population was only half a million; not until 1890 was the million mark topped. But by 1955, *mirable dictu!* the figures have jumped to around thirteen million! And the end is nowhere in sight.

In my childhood and youth the entire San Joaquin Valley seemed to be one vast wheat field, now completely transformed, by virtue of extensive irrigation systems, into a paradise of horticultural production with thriving cities here and there. Moreover, great expanses of desert have been reclaimed as if by the hand of magic, and made to flourish.

In this connection a significant change that I have witnessed at close range is the reclamation of the extensive swamp and tule lands on both sides of the lower Sacramento River, and the tens of thousands of acres of waste lands in the intricate delta of the Sacramento-San Joaquin river system. The "Lake Field" of the Hunt Ranch at Freeport was a small part of what has been thus transformed. The transformation of large areas on the west side (Yolo County) of the Sacramento, centering in the village of Clarksburg, is truly marvelous.

It was only after long, dogged struggle that adequate levees have been constructed, now topped by paved highways, and that below-river-level areas have been brought under intensive cultivation and made to produce enormous crops of sugar beets, asparagus, corn, barley, and other crops.

But what of industry? I moved to Los Angeles in 1908; large-scale industry was almost totally lacking. "Factories! factories!" was the cry. But now look! Senator Stephen M. White and associates created a splendid free harbor at San Pedro. Then came factories, singly and by troops, till we are hearing the plaint, "It is enough."

The far-flung petroleum industry, with the fabulous value of the "black gold," and refinements produced since 1895, so greatly exceeds that of the yellow metal as to make the comparison meaningless. Men of my time have witnessed the development also of rich metallic resources, such as silver, copper, lead, and iron, not to mention the long list of non-metallic resources.

But of all industries aviation, largely as a phase of the war effort, has seized an astounding lead. Outstripping everything else in capital investment and labor employment, it has gained unbelievable magnitude, unequalled anywhere else.

I can remember when the common labor day was twelve to fourteen hours for farm hands; it came near being from dawn to dark. But agitation for the eight-hour day brought results. The daily wage of my youth falls short of being an hour's pay today. Unheard-of workers' benefits — insurance, vacations, pensions, medical aid — have become commonplace. The day laborer has his automobile, his wife has her Frigidaire, the family enjoys television. Luxuries and wonderful new inventions have become necessities.

The plodding plowman is no longer seen following his sweating four-horse team; no longer does the farmer boy trudge wearily along behind the horse-drawn harrow. Farms have been completely mechanized and motorized. The work of weeks is compressed into a matter of hours. Farm help is of a very different sort now, when a mechanical picker does the work of forty men and when tractors are saving the farmers thousands of man-hours every season. Improvements are being introduced constantly.

Nothing could be more revolutionary than the changes I have witnessed in transportation. In 1854 my mother required three laborious months to make the trip by "prairie schooner" from Illinois to Sacramento; in 1954 I made the flight from New York to Los Angeles in a part of a single afternoon. When I was born the transcontinental railroad was not yet completed; of course there was no telephone, no electric light; the wireless and the radio, the automobile and even the bicycle were undreamed-of.

During my childhood California's first constitution, adopted in 1849, was still in effect. The constitution of 1879, never wholly satisfactory, has become a "crazy patchwork" because of the many and sundry amendments. But in the field of politics I have seen the elimination of the railroad "machine," and the establishment of the principles of direct legislation, as well as the granting of the franchise to women. There was the launching of the Lincoln-Roosevelt League by men like Chester Rowell and Edward Dickson.

I think no state has surpassed California in the number of its political isms and nostrums. With Henry George's Single Tax, Upton Sinclair's EPIC, Allen's "Ham and Eggs," and Dr. Townsend's more generous pensions for the aged, the political scene in California has been truly exciting.

Changes in the field of education have been many and startling. The state university was founded in the year of my birth. There was no system of high schools, or of normal schools, to say nothing of junior high schools, and state colleges, and junior colleges, now numbering in the scores. Most of the great leaders in education have appeared or done their best work in my time. I need only mention the names of John Swett, John and Joseph LeConte, David Starr Jordan, Benjamin Ide Wheeler, and Josiah Royce. It must be confessed, however, that the human brain has remained virtually unchanged since Plato and Aristotle. It has scarcely been able to cope with the great mass of new material that has emerged to confront it through the kaleidoscopic changes of recent years.

I have seen many changes — some amusing, some grotesque, many quite baffling — in fashions and styles. There were the extremes of the crinoline hoopskirt and the hobble skirt, with the bobbing bustle somewhere in between times! Little boys no longer wear short pants, and their fathers have suffered a loss of dignity by discarding their Prince Albert coats and well-groomed beards. But I must leave such items as cosmetics, and slacks, and the introduction of many new fabrics to the observation of my contemporaries — they are everywhere in evidence.

Social evolution has resulted in a greatly widened scope of governmental activity. The care of defectives, delinquents, and mentally ill had no counterpart in the days of my childhood. Humanitarian demands have enjoined this as a function of the state. It seems clear to me that in a populous community and dynamic society there cannot be a definite permanent line of demarcation between governmental activity and private initiative. I think of government as simply the machinery that enables the state to do its work.

This sketch of some of the changes in my time may be concluded with the observation that I see no slackening in the tempo of change now. I do see an accelerated application of atomic energy to peaceful pursuits, the startling introduction of automation in industry, the still further reduction of hours in the workday and of days in the work-week, and the increasing seriousness of the problems of leisure and an approaching "Robot Age" of leisure. I do perceive the necessity of dependable moral standards in the days ahead and the transcendent importance of developing and maintaining correct perspectives in the lives of individual citizens.

This section may be concluded by quoting the final lines from my essay "Demand for Moral Leadership," published not long ago:[1]

There must arise great moral leaders, towering like snow-crowned Shasta above the valley. The leader must be panoplied with

[1] *World Affairs Interpreter*, Vol. 25, No. 3 (October, 1954).

true religion, for otherwise the pressure is too great. Let him gain inspiration from the ancient prophets like Hosea and Isaiah; let him in all humility follow in the footsteps of Jesus, striving for his perfection, for He is the light of the world.

From my infancy I was under the religious influence of my devoted mother; father seemed quite content to leave the matter of religion to her. She had a simple faith, as expressed in the Methodist Episcopal Church, accepted the Bible as the Word of God, had never heard of "higher criticism," was extremely sincere in her worship and her aim to make practical application of the Christian gospel.

As I came to my youth and young maturity, my student habit naturally carried over into the realm of religion. Pure dogmatism was repugnant to my thinking, whether in philosophy or religion. The professions of some church members were confusing, sometimes appeared contradictory, to me. Likewise, the precise definition and application of terms like "salvation," "entire sanctification," "holiness," and "Christian perfection," by men and women sometimes of but slight education, did not seem to fit exactly into either my own experience, or my intellectual processes. Even my own sainted mother, brought up in a Christian home, could not point to the exact time and place of her own "conversion."

It was at times somewhat painful, as in an old-type "class meeting," to hear a certain man profess "Christian perfection," and exhort others, vocally, while his daily life obviously fell far short of the profession. There seemed to me — though I carefully concealed all such thought — to be some kind of boasting in such profession, even at times a species of selfishness, or egotism.

I gratefully accord full recognition to the importance and potency of religion as a factor in history and in my personal life. But theological and denominational terminology has never had a strong appeal to my matter-of-fact mind. It has seemed rather like a mold or pattern into which I could not readily be cast.

Therein lies one reason — not the principal one — why in my youth I did not respond to the suggestion to study for the ministry. I had been endowed with a mind of my own, which would have made it difficult, perhaps impossible, to "go along" with all of the statements and declarations then required or expected of ministers. When I heard one expound the doctrine of "entire sanctification," or declare the formula for the "third blessing," or insist on the absolute literal infallibility of the King James version of the Bible, I usually maintained a respectful silence, but had to live with my own mind. But I am quite willing to accord to others what I claim for myself, freedom of thought and obedience to individual conscience. In our search for truth there are many and devious paths.

Religion has been given a commanding place in my thinking since undergraduate days in college. In my published writings Christianity has been granted the position of suzerainty. When in college as an Orophilean, I chose as a title for my essay on the program competing against the Matheteia Society, in Napa, in 1889, "Stoic or Epicure?" in which I extolled the simple religion of Jesus above both Stoicism and Epicureanism. In my college graduating oration on "The Heritage of Culture," in 1890 these words expressed my student thinking:

> Pure religion is the disinterested perfection of the moral principle. A beautiful life is the result of the marriage of the moral and the spiritual. Talent, if divorced from rectitude, may prove more a demon than a god. Due recognition of spiritual life, and of the fact that spiritual life transcends all other phases, is a virtual recognition of man's exceeding great destiny.

Two of my early articles, on "Christ as a Social Reformer," were published in the *California Christian Advocate* in the spring spring of 1897. I made bold to state:

> We are taught that a vital relation exists, or should exist, between the legitimate pursuits of this life and the kingdom of God—between our trading and getting gain, our marrying, our *living*, and the eternal verities, the destiny of man, heaven, hell.

In the same essay I claimed, "There is no social problem to which the Gospel of Christ does not furnish the clue for a solution." From which I argued that the best reformer of our social life is "The Christian who is also the best student of the times and institutions, who has availed himself of all modern means and appliances."

I had been reading with absorbing interest and appreciation the writings of Lyman Abbott, Washington Gladden, Richard T. Ely, and Shailer Matthews, to be followed by those of Francis Peabody, Walter Rauschenbusch, and Graham Taylor. I was becoming quite enamored of what came to be known as the "Social Gospel," which insists that redemption cannot be complete unless and until it has been sincerely applied to all areas of life — economic, industrial, political, social — foreshadowed by such men as Charles H. Parkhurst and Josiah Strong. How could I doubt the vital future growth of the church and its increasing membership in the graces of goodness and godliness and the expanding service of social ministry? Were not all things ready at the opening of the twentieth century?

Here I must make a confession. In the perspective of the years I have experienced a sense of disappointment with reference to the high hope I entertained half a century and more ago. The utterances of consecrated prophets found expression in social creeds of churches, and in inspired magazine articles, of limited circulation, to be sure; but they did not find prevailing exemplification in the hearts and daily lives of the multitudes of believers or in the practices of many captains of industry, who professed Christianity. Some progress has been achieved, largely through tribulation; but I have only to look about me to see unlovely, even shocking, features of contemporaneous society, such as the slum districts and "skid rows" of certain cities, and numerous low-grade taverns, or saloons, totally repugnant to the principles of Christian ethics and the clear teachings of the Sermon on the Mount. For many years I have vigorously repudiated the dictum that "religion is irrelevant to the real problems of our day"; and just as vigorously have I held to the teaching that in true religion is to be found the best clue to the solution of even our greatest problems.

For the progress that has been achieved — and it is by no means negligible — I am grateful; but it is far from adequate. I have therefore raised my sights for a longer perspective, resolved to strive on, insisting still, however, that the wedding of Christianity and the social movement must be accepted by the church as a special behest by the Founder of Christianity himself. For only as we complete this assignment can practical Christianity be held up as "the consummation of the finest and truest of life's aspirations."

In the light of recently acquired information relative to the magnitude of newly-discovered galaxies and their incomprehensible distances from our earth, as well as the hitherto secret nature and constituents of the atom, I find any form of anthropomorphism quite inadequate in an attempt to describe the Deity. To think of God as possessing eyes, hands, ears, and heart — that is, to have some sort of physical attributes similar to man's — is quite inadmissible: yet how else can finite man think of infinite Deity? If I undertake to define God, I limit him — he is no longer God. It is only by an act of faith that I can have even the slightest apprehension of the infinite — and by faith I conceive God, as spirit, to be both infinite and omnipotent.

For many years I have been a teacher of economics. Economics has to do with the social ordering of wealth. In the area of religion the scene that presents itself is not always an exhibit of good economy. In California alone there exist well over 100 religious denominations. In a certain town of fewer than 3,000 souls there were found to be more than twenty different churches —and that town was by no means unique. The unseemly competition to maintain struggling churches at a bare subsistence level renders it impracticable for them to assume the aggresive leadership in a general movement for community betterment or any adequate forward-looking program.

With what assurance can such a divided and weakened Christianity face the heroic task of promoting fellowship and demonstrating brotherliness in a world torn with bitter strife between groups and individuals? How can a church denomination, compelled to struggle and compete with others for its very existence, avail in its pleading for world unity? Is it not high time for the church to take a leaf from the primer of economics? The movement toward church unity is laudable, but its tempo seems deplorably slow. A united Christianity could be an incalculable force in our quest for the goal of a united world. I am forcibly reminded of the famous quatrain of Edwin Markham, "Outwitted," for which I have long had great admiration:

> He drew a circle that shut me out—
> Heretic, rebel, a thing to flout.
> But love and I had the wit to win!
> We drew a circle that took him in.

Nothwithstanding all defects and shortcomings of the Christian Church, however, I am constrained to say with John R. Mott:

> It has done more to purify, enrich, and strengthen mankind than have all other movements. It is still the most powerful and beneficent agency for promoting the cause of morality and religion.

While I may not qualify as an "old man" —and I firmly deny any aspirations to attain that status—the very years I have accumulated must entitle me to indulge in retrospection in an attempt to answer the question, "What are some of the lessons that length of days has taught me?" It must be that "the swift unrolling of the web of time" has taught me something of value. Reflection has been added to experience. Even so, it is no easy task to set down in succinct phrases certain of the lessons graven on my heart.

I have never even attempted to spell out a complete philosophy of life; yet, like all truth-loving individuals, I must have such a philosophy implicit in my innermost being. Aware of the insufficiency of my words, I may at least set down divers thoughts and personal convictions that should afford a glimpse of what might be developed into an integrated philosophy. I do not command the artistry to complete the mosaic I can envision, but I can assemble the materials and commit them to the creative thought of the reader.

Both experience and observation have taught me the lesson of self-reliance, a conspicuous trait of my forefathers quite as essential today, though with different manifestations. A natural corollary is seen in the advantages of activity in industry and honest labor over indolence and supine dependence upon others.

I believe a major task of each individual is to live his own life and live it nobly. I am not simply an average man; I am myself, and there's no other quite like me. I am grateful for what others can do for me, but I am not bound to violate the inner voice of my own conscience even though the common mores are against me.

I have a mission in life, which challenges me to the fullest development of my God-given powers, to the end that I may make my best contribution to human welfare. Since I can dimly apprehend infinity when I contemplate the heavenly galaxies or marvel at the power of the atom, I dare to think that I am somewhat, mystically perhaps, linked up with infinity; and in

that linkage lies the quintessence of man. Life is intensely
practical; but without ideals the so-called practical is ineffective,
meaningless, for the most practical of all things is the ideal.

Translated into daily conduct, the experience of years, fructified
by a perennial idealism, has imparted certain specific lessons
which I hold to be true. Among these are the following: (1) It
is desirable always to have in mind more projects than I can hope
to bring to completion — this banishes *ennui* and insures fresh
zest to the art of living; (2) it is wise to avoid hurry, which is
the parent of confusion and too often the grandparent of chaos;
hurry impairs happiness, curtails usefulness, shortens life; (3) I
must attain and steadfastly maintain serenity of spirit; only thus
can I attain to inner peace and self-mastery; (4) this being a
friendly universe, time will be granted for everything I ought
to do; whatever is my duty, that I can do; whatever I ought to
do I must do; (5) to sustain and strengthen my moral principles
under all conditions I need the sanctions and inspiration of
religion; in this my own experience has, in its limited way,
reflected the light of human history.

In the preface to this book I refer to my long wait before
undertaking to write my autobiography. As I approach its
conclusion I am again hesitant. I cannot write the *finis* at the
close of my life, for the simple reason that the end has not come,
nor is it clearly in sight. But my present task is about to be
completed, and I am grateful for the strength and opportunity
to present its final chapter.

Although I am quite aware of my own limitations and the
slackening of my pace, it seems unrealistic to think of myself
as an old person. I have not lost my enthusiasm, I still have
zest for living, I am challenged daily with interests that engage
my thinking even to the ends of the earth — why call myself
an old man? I'd prefer to side with Emerson when he avers,

"We do not count a man's years until he has nothing else to count." Or, as he declared when enjoying a college reunion with Oliver Wendell Holmes, "Old Time is a liar! We're twenty tonight!"

When at eighty-six I entered my second retirement, I thought the first thing I should do would be "to prepare for old age — if any." But my retirement continues to be so active as to incline me now to postpone such preparation until my *third* retirement — if any! A friend remarked, the other day, "The third time it may take!"

Mine has been a full life. In it there have been deficiencies, deprivations, sacrifices, bereavements. But the measure of my blessings has been incomparably greater. My pioneer parents left me a rich heritage and lived on to my full maturity. I have had a good physique, unusually free from serious illness. Merely to suggest other items in the long account, I have had opportunity for good education; a happy family life has been mine, with daily comforts; congenial, devoted friends have made me rich; I have traveled in many lands and communed with my loved mountains; I have enjoyed happy and helpful relationships and associations as a layman in the church. To be sure, I have suffered heavy bereavement, particularly in the loss of my dear namesake, then of my life companion, but in my heart there resides no bitterness toward God or any man. Life has been good to me — I am profoundly, humbly grateful.

What has been my most important work in life? I do not know. It is impossible for me to judge. There is no known calculus by which to measure the influence in my own household, or in my teaching in various positions and institutions, or as an administrator, or writer, or by the spoken word, or as a leader in the field of religion.

Religion it is that has knit together and sustained all parts of my life pattern, and has in some mystical way related my own life to the great pattern of the universe. In many matters where human eyes could not discern, and human wisdom proved insufficient to point the way, the eye of faith has marked the trail. So it is in events that shake the world, however dark and forbidding today's outlook — through faith a brighter tomorrow beckons us onward and upward.

I have loved life. And now, at the sunset glow, I repudiate the generally accepted notion that age is "the most terrible misfortune that can happen to any man." My later years have been golden years, in which I have cultivated peace of mind and a serene spirit withal:

> The last of life for which the first was made.

Proficiency is good, but learning is to be prized above proficiency: competence is a worthy goal, but competence is not to be compared to wisdom.

> Happy is the man who gathers wisdom, the man who gains knowledge—we are told in the Proverbs of Solomon: "her profits are richer than silver, she brings in more than gold; she is more precious than rubies, no treasure can compare with her; long days are in her right hand, wealth and honor in her left; her ways are ways of tranquil ease and all her paths are bliss." [1]

Death seems still far away. To talk about it is like talking about a clear abstraction. Even in my realistic reflection on the brevity of time the end seems very remote. Far or near, it is for me to keep the faith. The sunset comes. Lines written by a friend and classmate of long ago, Lulu McNab, are to me now simply beautiful and beautifully simple:

---

[1] Proverbs, 3-13-17 (Moffatt)

SUNSET
Crimson melting into gray,
Rose and blue of dying day,
Lighting all the western sky
Where the gathering shadows lie.

As the sunset glories run,
So with Life, when Life is done,
Shadows dark and manifold
Turn at last to sunset gold.[1]

Of this I am resolved: that while it is yet day I shall not dwell always in the receding past, but shall continue to rejoice in the spirit of youth, inviting perennial springtime to find its dwelling place in my soul.

---

[1] Lulu McNab, in *Anthology* (Pacific Coast Women's Press Association, San Francisco, 1939).

PUBLICATIONS

I. BOOKS

1895 *The Genesis of California's First Constitution (1846-49)*
      Johns Hopkins University Press

1911 *California the Golden*
      Silver, Burdett & Co.

1926 *California: An American Commonwealth*
      Lewis Publishing Co.

1929 *A Short History of California* (with Nellie V. Sanchez)
      Thomas Y. Crowell Co.

      Oxcart to Airplane (with William S. Ament)
      Powell Publishing Co.

1930 *The First Half-Century* (University of Southern California)
      University of Southern California Press

1931 *California: A Little History of a Big State*
      D. C. Heath & Co.

1933 *New California the Golden*
      Silver, Burdett & Co.

1935 *California, the State Everybody Loves*
      Harr Wagner Pub. Co.

1942 *John Bidwell, Prince of California Pioneers*
      The Caxton Printers

1948 *California Ghost Towns Live Again*
      California History Foundation

      California Vignettes
      Exposition Press

1950 *California's Stately Hall of Fame*
      California History Foundation

1951 *History of the College of the Pacific*
     College of the Pacific
    A Vintage of Vignettes
     Exposition Press
1953 *California in the Making*
     The Caxton Printers

II. ARTICLES (Partial List)

1889   Stoic or Epicure
     Napa Classic, May
1890   Heritage of Culture
     Napa Classic, September
1893   The Province of Elocution in Oratory
     Proceedings, National Association of Elocutionists
1897   Christ as a Social Reformer
     California Christian Advocate, April 28, May 5
1898   Legal Status of California 1846-49
     Annals of American Academy, November
1901   Birth of the Commonwealth of California
     In Shuck, History of the Bench and Bar of California
     Golden Jubilee of the University of the Pacific
     Overland Monthly, May
1902   Local History as an Aid to the Study of General History
     Western Journal of Education, March
     Rationale of the French Revolution
     Methodist Review, July-August
     Thoughts on Socialism
     California Christian Advocate, October 9, November 6
1905   The Home and the School
     Western Journal of Education, October
1907   The Committees of Vigilance of California
     Overland Monthly, January
     Houses that Came Around the Horn for the Alameda Gardens
     Overland Monthly, March
     Camping Out in California
     Overland Monthly, September
1909   Eugenics: Nobler Breed of Men
     Twentieth Century, November

The Study of Our Local History
    Western Journal of Education, November
1910 The College Student and the Social Question
    Western Christian Advocate, January 12
Significant Events in California History
    Annual Publications Historical Society of Southern California
1911 Hubert Howe Bancroft: His Work and His Methods
    Annual Publications Historical Society of Southern California
1913 A California Calendar of Pioneer Princes
    Annual Publications Historical Society of Southern California
1914 Socialism and the Student
    California Christian Advocate, September 3
1915 Socialism and the Church
    California Christian Advocate, January 14, 21
Charity Organization Movement
    Second Annual Report Los Angeles Municipal Charities
        Commission
1916 Aspects of the Study of History
    Annual Publications Historical Society of Southern California
By Ox-team to California—Personal Narrative of Nancy A. Hunt
    Overland Monthly, April (edited)
Cornelius Cole, a California Pioneer
    Overland Monthly, September
1917 John Bidwell: A Prince Among Pioneers
    Annual Publications Historical Society of Southern California
Boyhood Days on the Banks of the Sacramento in the 'Seventies
    Overland Monthly, June
Thrift
    Thrift Magazine, December
1919 Problem of Economic Reconstruction
    Overland Monthly, February
Compensations of the Great War
    Overland Monthly, March
Golden Jubilee of the Pacific Railroad
    Overland Monthly, May-June
1920 National Conservation and Personal Thrift
    Overland Monthly, March
1921 Political Science and Practical Citizenship
    Educational Review, March

1922 Religion in Utopia
         Los Angeles Times Magazine, March 19
1923 Historic Spots in California
         Overland Monthly, May
1923 A Prize and a National Policy: The Contest for California
         Annual Publications Historical Society of Southern California
1924 History of the California State Division Controversy
         Annual Publications Historical Society of Southern California
1925 California and the Japanese Question
         Overland Monthly and Out West, April-May
1926 Picturesque Days of California: The Spanish Period
         Southern California Alumni Review, January
      The Doctor of Philosophy Degree
         School and Society, January
      Introduction to Land Economics
         University of Southern California Correspondence Study
            Department, Lesson 24
1930 The Semi-Centennial of the University of Southern California
         Overland Monthly, April
      China Is On the March
         The Cultural World, November-December
1932 Antecedents of the Great Depression
         Religion and Life, Autumn
1934 University Research and Its Functions
         Southern California Alumni Review, January
      Economics of Welfare Today and Tomorrow
         World Affairs Interpreter, January
      At Johns Hopkins University Forty Years Ago
         Johns Hopkins Alumni Magazine, November
1935 Have Faith in Democracy
         World Affairs Interpreter, January
1938 In Praise of Democracy
         World Affairs Interpreter, April
1939 The Good American Way
         World Affairs Interpreter, April
      A Vacation Trip to South America
         World Affairs Interpreter, October
1941 The Social Significance of Planning
         In *Los Angeles: Preface to a Master Plan*

1944 Toward Peace with Plenty
 World Affairs Interpreter, April
1946 Postwar Reflections on the American Way
 World Affairs Interpreter, April
1946 California in Perspective
 Annals of the American Academy, November
 Evolution of Transportation in California
  Quarterly Historical Society of Southern California,
   December
1947 In Search of Human Welfare
 World Affairs Interpreter, January
 These Were My Teachers
  The Phi Delta Kappan, March
 California's Centennial Celebrations
  Pacific Review, December
1948 California in Review, After a Century of American Control:
 Eight Centennial Lectures
  Extension Remarks LeRoy Johnson, H.R. April-May
 Some California Pioneers I Have Known
  Quarterly Historical Society of Southern California,
   December
1949 Pioneer Protestant Preachers of Early California
  Pacific Historical Review, February
 Thoughts on the Changing American Way
  World Affairs Interpreter, April
 Great Women of California
  Quarterly Historical Society of Southern California,
   September
 The Harvest of the Past
  Pacific Review, December
1950 Morality Is a World Affair
  World Affairs Interpreter, October
 The College of the Pacific, 1850-1950
  Western College Association Addresses, November 4
1951 Some Imperatives of American Citizenship
  World Affairs Interpreter, July
1952 Martin C. Briggs, "Methodist Trumpeter" of California
  Quarterly California Historical Society, March

Three M's: Mores, Morale, Morality
    World Affairs Interpreter, April
California Mountain Men of Another Breed
    Quarterly Historical Society of Southern California,
        September
Shredded Men and Desiccated Society
    Sociology and Social Research, November-December

1953   Impressions of Mexico
    World Affairs Interpreter, January
Zest After 80
    Today's Life, April-May
Educating for World Citizenship
    World Affairs Interpreter, July
Quest for Plenty
    World Affairs Interpreter, October

1954   Changes in California in My Time
    Quarterly Historical Society of Southern California,
        December

1955   Some Unfinished Business for U.S.A.
    World Affairs Interpreter, July

INDEX